Shifting Gears

Recalibrating Schoolwide Discipline and Student Support

A Restorative and Accountable Approach *for* Middle and High Schools

Engaging
SCHOOLS
Connect • Collaborate • Learn

Shifting Gears: Recalibrating Schoolwide Discipline and Student Support
A Restorative and Accountable Approach for Middle and High Schools

By Carol Miller Lieber, Michele Tissiere, and Nicole Frazier

Engaging
SCHOOLS
Connect ▪ Collaborate ▪ Learn

© 2015 Engaging Schools
Engaging Schools
23 Garden Street
Cambridge MA 02138
www.engagingschools.org

Edited by Jill Davidson and Denise Wolk
Book design by Walter Zekanoski / WZ DESIGN
10 9 8 7 6 5 4 3 2
Printed in the United States of America
ISBN 13: 978-0-942349-32-0

Shifting Gears

Recalibrating Schoolwide Discipline and Student Support

A Restorative and Accountable Approach *for* Middle and High Schools

Carol Miller Lieber

Michele Tissiere

Nicole Frazier

Engaging Schools is deeply grateful to The Atlantic Philanthropies, American Institutes for Research, The California Endowment, Lippincott Foundation, and an anonymous donor for the financial support that made this resource possible.

Contents

Foreword

I am grateful for this book and the guidance it will provide school leaders across our country. With a national spotlight now illuminating the need for school discipline reform, school leaders have a new opportunity to make sure every student gets the support she or he needs. This resource is an invaluable tool for leaders who want to place the highest priority on keeping children in school, safe, and learning.

The Children's Defense Fund (CDF) has been speaking out against school discipline policies that stack the odds against poor children and children of color since our founding. For our first report in 1974 on *Children Out of School in America*, CDF staff knocked on thousands of doors across the country to ask families why children were not in school after we learned from census data that two million children were out of school in America, including 750,000 between 7-13 years old. But census data did not tell us who they were and why they were out of school. We found that these were largely children with physical, mental, and emotional disabilities, but the second largest cause of children being out of school was school suspension and discipline policies. We reported that "If a child was not White, or was White but not middle class, did not speak English, was poor, needed special help with seeing, hearing, walking, reading, learning, adjusting, growing up, was pregnant or married at age 15, was not 'smart enough' or was 'too smart,' then, in too many places, school officials decided school was not the place for that child. In sum, out-of-school children shared a common characteristic of differentness by virtue of race, income, physical, mental or emotional 'handicap,' and age. They were for the most part, out of school not by choice but because they had been excluded. It is as if many school officials had decided that certain groups of children were beyond their responsibility and were expendable. They excluded them arbitrarily, discriminatorily and with impunity."

In 1975, CDF released a follow-up report, *School Suspensions: Are They Helping Children?* The answer was a resounding no. We found the vast majority of suspensions were for non-dangerous, nonviolent offenses. And while the largest numbers of suspended students were White, suspensions disproportionately hurt more children who were Black, poor, older, and male. We also found that the great majority of suspensions for truancy and tardiness and catchall terms like disruption, willful defiance, and disrespect served no demonstrated valid interests of children or schools. They pushed children and their problems out into the streets, causing more problems for them, their parents, and their communities and resulting in many dropping out of school.

Forty years later, too much of what we learned then remains true now. Children continue to be suspended for truancy and tardiness. I have never understood why we exclude children from school for not coming to school, rather than finding out why they are absent.

I believe the purpose of public schools is to educate all children, and to help identify and meet children's needs. Since denying a child an education is sentencing a child to social and economic death, huge reforms are required in school discipline policies and practices across our nation. School pushout has worsened in past decades and is contributing to the criminalization of children at younger and younger ages, aided and abetted by zero tolerance school expulsion and suspension policies which funnel children into the prison pipeline, often crippling them for life. Schools with higher suspension and expulsion rates have worse school climates, lower student academic achievement, and are often less safe. And poor children of color, especially Black males, bear the brunt of these exclusionary policies. One in three Black and one in six Latino boys will go to prison in their lifetime unless we change course.

There is encouraging news as more districts begin reviewing and reforming their discipline policies. More fundamentally, they are examining how they view and treat children by moving away from harsh and exclusionary policies toward more positive and restorative approaches that improve discipline outcomes, keep children in school, and enable them to get the preparation they need for college, work, and life.

We know what works for children. Engaged students, parents, and communities working with committed educators are showing that change is possible. It's way past time to end child exclusion in the indispensable lifeline of education for any except the most serious offenses, and begin referring children to appropriate help. No child is expendable and every child has a right to learn and grow up to be the best they can be.

We must increase the positive momentum building to educate all children, help meet their individual needs, and prepare them for the future. This book helps build that momentum by providing school and district leaders, key drivers of school change, with a deeper understanding of the underlying issues involved in school discipline and the research that supports alternatives to the current failed policies. It outlines a systemic approach to transforming the policies and practices that will reduce harsh and disproportionate discipline, promote educational equity, and foster fair, restorative, and accountable school discipline and student support. Bolstered by the positive momentum and this new tool, I am hopeful that district and school officials will lead the way to major reforms. Let's join in to ensure a level growing and a level playing field for every child everywhere in our nation, and create school climates that will help all our children strive and thrive. Their future and our nation's future depend on it.

Marian Wright Edelman
President
Children's Defense Fund

Preface

During the last five years, there has been a sea change in the understanding among educators and many in our communities about the extent and impact of the use, overuse, and disproportional use of punitive and exclusionary discipline in many districts and schools across the country.

In 2011, *Breaking Schools' Rules: A Statewide Study of How Discipline Relates to Students' Success and Juvenile Justice Involvement*, the landmark study of discipline in Texas, described findings that have been echoed in various national and local data and studies since.

- Nearly six in ten public school students were suspended or expelled at least once between 7th and 12th grade.
- African-American students and those with educational disabilities were removed from the classroom at a disproportionately higher rate for discretionary disciplinary reasons.
- Students who are suspended or expelled were much more likely to become involved in the juvenile justice system.

The recent publication from UCLA's Center for Civil Rights Remedies, *Are We Closing the School Discipline Gap?*, highlights the scope of the problem at the national level — nearly 3.5 million public school students were suspended out of school at least once in 2011–12, and 1.5 million of these students were suspended at least twice. Given that the average suspension is conservatively put at 3.5 days, US public school children lost an estimated 18 million days of instruction in just one school year because of exclusionary discipline. Moreover, recent estimates are that one in three students will be suspended at some point between kindergarten and 12th grade. Data from various sources tells us that African-American students are more than three times as likely to be suspended as their White peers and special education students more than twice as likely.

We know that overly punitive discipline has a cascading negative impact. For example, it results in greater school alienation and disengagement, loss of instructional time, and higher failure and drop-out rates.

In January 2014, the Federal Departments of Education and Justice issued *Guiding Principles: A Resource Guide for Improving School Climate and Discipline*. It framed three guiding principles and recommended action steps for each:

1. Create positive climates and focus on prevention.
2. Develop clear, appropriate, and consistent expectations and consequences to address disruptive student behaviors.
3. Ensure fairness, equity, and continuous improvement.

Districts and schools have begun to make progress to address these principles. For example, school districts are revising codes of character, conduct, and student support to limit the use of suspension and out-of-school suspension rates have begun to come down in some places. The PBIS framework is being used more broadly to organize behavior supports and interventions. Social and emotional learning (SEL) is being implemented in more districts and schools. The use of restorative practices is spreading.

However, each sign of progress is accompanied by continued challenges. Reduction in out-of-school suspension may be accompanied by increases in in-school suspension where students are still not getting the supports they need. The disproportionality of discipline is not changing much. PBIS' strength is as a framework and does not incorporate sufficient attention to day-to-day practices that need to change. It can encourage overuse of extrinsic rewards systems rather than building intrinsic motivation. SEL is more heavily implemented in elementary schools. Secondary schools are having a harder time figuring out how to integrate SEL into classrooms and the school. Although implementation of restorative practices holds great promise, these practices, by themselves, will not change the school culture.

Shifting Gears aims to help district and school leaders build on successes and address ongoing challenges. The authors address the need for integration of schoolwide discipline and student support in order to maximize each and every student's opportunities for success. The book's aim is to help district and school leaders address the issue holistically by reviewing and recalibrating the policies, systems, and practices that go into creating models that are respectful, fair, accountable, restorative, and viable. While *Shifting Gears* will be of value to anyone rethinking discipline and student support in middle and high schools, much of the information can be applied to recalibrate districtwide policies and practices as well.

Shifting Gears is rooted in Engaging Schools' long-standing recognition of the critical impact of a safe, respectful, and welcoming climate and learning-focused culture supporting students' success at school. It reflects Engaging Schools' belief that it is the job of schools to foster academic, social, and emotional learning and development, and cultivate the adult mindsets needed to support and sustain student success. It advocates that school staff members build a foundation of mutual trust, respect, and cultural competence in order to establish more personalized and positive relationships with students. Positive relationships are linked with student outcomes such as greater engagement, persistence, self-efficacy, and sense of well-being.

The authors recognize that successfully changing the policies, systems, and practices surrounding discipline requires all of the adults in the school building and community to play a role. *Shifting Gears* speaks to the roles of all staff from administrators, student support staff, and teachers to school safety teams. It also addresses the critical importance of collaboration with families and adult allies.

I am grateful for the important contribution that the authors, Carol, Michele, and Nicole have made to advance the field of schoolwide discipline and student support. They brought to the project many years' experience as school leaders and teachers combined with decades of experience consulting with districts and schools on these issues. I appreciate their collective wisdom, insights, and practical orientation, along with the comprehensive scope of their thinking.

I am confident that any district or school leaders who wish to make the shift to a more equitable, restorative, and accountable approach to schoolwide discipline and student support will find this book to be an invaluable "how to" guide.

Larry Dieringer
EXECUTIVE DIRECTOR,
Engaging Schools

Acknowledgements

The transformation of discipline and student support into a schoolwide model that is accountable, restorative, equitable and fair demands the investment of a committed and collaborative community. Because *Shifting Gears* is a call to all readers to consider new kinds of collaborations, we want to thank and acknowledge the generosity of a diverse national educational community of colleagues, students and Engaging Schools' staff members who co-labored with us to shed a spotlight on a topic of such significance. We are confident that the collective efforts of so many will result in more effective schoolwide discipline and student support models, contributing to the wellness of our school cultures and the healthy development of our youth across the country.

Many of the ideas and insights that informed this book were the result of decades of work with schools and districts all over the country. We mined the rich and textured experiences we have had with principals, assistant principals, teachers, ancillary staff, student support staff, and district leaders who demonstrated rigorous curiosity and discipline for stepping into this work. We thank them for their commitment to share their intellect, wisdom, and integrity and for their courage to engage in an ongoing complex dialogue about schoolwide discipline.

Knowing deep down the significant ways schools impact student lives, we believe it is critical to seek out student perspectives. We have listened to essential conversations with hundreds of students who have navigated the secondary school terrain - some with grit, grace and resilience, others with defeat, defiance and disillusionment. Their collective voices are invaluable. They asked penetrating questions, and shared poignant stories and real-time experiences, which compelled us to put in writing a schoolwide discipline and student support model that would help schools and districts cultivate a healthy school climate and culture where students can thrive and hold aspirations for a positive future. Their day-to-day circumstances fueled our energy and creativity.

Thank you to our dear colleagues, the Engaging Schools' consultants, who demonstrate an interminable strength, resilience and skillfulness in partnering with schools and districts to engage in this complex work. Sensitive and serious, thoughtful and spirited, we appreciate the sage counsel and advocacy they bring to district and school leaders, teachers, staff, students and families. We are grateful for the lively conversations inspired by this work, their personal stories from the field, and the opportunities to work through challenges with them. Our working partnerships with them have led to incisive ideas, frameworks, and strategies that inform an effective schoolwide discipline and student support model.

We are also grateful for the generosity of the many people who reviewed and commented on portions of the manuscript. We benefitted from their knowledge and critical perspectives, which motivated us to read, re-read, rethink and reconsider.

Our reviewers included:

- Sheila Donahue, START Team and Behavior Specialist with Syracuse City Schools District, Syracuse, NY.
- David Osher, Vice President, AIR Institute Fellow, Senior Advisor to the Health and Social Development Program. American Institutes for Research.
- John Hudson, Education Consultant specializing in Attendance, Truancy, Dropout Prevention, and Recovery, Killeen, TX.
- Erica Hasenbeck, Social-Emotional Systems Support Coordinator, Fresno Unified School District, Fresno, CA.
- Jaye Murray, Senior Administrator of Guidance and School Counseling, New York City Public Schools.
- Pedro Noguera, Distinguished Professor of Education in the Graduate School of Education and Information Sciences, UCLA.
- Pilar Vazquez-Vialva, Principal, Theodore Roosevelt High School, Chicago, IL.

Finally, we could not have done this work without the exhaustive support from the Engaging Schools' staff and work-study students from Harvard University in Cambridge. Their flexibility, sense of humor and enduring patience was ever present in the midst of a complex two-year project.

Our enduring thanks to all of you for the interdependent network of support you have generously offered us as a writing team. You inspired us and gave us hope to write a book that we feel will help district and school leaders reflect on and reshape their schoolwide discipline and student support model from within — in the service of each and every student in their care.

Shifting Gears: A Reader's Guide

What is Our Vision for *Shifting Gears*?

If you purchased this book, you are likely faced with discipline challenges in your district or school and are looking to both understand your situation and identify a coordinated approach to solve a complex and layered problem. Headlines like *"District Discipline Practices Under State Investigation"* and *"How Bad is the School to Prison Pipeline?"* are drawing attention to the reality and the results of far too many schools that are struggling with the complex challenge of getting discipline right. We wrote this book to provide middle and high school leaders—whether they be district administrators, school based leaders, student support staff, or teacher leaders—with a practical guide that will help them look critically at each aspect of their schoolwide discipline and student support model and provide ideas and solutions to recalibrate each of these critical components. Our goal? Schools that are designed and equipped to support each and every student to succeed in school, achieve academically, and graduate with the skills and dispositions that set them up for success in college, careers, and life.

We titled this book *Shifting Gears* and use the gears metaphor throughout the book because we see effective discipline as an intricate system with multiple moving and interrelated parts. A simple search on the Internet will reveal hundreds of "discipline" books focusing on classroom management, and yet a search for secondary schoolwide discipline yields a scant few resources. While we recognize the importance of effective classroom management, the complex discipline challenges we are facing in our schools need to be addressed holistically with coordinated schoolwide efforts. This book is designed to address all aspects of a comprehensive effort (including classroom practices) to promote safe, civil, nurturing, and orderly communities; prevent common misbehaviors and disruptions to learning; and provide accountable and restorative interventions for students who need additional and targeted support.

Much of what you will find between the covers of this book is a result of work we have done with districts and schools around the country. The good news is that focused and planful leaders within districts and schools who face significant challenges are able to turn the tide through strategic efforts to recalibrate their discipline and student support model.

Who is the Intended Audience?

Shifting Gears was designed as a resource to help district and school leadership teams explore the rationale for an accountable and restorative discipline approach, assess the strengths and needs of the existing discipline and student support systems, and identify ways to improve and strengthen a revised model. In addition, we anticipate that leadership teams might identify excerpts from the book that might be read and discussed in faculty meetings or professional development sessions to foster shared understandings around the goals for discipline and the best practices and systems that support students to become more self-disciplined.

We anticipate that depending upon their role within the school or district, readers will find some chapters or "gears" more relevant to their particular scope of work. For example, an administrator or student support team member who is in charge of designing and implementing interventions for struggling students will likely want to dig into Chapter 11: Interventions and Case Management. Likewise, those responsible for planning and designing teacher professional development might find Chapter 10: Classroom Practices particularly useful. Even though you might be drawn to a particular chapter, it is critical that all constituent groups develop a deep understanding of the whole model and each other's roles.

Knowing that all districts and schools have their own particular circumstances, *Shifting Gears* was written with a variety of school contexts in mind. Ours is not a one-size-fits-all formulaic discipline program; rather, it is a comprehensive approach to discipline and student support that encompasses a research and theory based model, proven and promising best practices, guidelines, and considerations. So whether you are a district leader, a new principal, seasoned school leader, teacher or student support team leader, working in large comprehensive middle and high schools, small secondary schools, or public charter schools, the concepts and ideas we put forth will apply, though they will inevitably need to be adapted to each district's/school's needs and interests.

We know that schools approach the work of improving discipline and student support from different points on continuums of readiness, urgency, and current effectiveness. *Shifting Gears* can be used with different goals and intentions in mind.

- For new district and school administrators, new school start-up teams, study groups, and planning teams who have the opportunity to fully re-imagine an alternative model of discipline and student support
- For district and school administrators and teams who want to rethink and revise current school policies and practices that help move the district or school in the direction of a model that better supports the healthy growth and development of every student
- For district and school administrators and teams who want to reorganize and reconfigure staff roles and responsibilities in order to create a more coherent and integrated system of discipline and student support
- For district and school administrators and teams who want to ramp up the use of more effective processes and interventions at the school and classroom level

- For district and school administrators and teams who want to replace a more punitive model of discipline and student support with a more accountable and restorative model, particularly in "turn-around" schools, innovation and pilot schools, or schools assigned other designations that require them to overhaul their entire discipline and student support system

How is the Book Organized?

For those charged with improving school discipline and student support, time to think through big ideas as well as the small details is at a premium. While this book is designed to be a comprehensive tool for re-imagining, revising, ramping up, or redesigning a school's discipline and student support systems, we have organized it into two parts so that busy practitioners can find information they need easily and efficiently.

Section 1 of the book (chapters 1 through 4) sets the stage by providing foundational background information about the discipline problem, features of an effective discipline model, the research behind those features, and the importance of understanding adolescent development and how it can shape more effective disciplinary policies and practices for middle and high school students. This section lays out both the vision and the details of an accountable and restorative approach to schoolwide discipline and student support. While some readers might be tempted to skip ahead, a close read of Section 1 lays out critical concepts that inform the specific changes in a recalibrated model. These chapters also provide rich material for school culture, discipline, and student support planning teams in search of short readings, pithy quotations, research references, and "boiler plate" language that will help teams defend their recommendations, galvanize broad support for change, and explain the nuts and bolts of new policies and practices. We absolutely encourage readers to comb these chapters for texts and specific language that will resonate with your school's goals and your team's needs and priorities.

Section 2 of the book (chapters 5 through 12) takes a deep dive into each component or gear of an accountable and restorative schoolwide discipline and student support model. It begins with a chapter on the importance of aligning a clearly articulated school vision to discipline redesign, followed next by a chapter that details essential features of a quality code of character, conduct, and support. Successive chapters provide information on establishing essential teams, collecting and using the right data, implementing schoolwide promotion and prevention initiatives, and classroom practices that support the schoolwide model, interventions, and case management systems to support students who struggle, and strategies for engaging families and adult allies in supporting their children's academic, social, and emotional growth and development. In summary, Section 2 is the practical "how-to" guide for recalibrating the schoolwide discipline and student support model or implementing targeted improvements in the model.

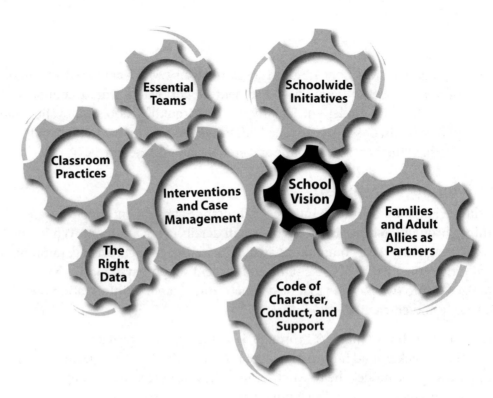

Each chapter begins with a guiding question and a chapter outline to support the reader with navigating the text purposefully and efficiently.

The Appendices include a targeted set of resources and tools to use as is or modify to fit individual school contexts.

Our primary intention with this resource is to offer perspective and illuminate practices that will support the effective development of a schoolwide discipline and student support model. We hope that *Shifting Gears* offers you and your colleagues a wealth of information to consider, discuss, and use to support your efforts and actions in implementing an accountable and restorative schoolwide discipline and student support model. We invite and encourage you to lean in and learn with each other. We are confident that an ongoing dialogue will help you strengthen the complex and critical work in which you are engaged.

Section 1

Foundational Understandings about Discipline and Student Support

1

The Discipline Problem

What are some of the impacts of ineffective and inequitable schoolwide discipline policies, practices, and structures on our students, their families, staff members, and the school culture and climate?

CHAPTER OUTLINE
Introduction
The Problem With Exclusionary Punitive Sanctions
Conditions That Influence Disparate Impact
School Conditions That Produce Ineffective Disciplinary Policies

Introduction

There are multiple problems and conditions that pose challenges to creating effective schoolwide discipline and student support models. The subject of public school discipline has surfaced recently as an urgent issue in national and local media. This has prompted a call to action from civil rights organizations, the United States Department of Education, state and district boards of education, district and school leaders, families, community organizations, and students concerned about their discipline policies and practices. The problems surrounding school discipline have a long and protracted history. These issues live on the ground at the school level — and the local school is where real students are adversely impacted by ineffective and inequitable disciplinary policies and practices. Staff, students, and families can feel demoralized, disengaged, and uninspired to partner with each other in a school culture where the schoolwide discipline system is dysfunctional and ineffective. This inhibits their collective capacity to create a school climate that feels stable and cohesive, inspiring and engaging, and welcoming and affirming.

Schoolwide discipline is complex. After the US Department of Education presented guidelines for improving school climate and discipline in 2014, a 2015 follow-up report, *Addressing the Root Causes of Disparities in School Discipline,*[1] calls upon districts and schools to "look across multiple domains" to get a full picture of the discipline problem through the examination of disciplinary policies, procedures, and practices; perceptions of school climate; the dominant norms, beliefs, and assumptions that inform the school culture; systemic factors that influence a student's educational opportunities; and staff attitudes and beliefs. (pp. 11–12 of cited DOE report) We have clustered these aspects of the problem into three areas to support your efforts to assess the current reality in your setting:

- The problem with exclusionary punitive sanctions
- Conditions that influence disparate impact
- School conditions that produce ineffective disciplinary policies

The Problem With Exclusionary Punitive Sanctions

The use and overuse of suspensions

Investigations into suspension practices pose this question to test out justifiable use: "Is there evidence that suspension is an educationally sound and justifiable practice as it is currently used?" The rationale for suspension typically rests on assumptions that time out of school will improve a student's behavior, deter other students from engaging in similar behaviors, and ensure that classrooms will be more orderly and conducive to teaching and learning.[2] Suspension, by itself, generally achieves none of these objectives. In fact, researchers who examine the use of suspension, classroom removal, and detention find that exclusionary punitive sanctions are least effective with students who engage in persistent unwanted behaviors.[3] The Academy of American Pediatrics recently concluded that "out-of-school suspension and expulsion are counterproductive to the intended goals, rarely if ever are necessary, and should not be considered as appropriate discipline in any but the most extreme and dangerous circumstances, as determined on an individual basis rather than as a blanket policy."[4]

When students are suspended out of school or expelled, loss of instructional time is often compounded by the absence of adult supervision during the very hours that teens are most likely to get in trouble with their peers.[5] Physical removal of students from the classroom, whether or not it leads to suspension, produces negative effects that reach far beyond lost learning opportunities. Classroom removal is a public act in front of peers that often exacerbates distrust and animosity that may already taint the student-teacher relationship. When students are "put out" with no resolution of the conflict between student and teacher, the process of re-entry and recovery is immensely challenging for both the adult and the adolescent. The likely result, at its best, is a stony stalemate. At its worst, mutual hostility festers, disengagement grows, and unacceptable behaviors persist.

Daniel Losen, of the UCLA Civil Rights Project, reports in *Discipline Policies, Successful Schools, and Racial Justice,* that "Suspended students are less likely to graduate on time and more likely to be suspended again, repeat a grade, drop out of school, and become involved in the juvenile justice system. When carried out in connection with zero-tolerance policies, such practices can erode trust between students and school staff, and undermine efforts to create the positive school climates needed to engage students in a well-rounded and rigorous curriculum."[6] From an academic perspective, higher suspension rates also appear to be associated with lower schoolwide achievement and standardized test scores.

The use of suspension varies widely across states, districts, schools within in a district, and across individual schools with suspension rates of less than two percent to rates of more than 25 percent of total enrollments. Suspension also varies by grade level. Nationally, students are two to four times as likely to be suspended in middle and high schools as compared to elementary schools. This has the potential to contribute to school disengagement, lost opportunities to learn, and dropping out.[7] "There are no data showing that out-of-school suspension or expulsion reduce rates of disruption or improve school climate; indeed, the available data suggest that, if anything, disciplinary removal appears to have negative effects on student outcomes and the learning climate."[8]

The overuse of suspension has been well documented over the last several decades. In raw numbers, suspensions have increased for all student groups since the mid-1970s. In a national sample of approximately 2,000 secondary schools, nearly 30 percent of middle and high schools suspended more than 20 percent of their total student enrollments. Drawing from 2009–2010 data from all United States schools, more than 2,600 secondary schools suspended more than one-fourth of their total enrollments.[9]

Conventional wisdom assumes that out-of-school suspensions are reserved for the most serious offenses that jeopardize school safety and order. Nationally, however, fewer than 10 percent of suspensions are categorized as "criminal, drug- or tobacco-related, or extremely dangerous or violent incidents." The vast majority of suspensions, often referred to as discretionary suspensions, are the result of incidents categorized as "disruptive behavior" and "other."[10] These categories of suspension are open to vast differences in interpretation and judgment that inform what exactly warrants a suspendable offense. Within these broad categories, district and school codes of conduct across the country use the following descriptors to identify suspendable offenses: obscenity, defiance, stubbornness, disruption to public order, disrespect, refusal to comply or follow directions, insubordination, disobedience, failure to act with courtesy, multiple tardies or class cuts, repeated failure to wear ID badge, and refusal to attend required detention.

We are clear that these behaviors must be dealt with immediately and effectively and that suspension is not the route to supporting more skillful behaviors in students. Consequently, an urgent priority is to support leaders at the district and school level, as well as teachers, to expand their repertoire to go beyond punitive responses for behaviors of this sort. This means fine-tuning policies and practices that encourage and support students to take responsibility for understanding the reasons behind their behaviors, correcting their behaviors, making amends, repairing the harm they caused, and restoring their good standing with peers, teachers, and other adults.

It is worth noting that the overuse of discretionary suspension, particularly in middle and high schools, arises most often from student-teacher interactions in which students are first removed from a classroom via an office disciplinary referral and then assigned suspensions for behaviors that disrupt the learning environment. Thus, schoolwide disciplinary policies and practices are directly impacted by teachers' disciplinary practices in the classroom. "Classroom disruptions tend to increase or decrease with the skill of the teacher in providing engaging instruction and in managing the classroom—areas many teachers say they would like help improving. Researchers find a strong connection between effective classroom management and improved educational outcomes" that point to "an inverse relationship between student misbehavior and a teacher's ability to engage students. As engagement goes up, misbehavior and suspensions tend to go down."[11]

Disproportional use of suspension

Disproportional suspension has become the subject of state subpoenas, grievances submitted by the federal Office of Civil Rights, and lawsuits on behalf of students and parents because of suspension's disparate impact on students of color and students with disabilities. In United States employment law, the doctrine of **disparate impact** holds that practices may be considered discriminatory and illegal if they have a disproportionate **adverse impact** on members of a minority group.[12] This doctrine prohibits the use of practices that, on face value, are neutral and non-discriminatory, but produce a discriminatory effect, or unjustified adverse impact, on members of a protected class. Disparate impact is unintentional, whereas disparate treatment is an intentional decision to treat people prejudicially based on their race or other protected characteristics.

In the research, disproportional use of suspension exists when the percent of suspensions within a specific student group reaches a rate that is more than 20 percent above the percent of that specific group within the total enrollment of a school or district. For example, if 100 Black students comprised 20 percent of a school's total enrollment of 500, a proportional rate of suspension would be 20 percent. However, if Black students received 37 of a total number of 100 suspensions, the rate of suspension for Black students would be 37 percent, or almost twice the rate (nearly 50% higher) than would be proportional to the number of Black students in the school.

National data on the use of suspension clearly show that students of color and students with disabilities are disproportionately impacted in comparison to other student groups. National suspension rates for Black and Latino students have doubled over the last 40 years and suspension rates for students with disabilities have increased by over 50 percent during this same period. "African-American students without disabilities are more than three times as likely as their White peers without disabilities to be expelled or suspended. Nearly a quarter of Black students across the country were suspended during the 2009–10 school year compared to just 7.1 percent of White students. Twelve percent of Latino students were suspended in the same year."[13] Most alarmingly, schools and districts identified as having disproportionate disciplinary practices show suspension rates for Black male students with disabilities as high as 40 percent.

Although students who receive special education services represent 12 percent of students in the US, they make up 19 percent of students suspended in school (compared to 6.6 percent of students without disabilities), 20 percent of students receiving one out-of-school suspension, 25 percent of students receiving multiple out-of-school suspensions, and 19 percent of students expelled."[14] Special education students are already at risk for facing a lifetime of inequality. Often suspensions are triggered by the student's disability and reflect a lack of knowledge about effective strategies for teaching and supporting these students. Disproportional use of suspension deprives them of receiving systematic behavioral, emotional, social, and academic supports and interventions needed to ensure their success at school and in life. "Because suspension increases a young person's probability of both dropping out and becoming involved with the criminal justice system, it is difficult to justify, except in extreme situations where safety, or the educational process of the school, is directly and seriously threatened. For the vast majority of cases, however, the challenge is to find a way to address the situation with better practices, more alternatives, and more effective training of school personnel."[15]

In our work with districts and schools where disproportional use of suspension is deeply embedded in the school culture and/or district, we recognize the strategic steps that need to be taken to open the door to a critical conversation about the data narrative and the current reality for teachers, students, and their families. Rethinking school discipline and the disproportional use of suspension takes relentless commitment from a variety of stakeholders: school board members, district and school leaders, teachers, school safety staff, school student support staff, families and adult allies, community leaders and, importantly, students themselves.

Conditions That Influence Disparate Impact

Cultural mismatch

Cultural mismatch or **incompatibility theory** suggests that the classroom culture, and more specifically the norms, attitudes, and values of the teacher, can be at odds with the prevailing cultural and communication norms of specific student groups.[16] When school and home cultures are at odds, the result is a cultural clash that gets in the way of student learning.[17] Student-teacher mismatch may be a contributing factor when classroom disciplinary referrals, which are the source of the majority of suspensions, describe students' behavior as defiant or non-compliant. These are often "violations of implicit interactional codes," in which students call into question established classroom practices or the teacher's authority.[18]

When students and teachers perceive significant disconnects between each other's norms and values, feelings of distrust, frustration, and discomfort can surface. For example, students who negotiate life outside of school by using a "code of the street" may find it more difficult to adjust to a different set of norms in their interactions with peers and teachers in school settings.[19]

Culture clashes are most likely to occur over differences in styles of communication and personal expression;[20] beliefs about how to earn respect, resolve conflicts, handle frustration, and respond to mistakes; and educational values and aspirations. In a groundbreaking study from Stanford University, researchers concluded that the more adolescents' worlds of family, peers, and school were dramatically different from each other, the more adolescents were likely to experience difficult transitions and less success at school.[21]

Implicit bias, stereotype, and low expectations

Implicit bias, also known as hidden or unconscious bias, explains how discrimination and selected targeting continue to exist, even when people consciously reject stereotypes and perceive themselves to be unprejudiced. "Implicit bias is defined as the mental process that causes us to have negative feelings and attitudes about people based on characteristics like race, ethnicity, age, and appearance. Because this cognitive process functions in our unconscious mind, we are typically not consciously aware of the negative racial biases that we develop over the course of our lifetime."[22]

Our unconscious mind clusters things, as well as people, into schemas that make it easier to recognize and remember what we see and experience in the world. These schemas become stereotypes when we begin to associate a specific set of characteristics with a specific group of people. Prejudicial stereotypes exist when we hold mostly negative associations with a particular group. In other words, unconscious biases can generate stereotypes that may influence our conscious attitudes, reactions, and behaviors toward a specific group of people.[23] For example, if implicit biases trigger associations of dangerous behavior, aggressiveness, or irresponsibility with Black boys, teacher behaviors toward Black boys might be unconsciously driven by feelings of fear and discomfort that may influence the degree to which they care about or disregard this group of students.[24]

Teacher expectations, which are one of the most powerful predictors of student success in school, can be influenced by implicit bias as well as explicit prejudicial mindsets.[25] If teachers make unconscious associations that some student groups are unable to learn curricular content or cannot behave appropriately, these lowered expectations may result in teachers treating students of color and students with disabilities prejudicially by providing less praise and encouragement and by assigning harsher and more frequent disciplinary sanctions.[26]

Personal stressors, trauma, family conflict, and poverty

So often, behaviors such as acting-out and withdrawn behaviors are symptoms of underlying issues that urban adolescents are dealing with at school, at home, or in their communities. We all hold a collective responsibility to unpack the surface issues that students present to us and get to the heart of the problem. "We need community-school partnerships and caring and compassionate adults at schools, especially counselors and mental health professionals, to give children and educators the best chance to succeed. Many of the troubles that children experience at home and in their communities have their origins in adverse childhood experiences, bringing us back to the urgent need to prevent them in the first place and to build resiliency in children and families so they can survive the traumas of life when they do occur."[27]

Since the 1980s, risk and resiliency researchers have pointed to a multitude of factors, both positive and negative, that influence the health and well-being of adolescents. Risk factors like early aggressive behavior, developmental delays associated with impulsiveness, poor judgment, poor social skills, limited parental supervision and support, substance abuse, family conflict, abuse, and serial family crises can contribute to less-than-ideal outcomes and can diminish the likelihood of successful development. While they do not predict or guarantee a particular outcome, risk factors can result in long-term stressors that threaten young peoples' positive life chances and impacts students' positive attachment to school, their capacity to bond with adults and peers in healthy ways, their academic performance, and their personal and social efficacy.[28]

The emerging field of trauma research corroborates these earlier findings that show an adverse relationship between trauma and healthy development and school success. Researchers point out that "trauma is not an event itself, but rather a response to one or more overwhelmingly stressful events where one's ability to cope is dramatically undermined."[29] The Adverse Childhood Experiences (ACE) study found that just over 50 percent of adults surveyed reported having experienced at least one form of childhood adversity including "verbal, physical, or sexual abuse, as well as family dysfunction (e.g., an incarcerated, mentally ill, or substance-abusing family member; domestic violence; or absence of a parent because of divorce or separation)."[30] These experiences in childhood can lead to a cascade of social, emotional, and academic difficulties. As students get older, exposure to traumatic experiences can also lead to the adoption of self-medicating behaviors such as substance abuse, smoking, and overeating. All of these responses to traumatic events can interfere with a child's ability to learn at school."[31]

Recent neurobiological and psychological studies have shown that traumatic experiences in childhood can diminish concentration, memory, and the organizational and language abilities children need to succeed in school.[32] "For some children, this can lead to problems with academic performance, inappropriate behavior in the classroom, delays in social skill development, and difficulty forming healthy relationships with peers and adults. Many of the effects of traumatic experiences on classroom behavior originate from the same problems that create academic difficulties: the inability to process social cues and to convey feelings in an appropriate manner."[33]

Moreover, the area of a child's brain that is associated with the fear response may become overdeveloped, causing a child to overuse the fight, flight, or freeze response when triggered by a trauma reminder, even when there is no actual threat of fear.[34] Putting on a "tough front" to avoid future victimization and gain a measure of control can serve as a student's self-protective shield.[35] A student's need for safety and control, whether expressed externally by acting out or internally through withdrawal, may be misunderstood by teachers, evoking open frustration and "exasperated reprisals, reactions that both strengthen the child's expectations of confrontation and danger and reinforce a negative self-image."[36]

While any student may experience personal stressors or trauma at some point during adolescence, students from families who live below the poverty line often have more limited access to resources, making it more challenging to meet students' individual needs. Children living in poverty may experience food insecurity, limited exposure to literature and language, and a lack of hope and optimism. Many of these children have inconsistent adult supervision and stressed relationships with caregivers. Three-quarters of all children from poverty have a single-parent caregiver.[37] These students enter school already at risk and disproportional disciplinary practices exacerbate their capacity to sustain their engagement in school and develop healthy relationships with their peers and teachers.

School Conditions That Produce Ineffective Disciplinary Policies

Code of conduct and enforcement problems

The ways that rules are written in the code of conduct and the ways that rules are enforced are often the source of inequitable and ineffective disciplinary policies and practices. When rules state neither the specific positive behaviors expected of students nor the specific behaviors that are unacceptable, school staff members may interpret rules and determine consequences for rule violations very differently from one another. Some school districts, for example, assign a suspension of one to five days for all types of rule violations, from fighting to insubordination, without delineating specific conditions and actions that warrant a one-day versus a five-day suspension. Although this omission may seem trivial, it can set the stage for implicit bias to play out and result in the application of inconsistent consequences and sanctions for the exact same student behavior. We have worked with discipline deans within the same school who use different criteria to determine whether a student will be suspended and the length of time for a suspension. When common criteria for assigning suspension focus only on harsh, punitive sanctions or common criteria are absent altogether, the stage is set for implicit bias to drive the overuse of suspension that, too easily, can become a school norm.

In addition, the chasm between written rules and the degree to which the rules are enforced creates much of the confusion, frustration, and ineffectiveness around school discipline. A common complaint that we hear from teachers centers on the inconsistent enforcement of school rules. Inconsistent rule enforcement can result when most adults choose to enforce some rules and not others, or different adults choose different rules to enforce, or a substantial number of adults choose not to enforce most rules altogether. In any of these circumstances, students receive a terrible mixed message that blurs the clarity of school norms; and they pay the price of disparate treatment.

Zero tolerance policies

Zero tolerance policies, which are most often linked to long-term suspension or expulsion for a single behavior violation, result in neither improved school safety nor improved student behavior, especially for adolescents most likely to experience disciplinary problems.[38] The term "zero tolerance" became widely adopted in schools in the early 1990s as a philosophy or policy that mandates the application of predetermined consequences, most often severe and punitive in nature, that are intended to be applied regardless of the gravity of behavior, mitigating circumstances, or situational context.[39] Although these policies were originally intended to apply exclusively to dangerous or threatening offenses involving weapons, drugs, or violence, many schools gravitated to assigning harsher and more inflexible punishments to minor behavior incidents as well, resulting in increased discretionary suspensions.

Researchers who have studied "get tough" discipline policies over the last twenty years point to an increase in the use of suspension and expulsion, but find no evidence that zero tolerance policies serve as an effective deterrence to disruptive behavior; nor does it improve school climate, reduce levels of violence, or deliver more equitable consequences.[40] From a developmental perspective, many rule violations are a result of students' immature executive brain functioning: poor judgment, lack of impulse control, and inability to predict risk and consequences accurately. Except in situations that pose a severe threat to safety, the use of harsh and arbitrary punishments to combat developmental immaturity appears to be an uninformed or unskillful choice of disciplinary strategy. These punishments have the potential of doing much harm and creating a long lasting impact on the student's ability to feel in charge of himself, his thinking, and his ability to feeling connected to his peers and adults and develop trusting relationships.

The capacity problem

Insufficient capacity to manage schoolwide discipline effectively cuts across all school staff, beginning with principals who may not see their direct involvement in organizing and resourcing effective discipline and student support structures and systems as a primary responsibility. This includes allocating adequate time for professional learning to enhance the teaching faculty's classroom management and discipline skill set and their capacity to engage all learners. Equally important, school leaders in their evaluation roles may not always identify effective classroom management and discipline skills as a first priority for classroom observation rounds in order to intervene early with teachers who need greater support and coaching.

Administrators also need to provide adequate time and resources to establish effective Student Support Teams. The disappearance of robust numbers of counselors, and student support and youth development staff, has become commonplace in many secondary schools. The shrinkage could not come at a worse time, when physicians, research scientists, and mental health practitioners are noticing an alarming rise in the numbers of children and young people who are failing to thrive and flourish in their communities.[41] The continual hemorrhaging of student support positions in schools makes it extremely difficult to follow-up and follow-through with students whose behavior problems require more intensive interventions, and not just the assignment of a Schools Sanctions/Consequences.

Overloaded deans and student support staff have reported that they have increasingly limited time to offer timely interventions. Also, many have shared that they do not feel that they have a sophisticated skill set, nor have they had professional learning opportunities, to provide the kind of attentive, effective interventions that would make a difference for students at greatest risk for succeeding in school, socially, academically, and behaviorally.

In some instances, inadequate numbers of student support personnel reach a crisis proportion in schools that have unusually high numbers of students who are chronically absent, disengaged in the classroom, frequently skipping classes or hall walking, or persistently demonstrating defiant or aggressive behaviors. In these contexts, incidents pile up, reports do not get processed immediately, and the school simply does not have the capacity to insist on and support students to change behaviors that have become barriers to succeeding academically and behaving responsibly. Promoting authentic student accountability becomes an elusive proposition, students get the message that nothing will really happen, and the adults feel overwhelmed and at a loss as to how to strategically navigate the situation.

Systems break-down across discipline and student support structures

Too often, discipline and student support policies and practices are developed and implemented in different silos by different people resulting in inconsistent follow-through, randomly applied consequences and interventions, and an incoherent case management system for tracking and monitoring students with the most problematic behaviors. However well intentioned, this mix of hit and miss responses does little to actually improve student outcomes.

The breakdown in the system is often a result of well-intentioned staff members not being clear about their roles or not having sufficient data to view problems holistically. Ignoring the interdependent nature of everyone's responsibilities for supporting a safe, orderly, and disciplined learning environment can have an adverse impact on students, staff, and school morale. Here are some examples:

- **Administrative Presence:** When administrators are not visible in the hallways at passing time, teachers are much less likely to see their own presence in public spaces as a critical prevention strategy that supports a safe, civil, and orderly learning community.

- **Classroom Practices:** When teachers are not using promotion and prevention strategies and practices to handle the vast majority of discipline problems, referrals for minor infractions begin to clog up the system, making it much more difficult to deliver more intensive interventions to students with more serious problems.

- **Timely Interventions:** When students with persistent aggressive and non-compliant behaviors do not receive the timely interventions they need to turn around unacceptable behaviors, teachers get demoralized and become far less likely to engage in promotion and prevention strategies and practices.

- **Data Systems:** When disciplinary, attendance, and academic data are not recorded, analyzed, and summarized on a weekly basis, the case management team does not have the requisite data to review the status of high needs students or determine interventions that need to be in place for specific students.

- **Data Review:** When the leadership team does not routinely examine disciplinary data looking for positive and negative trend lines; disproportional assignment of suspensions and referrals by student group; disproportional submission of referrals by individual teacher; or unusually high numbers of specific kinds of incidents or referrals, the team is unable to make informed decisions about action steps that will address their concerns.

They might be seeing parts of a problem or working on the problem with colleagues in isolation to come up with short-term solutions that are not holistically serving the students, families, the staff, and the community at large.

The culture of blame

When pressures to reduce suspensions and chronic incidents of bad behavior collide, blame can become an insidious element of an individual school culture or district-wide communication. Creating or refining a schoolwide discipline and student support model is difficult when key constituencies take on polarized stances about who is to blame for poor discipline in schools. When working with schools we often hear from teachers that they are struggling with classroom management and discipline and do not know how to navigate an array of challenging student behaviors. Teachers often share that they do not feel supported by administration and tend to blame students and their parents for bad behavior in the classroom. Many administrators place the blame on teachers and share their complaints and frustrations about teachers' reluctance to address problematic behaviors in the moment and their overreliance on disciplinary referrals. Social workers, counselors, youth advocates, behaviorist researchers, civil rights advocates, and parents tend to blame the school, the teachers, and the union. A culture of blame results in conversations fraught with highly charged emotions and loaded language. In this kind of adversarial climate, people have a very tough time moving beyond their positions to work as collaborative partners who take collective responsibility for solving the discipline problem.

Empirical evidence and common sense tells us that students' behavior problems do not originate from a single source. Research indicates that the wide variation in student behavior can be attributed to the following factors in descending order: (1) among individual students, differences in temperament, emotional expression, self-regulation, attentional control, and sociability; (2) classroom factors such as student-teacher relationships, behavior management skills, and clarity of expectations; (3) parenting practices and supervision; and (4) principal leadership and schoolwide climate and discipline policies and practices.[42]

A lack of balance between standards-based and supports-based reform

A lack of balance between standards-based and supports-based reform is an obvious oversight to people who actually work in schools. However, those who make educational policy and distribute funding are not currently leading the charge for greater balance between these two reform strategies. More dollars devoted to data accountability, test prep, assessments, and the technology associated with a standards-based curriculum mean fewer dollars for supports-based reforms.

Supports-based reform involves all dimensions of supporting students' academic success and healthy development. This includes providing wraparound social, physical, and mental health services within all schools; employing more trained counselors, student support and mental health specialists, youth advocates, and graduation coaches; embedding more targeted academic and behavior supports within the school day; and balancing standards-based instruction with more student-centered learning and a more developmentally appropriate pedagogy.

ASCD's Whole Child Campaign was a pioneer initiative in this movement and many educational thought leaders are now calling for increased funding for and attention to supports-based reforms that help meet students' academic and developmental needs. The Opportunity to Learn (OTL) Campaign unites a growing coalition of advocates and organizers from across the country working to ensure that every student has access to wraparound academic, social, emotional, and health supports, highly prepared and effective teachers, and effective school discipline.

John H. Jackson, president of the Schott Foundation for Public Education, wrote this in a 2013 commentary: *"In the past decade, federal and state education policies have focused primarily on efforts to raise standards, improve assessments, and evaluate teachers. While each of these issues warrants attention in the landscape of education policy, they are not effective drivers toward significantly changing the conditions for students across the country. The standards-based reform agenda has made it virtually impossible for educators to give all students the varied attention and resources needed to engage them in a meaningful learning process. Now is the time to focus on providing the necessary supports to better engage young, low-income Black and Latino students and truly close those gaps."*[43]

Dr. James Comer, Director of the Yale Child Study Center, a longtime advocate for whole child development and member of the newly formed President's Advisory Commission on Educational Excellence for African-Americans, has raised the alarm that current reform efforts reveal "an absence of understanding of brain growth and maturation–of the social, emotional, moral, ethical and linguistic development of children."[44] Comer urges a more balanced focus on "what students need to know," "what kind of experiences they need to be successful adults," and what kind of supports are needed to foster "continual development from birth to maturity."

A behaviorist model of schooling

With the launch of the No Child Left Behind Act in 2001, behaviorist principles and pedagogy have quietly saturated the urban school reform agenda with little vocal opposition. Behaviorism assumes that the cause of all behavior exists outside the child in the environment. Consequently, how children think and feel internally is irrelevant to both behavior analysis and subsequent interventions that focus exclusively on what is observable and measurable. Behaviorism rests on the idea of external control. It is, after all, the "science of controlling others,"[45] reflecting a carrot and stick approach of rewards and positive reinforcement in addition to punishment and negative reinforcement. Yet, a review of raw data of suspensions and office disciplinary referrals over the last two decades would suggest that an overreliance on punishment, rewards, and external control has generated an increase, rather than a reduction, in classroom disruptions.[46] A punishment-reward orientation also has potential to cast a lingering shadow over the entire school climate through tacit permission to use admonishment and student removal as primary strategies for addressing discipline problems in the classroom.

Other factors may also limit the effectiveness of behaviorist approaches for adolescents. For older students, internal factors like will and motivation play a much larger role in behavior that may diminish effectiveness of strategies that depend solely on external control. Second, although the use of aversive or punitive consequences can inhibit the occurrence of problem behavior in students who are already relatively successful at school, researchers have concluded that these practices tend to be least effective for students with the most problematic behaviors.[47] Punishment rarely produces sustained improvements in the behavior of students who tend to monopolize the time and attention of assistant principals, deans, and support staff. Moreover, punitive approaches tend to exacerbate bad behavior, intensify feelings of anger and alienation, worsen relationships between teachers and students, and generally precipitate poorer academic performance.[48]

Finally, a behaviorist paradigm comes with the underlying assumption that quantitative data are the only reliable measure of success or failure. Numbers alone cannot reveal a school's commitment to children's healthy development within a community that values caring and empathy. And therein lies the dilemma. We are educating children in a time when only what is measured is what is valued.

In unpacking the discipline problem in our districts and schools we come to the conclusion that it is never just one problem. The many complexities of identifying the barriers to an effective schoolwide discipline and student support model require patience and thoughtfulness and the capacity to invite in all perspectives within the school community. We hope the array of problems we have presented in this chapter provide entry points for your own study, analysis and problem-solving.

[1] Osher, D., Fisher, D., Amos, L., Katz, J., Dwyer, K., Duffey, T., & Colombi, G.D. (2015). Addressing the root causes of disparities in school discipline: An educator's action planning guide. Washington, DC: National Center on Safe Supportive Learning Environments.

[2] Losen, D., & Martinez, T. (2013, April 8). Out of School & Off Track: The Overuse of Suspensions in American Middle and High Schools. The Center for Civil Rights Remedies/The Civil Rights Project. Los Angeles, CA.

[3] Sugai, G., Horner, R. H., Dunlap, G., Hieneman, M., Lewis, T. J., Nelson, C. M., & Ruef, M. (2000). Applying positive behavior support and functional behavioral assessment in schools. Journal of Positive Behavior Interventions, 2(3), 131–143.

[4] American Psychological Association Zero Tolerance Task Force. (2008). Are zero tolerance policies effective in the schools?: an evidentiary review and recommendations. The American Psychologist, 63(9), 852.

[5] National Institute on Out-of-School Time at the Wellesley Centers for Women at Wellesley College (2009) Making the Case: A 2009 Fact Sheet on Children and Youth In Out-of-School Time.

[6] Losen, D. (2011, October 5). Discipline Policies, Successful Schools, and Racial Justice. Office of Civil Rights Report, NEPC.

[7] American Academy of Pediatrics, 1998; Morrison et al., 2001; Osher, Morrison, & Bailey, (2003); Gregory, A., Skiba , R. J. & Noguera, P. A. (2010). The achievement gap and the discipline gap: Two sides of the same coin? Educational Researcher, 39, 59–68.

[8] American Psychological Association Zero Tolerance Task Force. (2008). Are zero tolerance policies effective in the schools?: an evidentiary review and recommendations. The American Psychologist, 63(9), 852.

[9] Losen, D. J., & Martinez, T.E. (2013) Out of School and Off Track: The Overuse of Suspensions in American Middle and High Schools. The Center for Civil Rights Remedies/The Civil Rights Project. Los Angeles, CA.

[10] Skiba, Chung, Trechok, Baker, Sheya, Hughes. "Where Should We Intervene?" (2015) Closing the School Discipline Gap, Teachers College Press, p. 133.

[11] Losen, D.J. (2011). Discipline Policies, Successful Schools, and Racial Justice. Boulder, CO: National Education Policy Center. Retrieved from http://nepc.colorado.edu/publication/discipline-policies.

[12] EEOC v. Sambo's of Georgia, Inc., 530 F. Supp. 86, 92 (N.D. Ga. 1981).

[13] Losen, D. J., & Martinez, T.E. (2013) Out of School and Off Track: The Overuse of Suspensions in American Middle and High Schools. The Center for Civil Rights Remedies/The Civil Rights Project. Los Angeles, CA.

[14] Data collected by the Civil Rights Data Collection (CRDC) for the 2011–12 school year as of January 8, 2014. Additional information and publicly available data from the CRDC can be found at http://ocrdata.ed.gov.

[15]   Losen, D. and Gillespie, J. (2012) Opportunities Suspended: The Disparate Impact of Disciplinary Exclusion from School. The Center for Civil Rights Remedies/The Civil Rights Project. Los Angeles, CA.

[16]   Townsend, B. L. (2000). The disproportionate discipline of African-American learners: Suspensions and expulsions. Exceptional Children, 66, 381–391. Irvine, J. J. (2002). In search of wholeness: African-American teachers and their culturally competent classroom practices. New York: Palgrave.

[17]   Nieto, S. (2009) Language, Culture, and Teaching: Critical Perspectives. Routledge.

[18]   Skiba, R. J., Michael, R. S., Nardo, A. C., & Peterson, R. L. (2002). The color of discipline: Sources of racial and gender disproportionality in school punishment. The urban review, 34(4), 317–342.; Gregory, A., Skiba, R. J., & Noguera, P. A. (2010). The Achievement Gap and the Discipline Gap Two Sides of the Same Coin?. Educational Researcher, 39(1), 59–68., Vavrus, F., & Cole, K. (2002). "I didn't do nothin'": The discursive construction of school suspension. The Urban Review, 34(2), 87–11.

[19]   ibid

[20]   Kochman, T. (1981). Black and White styles in conflict. University of Chicago Press.

[21]   Phelan, P., Davidson, A. L., & Yu, H. C. (1998). Adolescents' worlds: Negotiating family, peers, and school. Teachers College Press.

[22]   Rudd, T. (2014, February 1). Racial Disproportionality in School Discipline Implicit Bias is Heavily Implicated. Retrieved from http://kirwaninstitute.osu.edu/wp-content/uploads/2014/02/racial-disproportionality-schools-02.pdf

[23]   Kang, J., & Banaji, M. R. (2006). Fair measures: A behavioral realist revision of" affirmative action". California Law Review, 1063–1118.

[24]   Dovidio, J. F., Glick, P. E., & Rudman, L. A. (2005). On the nature of prejudice: Fifty years after Allport. Blackwell Publishing.

[25]   Hattie, J. (2012). Visible learning for teachers: Maximizing impact on learning. Routledge.

[26]   Rudd, T. (2014, February 1). Racial Disproportionality in School Discipline Implicit Bias is Heavily Implicated. Retrieved from http://kirwaninstitute.osu.edu/wp-content/uploads/2014/02/racial-disproportionality-schools-02.pdf

[27]   Robert K. Ross, president and chief executive of The California Endowment, Letter to the editor in response a 2013 New York Times article. Retrieved from http://acestoohigh.com/2014/01/09/new-federal-guidance-should-help-slow-the-flow-in-school-to-prison-pipeline-but-much-work-remains/

[28]   Hawkins, J. D., Catalano, R. F., & Miller, J. Y. (1992). Risk and protective factors for alcohol and other drug problems in adolescence and early adulthood: implications for substance abuse prevention. Psychological bulletin, 112(1), 64.

[29]   Trauma and Learning Policy Initiative. http://massadvocates.org/tlpi/

[30]   Center for Disease Control and Prevention. Adverse Childhood Experiences Reported by Adults — Five States, 2009 December 17, 2010 / 59(49); 1609–1613.

[31]   Trauma and Learning Policy Initiative. http://massadvocates.org/tlpi/

[32]   ibid

[33]   ibid

[34]   ibid

[35]   Gregory, A., Skiba, R. J., & Noguera, P. A. (2010). The Achievement Gap and the Discipline Gap Two Sides of the Same Coin?. Educational Researcher, 39(1), 59–68.

36 Trauma and Learning Policy Initiative. http://massadvocates.org/tlpi/

37 Jensen, E. (2013). How poverty affects classroom engagement. Educational Leadership, 70(8), 24–30.

38 Skiba, R. J., & Knesting, K. (2001). Zero tolerance, zero evidence: An analysis of school disciplinary practice. New directions for youth development, 2001(92), 17–43.

39 American Psychological Association Zero Tolerance Task Force. (2008). Are zero tolerance policies effective in the schools?: an evidentiary review and recommendations. The American Psychologist, 63(9), 852.

40 ibid

41 Commission on Children at Risk, Institute for American Values, YMCA of the USA, & Dartmouth Medical School. (2003). Hardwired to Connect: The New Scientific Case for Authoritative Communities. Broadway Publications.

42 Bear, G. G. (1998). School discipline in the United States: Prevention, correction, and long-term social development. School psychology review.

43 Jackson, J.H. Moving From Standards to Supports. Education Week May 7, 2013. http://www.edweek.org/ew/articles/2013/05/08/30jackson.h32.html

44 Bailey, M. Comer To Obama: Look Beyond Test Scores. New Haven Independent. February 21, 2014. http://www.newhavenindependent.org/index.php/archives/entry/comer_named_to_advise_president/

45 Bredo, E. (2002). How can philosophy of education be both viable and good?. Educational theory, 52(3), 263–271.

46 Hoffman, L. L., Hutchinson, C. J., & Reiss, E. (2009). On Improving School Climate: Reducing Reliance on Rewards and Punishment. *International Journal of Whole Schooling, 5(1), 13–24.*

47 Sugai, G., Horner, R. H., Dunlap, G., Hieneman, M., Lewis, T. J., Nelson, C. M., & Ruef, M. (2000). Applying positive behavior support and functional behavioral assessment in schools. Journal of Positive Behavior Interventions, 2(3), 131–143.

48 Alberto, P. A., & Troutman, A. C. (2012). Applied behavior analysis for teachers. Pearson Higher Ed.

2

Essential Features of an Effective Model

What needs to be understood, believed, refined, and implemented in order to establish an effective schoolwide discipline and student support model?

CHAPTER OUTLINE

Introduction
Why Climate and Culture Matter
A Caring, Civic Community Built on Relational Trust
Qualities to Strive For
The Gears in the System
The Critical Need for Shared Responsibility of Student Discipline

Introduction

In January of 2014, the US Department of Education published a set of guidelines to help schools to improve discipline policies and practices.[1] The three guiding principles shown in Figure 2.1 are supported by a robust research base, and serve as a guide for identifying some of the big ideas that need to be evident and functioning in an effective, non-discriminatory schoolwide discipline model. While these guiding principles are helping to drive important reforms in schools around the country, they are not a comprehensive "how to" guide.

Taking on the all too common problems with school discipline outlined in Chapter One and achieving the goals put forth in the federal guidelines might seem daunting, yet we know it can be done. Moreover, it will be worth the effort. Schools that commit to assessing and recalibrating their schoolwide discipline and student support policies and practices see results in reduced disciplinary incidents, increased teacher efficacy, improved school climate, and increased student achievement. Creating complex change in a school setting requires a nuanced approach, a deep awareness of what it takes to create and sustain a shared vision, and the skills and knowledge to take the specific steps necessary for transformation.

The goal of this chapter is to set the stage for the rest of the book by providing an overview of an effective schoolwide discipline and student support model. Through our work with districts and schools across the country, Engaging Schools has identified key features of a caring and civic community, the qualities that create a fair, respectful, accountable, restorative, and viable model, and the critical shifts that generate effective and sustainable change. Along the way, we discuss why school climate and culture matter, highlight the significant differences between traditional approaches to school discipline and our own model, and introduce the key components or "gears" that make the model work. We close the chapter with a call for schools to develop a shared responsibility for student discipline. We aim to help you construct and clarify your school's vision of an improved and more effective schoolwide discipline and student support model.

Figure 2.1

Excerpts from Guiding Principles: A Resource Guide for Improving School Climate and Discipline

Principle 1: Create positive climates and focus on prevention
Schools that foster positive school climates can help to engage all students in learning by preventing problem behaviors and intervening effectively to support struggling and students at risk.

Principle 2: Develop clear appropriate and consistent expectations and consequences to address disruptive student behaviors
Schools that have discipline policies or codes of conduct with clear, appropriate, and consistently applied <u>expectations</u> and <u>consequences</u> will help students improve behavior, increase engagement, and boost achievement.

Principle 3: Ensure fairness, equity, and continuous improvement
Schools that build staff capacity and continuously evaluate the school's discipline policies and practices are more likely to ensure fairness and equity and promote achievement for all students.

Why Climate and Culture Matter

An ever-increasing body of research indicates what educators know intuitively: school culture and school climate have a significant impact on student achievement.

To tackle the discipline challenge, we must recognize that schoolwide discipline and student support live within the larger domain of school climate and culture. **School Climate** is related to the collective perceptions, mood, and morale of the staff members, students and their families. **School Culture** permeates schoolwide discipline and student support systems because it is the beliefs, values, norms, and shared practices that communicate, "This is the way we do things around here."[2] In *Shaping School Culture: Pitfalls, Paradoxes, and Promises*, Terry Deal and Kent Peterson suggest that "highly respected organizations have evolved a shared system of informal folkways and traditions that infuse their work with meaning, passion, and purpose."[3] Put simply, a coherent school culture communicates:

- This is how we do school.
- This is what we expect of you and expect of ourselves.
- This is how we present and express ourselves to others.
- This is how we treat each other.
- This is how we work and learn together.
- This is how we correct mistakes, get back on track, repair harm, restore community, and make things right.

The way students, teachers, and administrators feel about school influences their actions and behaviors. We know that safe, supportive environments and positive relationships among adults and peers strengthen attachment to school and enhance adolescent resiliency and healthy development. On the other hand, when perceptions of school are dominated by adversarial, "us vs. them" relationships and feelings of anonymity, anxiety, distrust, and discouragement, students are more likely to experience school apathy and academic failure, emotional distress, and other risk behaviors.

A study of 15 urban districts commissioned by the National School Boards Association cautioned educators about focusing exclusively on instruction and testing at the cost of ignoring school climate factors that directly influence academic performance. "Good student development and academic learning are inextricably linked. Students care very much about what it feels like to be at school. Is the school safe and clean? Can they trust their teachers? And do teachers believe in and respect them? These feelings influence how students feel about themselves — how confident they are, what they think of themselves as learners, and what kind of future they see. Students cannot learn well and are not likely to behave well in difficult school environments."[4]

A Caring, Civic Community Built on Relational Trust

Developing and sustaining a **sense of community** among all students and adults within a school is a conscious act that requires time, attention, and intention. "A community exists when a critical mass of stakeholders are committed to each other and to the organization's goals and values and exert effort to achieve their goals and maintain relationships with each other. A perception of community is shaped by daily experiences and probably is best engendered when a person feels welcomed, supported, nurtured, respected, liked, and connected in reciprocal relationships with others, and contributes actively to the collective identity, destiny, and vision."[5]

Schools that cultivate a **caring community** emphasize a relational view of community that puts caring relationships front and center. Nel Noddings, who has taught and written extensively on the ethics of care, posits, "To care and be cared for are fundamental human needs. All human beings need to be understood, received, respected, and recognized."[6] Through the reciprocal attention and responsiveness of being "cared for," we learn how to "care about" the conditions and treatment of others. A caring community provides the conditions that make it possible and compelling to respond in a caring manner to others. "We show them how to care. Children educated in this way gradually build an ethical ideal, a dependable caring self."[7]

Schools that see themselves as a **civic community** treat the idea of balancing individual rights with civic obligations as a serious school endeavor. If education is supposed to be preparation for life and citizenship, then educators must play a role in equipping students to take part in the democratic process.[8] Educational philosopher John Dewey argued that schools are democracy's laboratory, "a mode of associated living, of conjoint communicated experience" that requires the school community to find common interests and values through "an equitable opportunity to receive and to take from others through a large variety of shared undertakings and experiences."[9] The most important of these shared undertakings is learning how to live within a community of rights, responsibilities, and rules.

Strong relational trust is the bedrock that grounds a school's climate and enables a school to become a caring and civic community. Effective schools promote and model mutual respect, high quality professionalism, and transparent accountability based on relational trust among and between administration, staff, students, and families. Shame and blame are not part of the culture. In their longitudinal study of trust in schools, researchers Anthony Bryk and Barbara Schneider found that the degree of relational trust between and among administrators, staff, students, and parents not only impacted people's general sense of purpose, well-being, and hopefulness in the daily life of the school; but relational trust also influenced the degree to which school reform efforts actually increased student achievement. Schools with low relational trust were three times less likely to produce improved outcomes from their reform initiatives.[10]

If there are few opportunities for people across roles and responsibilities to talk, learn, and work together authentically, relational trust is an elusive proposition. Trust emerges from interactions in which people's interdependent relationships are made visible and expectations are clear and agreed upon by all parties. People know what they can count on from each other, they know how they will be treated, and, most importantly, they know that others will take them seriously and take their interests to heart. For students, this means that adults communicate "I'm on your side" as well as "I'm on your case" when they make mistakes. For teachers, it means that their important concerns about student discipline and support will be addressed. For administrators, it means that they can count on all adults to enforce important rules and policies. For parents, it means that they have confidence in the administrators and staff to apply disciplinary rules and policies fairly, without favor toward or prejudice against particular students or particular groups of students. More than anything, strong relational trust communicates the shared belief in people's good intentions and their capacity to do the right thing. The result is a good will commitment to do the work that needs to be done to accomplish the goals the school aims to achieve.

Building a caring and civic community that results in high levels of relational trust is neither fast nor easy. A first step might be to have a leadership team do a frank assessment of their school's climate and culture, teacher and student morale, and major disciplinary challenges. To uncover schoolwide trends, consider having staff and students complete a valid and reliable climate and culture survey. What actions have we taken as a school community to ensure all adults have a shared vision for the school? What evidence exists that teachers feel supported by the Administrative Team? What actions have we taken to understand how students feel about how they are disciplined? What quantitative and qualitative data exists around students being sent out of class, and the way serious discipline incidents are being handled? What steps have we taken as a school community to communicate with parents about our efforts to ensure their children are getting the supports they need?

Having an independent party facilitate teacher and student focus groups can also shed light on issues that need to be addressed. Keep in mind, just as teachers need to depersonalize a student's display of negative emotions, administrators need to avoid getting defensive about the current status of their school's climate and culture. Accurate diagnosis is a necessary first step on the path to change. Often the simple act of acknowledging and wanting to understand what is not working builds trust and credibility. It also typically reveals what might be the best next planning and problem solving step, such as inviting faculty to develop a shared school vision as described in Chapter Five or generating a few important schoolwide rules as described in Chapter Six.

Qualities to Strive For

An effective schoolwide discipline model should be: respectful, fair, accountable, restorative, and viable. Each of these qualities goes a long way to counter the list of complaints and grievances that surround more traditional models of school discipline. Many schools capture some of these qualities in their discipline policies and practices, but most schools do not make all five of these qualities transparent to everyone in the school community. We believe that all five of these qualities are essential if schools are committed to meeting the needs and interests of multiple stakeholders — from the school principal, to the parents of a student with disabilities, the district lawyer, the community activist, the teacher union representative, and a high school student. Interactions between and among district and school staff, students, and parents communicate respect, protect the dignity of each individual, and ensure a tone of decency when these qualities are evident.

This set of qualities also provides a kind of litmus test for school teams who are considering changes to current policies and practices. Throughout a revision and planning process, teams can use the following question to assess whether they are on track for developing more effective policies and practices: "Does the recommended change to this specific policy or practice help our model become more respectful, fair, accountable, restorative, and viable?"

Essential Qualities of an Effective Discipline and Student Support Model

Respectful

Respect affirms each person's identity, value, and dignity by appreciating what each person brings to the school community. Respect begins by calling people by name, acknowledging their presence, and listening to them attentively. It is nurtured though cultural responsiveness by welcoming, noticing, and learning about the diversity of students, staff, and families within the school and every classroom. Adults create a climate of mutual respect through asking thoughtful questions and inviting and listening to students' different perspectives. Adolescents overwhelmingly corroborate that they want to be listened to and taken seriously. When we work with districts and schools to recalibrate schoolwide discipline and student support programs, student voices are always involved in the initial needs assessment through survey data and focus group interviews.

Adults' direct modeling of respectful behaviors sets the stage for students to communicate respectfully. Particularly when dealing with discipline issues, we need to remind ourselves that our response will always shape the student's response. On that note, it is worth unpacking why "being disrespected" is the source of so many adult-adolescent conflicts. Developmentally, young people are hypersensitive when it comes to the question of respect. They tend to label any adult comments and actions that diminish their self-worth, discount their feelings, or use embarrassment or sarcasm to communicate disapproval or disappointment as disrespect — and once named, will likely heighten students' feelings of anger and agitation. We see respectful adult-to-student communication as the cornerstone for all disciplinary practices.

Fair

In addition to respect, fairness is the other quality that students care most about. For students, fairness is about when and how adults choose to engage in conversations about discipline and the way adults respond to discipline incidents. This includes assigning consequences and interventions that fit the severity and frequency of behavior violations, saving more serious responses for the incidents that most seriously jeopardize students' safety. Students quickly abandon their good will with teachers who make a big deal over the student without a pencil or toss a student out of class for talking. Adolescents let us know that "we are supposed to make mistakes — we're teenagers." Thus, it is critical to create opportunities where they can reset and make a fresh start when they make a mistake. Being fair means adults treat students reasonably, interact with students respectfully, avoid favoritism that feels arbitrary, and claim the middle ground between harshness or humiliation and permissiveness or doing nothing.

As much as students want adults to respond consistently when they get in trouble, students also want to be reassured that adults will exercise a degree of judiciousness when the particulars of a situation should factor into a determination of the most appropriate consequence. Differentiated responses, however, must reside within a larger framework of equitable practices under which all students are treated fairly without favor toward or prejudice against any one group of students according to ability, talent, age, gender, developmental and acquired disabilities, race and ethnicity, socio-economic status, religious and spiritual orientation, national origin and home language, sexual orientation, and indigenous heritage. In practical terms, this means that: (1) in a multi-tiered system of supports (MTSS), all opportunities and interventions must be accessible to every student, (2) Tier 2 and Tier 3 consequences and interventions must be consistently applied across all groups of students with fidelity and integrity, (3) culturally competent and responsive practices are embedded throughout the educational program; and (4) data must be transparent to determine the use and efficacy of all consequences and interventions, paying particular attention to indicators of disproportionality among various student groups.

Accountable

Accountability involves an obligation or willingness to accept and account for one's actions to others. We have never met an educator or parent who did not want young people to be accountable for their behavior. However, when schools choose to take on the mantle of an accountable approach to discipline and student support, they need to consider the degree to which accountability is perceived as supportive and collective. Does the school leadership team operate from a more supportive or punitive stance? Punitive accountability is about "dinging" students, staff, parents, and schools when they get it wrong and, most likely, attaching punitive sanctions to wrongful actions or bad results. In contrast, supportive accountability creates an environment free from harsh criticism, blame, and shame, so people are more willing to own their mistakes and missteps and make good faith attempts to correct things and get it right.

For example, if the entire faculty agrees to be at their doors and in hallways during the change of classes, and some staff members are noticeably absent, punitive accountability would translate into a principal's "gotcha" message directed to non-compliant staff: "Mr. Green, Ms. Brown, and Mrs. Grey, this is the second week you've been AWOL in the hallways. One more week of no shows and I will need to write you up." On the other hand, a principal who believes in supportive accountability might use constructive feedback to share observable data with the whole staff. "On hall walks this week, 80 percent of staff were present in wings A and D during transitions. Less than half of the staff on B and C wings were out and about. Folks, let's everyone ramp it up to 90 percent next week. Thanks in advance for helping make good on our agreement." School leaders who push for supportive accountability do three other things. They expect some imperfection. "Well that didn't go well, but it's not the end of the world." They are optimistic and solution-oriented. "This is fixable." And they communicate their confidence in adults' and students' capacity to change. "You can do this."

Being held accountable generates a more positive response when it is perceived as a collective endeavor. We cannot ask students to rise to the occasion and own their behavior if we are reluctant to call on adults to step up their own accountability for their words and actions. Collective accountability for establishing an effective schoolwide discipline and student support model calls on all stakeholders to accept the following obligations:

- **The School Administration** has the obligation to serve as champions of promoting a positive school climate and overseeing and supervising all personnel, systems, and structures associated with discipline and student support.
- **Teachers** have the obligation to treat all students respectfully and fairly; promote positive behaviors by teaching habits of learning and self-discipline; provide clear academic and behavioral expectations, routines, and procedures; increase students' engagement in learning; prevent and defuse conflicts and confrontational behaviors; and use restorative strategies to help struggling students get back on track.
- **The Student Support Team** has the obligation to maximize its capacity and expertise in order to provide timely and effective interventions that will help students get back on track and function more successfully at school.

- **Students** have the obligation to accept assigned school sanctions/consequences and fully participate in the interventions designed to address specific behaviors or disciplinary incidents.
- **Parents/Guardians/Caregivers** have the obligation to partner with school staff to support their child's success in school and their healthy development and well-being.

Restorative

A restorative approach to discipline is based on the belief that students are resilient, capable of turning around adverse situations, and can restore themselves and their relationships with the understanding and guidance of caring adults. As illustrated in Figure 2.2 a restorative approach moves beyond punishment by providing interventions and supports to mitigate future misbehavior. More traditional school discipline focuses singular attention on the processing, assignment and delivery of a punishment when students misbehave. This "eye for an eye" principle is rooted deep in human history; however, the reality reminds us that punishments and the threat of punishments do not deter or reduce most misbehavior in schools. Students who are repeatedly removed from classrooms, sent to the dean's office, or assigned detention and suspension are caught in a cycle that makes it difficult for them to change direction and for teachers to step back and try more effective responses.

Figure 2.2

Comparison Between a Punitive and a Restorative Approach

	Punitive Approach	Restorative Approach
Intention	Punishment is an end in itself intended to inflict sufficient discomfort, unpleasantness, or undesired consequence in order to decrease the unwanted behavior.	A restorative intervention is a learning opportunity in which a student must account for his/her behavior and take some action to repair the harm done, make amends, self-correct, right oneself, problem solve, learn new behaviors, or restore one's good standing.
The Process	Actions are done to a student through external control and authority. The needs and feelings of those harmed in an incident are often ignored. Blame and faultfinding are central. Perceived as confrontational or adversarial. Perceived as win-lose.	Actions are done by a student with the support of caring adults. When an incident has harmed others, their needs and feelings are central to the process. Problem analysis and problem solving are central. Perceived as supportive, collaborative and learning-focused. Perceived as win-win using fair process.
Parties Involved	Student and district authority or school administrator.	Student, administrator, a Student Support Coach, and parties affected by the incident.
Focus	Primary focus on the past (What did you do?)	Primary focus on the present (What are you thinking now?) and the future (What can you do to make it right? When a situation like this comes up again, what actions might you take next time?)
Accountability	Involves "doing time" through the assignment of a punishment or penalty.	Involves "owing time" to account for one's actions, take personal responsibility, reflect on the impact of one's behavior, and engage in some action to make it right.
Effects on the Student	Tends to encourage lying, blame, and defensiveness, intensify feelings of anger, resentment, hostility, and alienation resulting in low motivation to change.	Tends to encourage candor and truthfulness, defuse anger, generate feelings of being cared for and respected, support personal agency, insight, and competence resulting in greater motivation to change.
Effects on Relationships and Community	Relationships tend to worsen or remain adversarial.	Supports maintenance and/or repair of relationships. Supports restoration of one's good standing in the community.
Re-entry if Exclusionary Sanctions are Still in Use	Planned re-entry is often absent.	Re-entry to school community involves consistent protocols and processes that are carefully planned and monitored.

A restorative approach ensures that assigned school sanctions/consequences are aligned to appropriate interventions. Moreover, it places a greater emphasis on the intervention phase of a disciplinary incident than the consequence phase. The intervention phase signals to students that they will be asked to own the problem, reflect on the impact of their behavior on themselves and others, understand *why* the behavior was inappropriate, unacceptable, or unskillful, and engage in some action with the support of a caring adult to right oneself, learn new skills and practice different behaviors, or repair the harm and make it right. Human beings are more cooperative, responsive, and more likely to make positive changes in behavior when others do things with them, not to them or for them. Interventions are likely to include restorative practices like problem solving and planning conferences, mediation, and Restorative Group Conferences for high impact incidents when students experience interpersonal conflicts. Other interventions like counseling, replacement behavior sessions, and progress monitoring support students' development of new skills and mindsets that strengthen their personal and social efficacy.

To be absolutely clear, a shift to a restorative approach does not eliminate the consequence phase of a disciplinary incident. Nor are punishments eliminated altogether. Most states and school districts have mandated punitive sanctions for the most serious behavior violations and these mandates are unlikely to change in any model. However, a restorative approach does aim to reduce and even eliminate the use, overuse, and disproportional use of exclusionary sanctions through implementation of more restorative strategies in the classroom, greater use of in-school interventions, and clearer and fewer conditions under which classroom removal and suspension may be used.

Viable

This last quality is often ignored at a district's or school's peril. It is critical to ensure that all stated rules and policies are feasible and capable of working successfully. This requires that 95 percent of adults in the school are willing to do what is required to support and enforce the rule or policy. It also necessitates that all consequences and interventions are doable which means the school has the capacity in time, numbers of personnel, and expertise to manage, process, and deliver desired consequences and interventions to all students who need them. Schools want to avoid making the mistake of promoting a rule or policy that is unenforceable or offering an intervention that is never likely to be available to all students who need it. A few cautionary guidelines and examples may help teams analyze the viability of their rules and policies, sort out what to keep, what to eliminate, and what might require adjustments.

- Avoid rules and policies that require too many steps to enforce. (An electronic device policy that requires adults to confiscate all devices that are seen or heard, bag and tag the device, and then take the device to the office to be placed in the school safe is not feasibly enforceable.)

- Avoid expectations that are humanly impossible to meet. (The expectation that every single disciplinary incident will be investigated [vs. insisting on investigation for all incidents that meet certain criteria] is a promise that cannot be kept.)
- Avoid rules that will not generate at least 95 percent compliance from the staff to enforce them. (A tardy policy that expects teachers to contact a parent every time a student is late is unlikely to be enforced consistently.)
- Avoid consequences for which the time, processing tasks, and communication points required to deliver it are disproportional to either the severity of the violation or the effectiveness of the consequence. (Assigning after school detention for each tardy or minor disciplinary incidents involves an exhaustive number of steps, time, and personnel to ensure compliance to the rule. If there is no back up protocol when students do not show up, the policy becomes a joke to students.)
- Be cautious about introducing interventions for which you do not have adequate personnel to deliver. (Even though a comprehensive re-entry plan would be ideal for any suspension, it may only be viable for students returning from long-term suspensions.)

The Gears in the System

In *Leadership and the New Science,* Margaret Wheatley eloquently describes the challenges of implementing and sustaining organizational change. "How do we create organizational coherence…how do we create structures that move with change, that are flexible and adaptive…that enable rather than constrain? How do we resolve the need for personal freedom and autonomy with organizational needs for prediction and control?"[11]

We have identified eight gears — system components and important shifts that help schools recalibrate a schoolwide discipline and student support model in ways to maximize students' success in school; foster students' academic, social, and emotional development; and maximize adult effectiveness in supporting all students. Each gear has multiple moving parts and is an essential component of the whole model. All of the gears are interdependent. The word interdependent implies that all staff members are dependent on the efficacy of each other's actions and work collaboratively to make the model function. Making changes in any of the gears will require significant shifts in adult mindsets, development of new structures and programs, and implementation of a different set of practices used by administrators, teachers, and student support staff.

As teams identify needs and begin implementing changes with individual gears, they will find that it is important to review and fine-tune the other gears to make sure each part of the system is aligned and compatible. Consider systems change as a gestalt process where the whole is greater than the sum of its parts. The graphic depiction in Figure 2.3 provides a visual overview of the eight gears that make the model work.

Figure 2.3:

Gears in the System

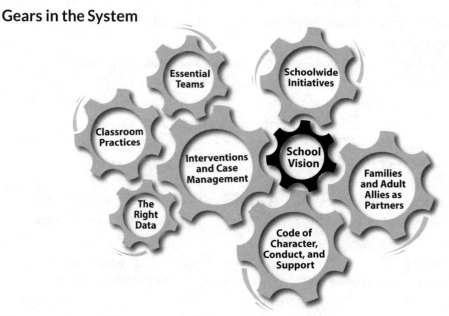

These gears will be explored in detail in Section 2.

School Vision, Chapter Five

A school's vision encompasses its mission, core values and beliefs and makes up a central "gear" in the model. A foundational step for any school looking to improve their discipline practices is to start by examining and articulating beliefs around discipline and ensuring that disciplinary practices are aligned with the school vision.

Code of Character, Conduct, and Support, Chapter Six

One of the three key principles in the federal guidelines for improving school climate and discipline centers on the development of "schoolwide disciplinary policy that sets high expectations for behavior, provides clear rules and developmentally appropriate and proportional consequences that are consistently applied, and uses disciplinary incidents to help students learn from their mistakes, improve their behavior, and meet high expectations."[12] For most districts and schools, meeting these standards will require close examination and changes to their code of conduct.

Essential Teams, Chapter Seven

Our work in middle and high schools has revealed the necessity for establishing four distinct teams that drive the work involved in implementing effective policies and practices related to discipline and student support. They are: (1) the Administrative Team, (2) the School Climate-Discipline Team, (3) the Student Support Team, and (4) the School (or grade level) Intervention Team. Each team has clearly delineated roles and responsibilities and uses structured protocols to organize and manage the work of the team.

The Right Data, Chapter Eight

Collecting, disaggregating, analyzing, and using the right set of data is an essential first step to improving school climate, assigning the right consequences and delivering the right interventions, and ultimately improving students' overall behavior and academic performance. Data must also be integrated in ways that capture a holistic portrait of each student with the capacity to generate weekly individual student reports. Equally important is making data transparent and accessible with particular attention to indicators that reveal overuse of exclusionary sanctions and disproportionality among various student groups.

Schoolwide Initiatives, Chapter Nine

An effective discipline and student support model focuses equal, if not more, time and effort on promotion and prevention measures as it does on reactive responses to discipline incidents. Schoolwide initiatives promote a positive school climate through activities and practices that increase student voice; maintain a safe, orderly, and attractive physical environment; and foster caring and civil communication among and between adults and young people.

Classroom Practices, Chapter Ten

Teacher mindsets, knowledge, skills, and practices impact school climate and culture. They play a critical role in schoolwide discipline. This gear highlights the importance of implementing some core universal classroom practices that align with the school's goals for discipline, create orderly and engaging classrooms, support students to develop greater self-discipline, prevent most discipline problems, and use restorative processes to intervene when behavioral concerns persist.

Interventions and Case Management, Chapter Eleven

Two notable changes in the federal guidelines center around interventions and case management: (1) a stronger push for schools to develop more articulated supports and interventions; and (2) a push to increase the numbers and the capacity of school-based behavior and mental health specialists to meet the needs of students who are experiencing academic, behavioral, and mental health challenges. Anyone familiar with PBIS (Positive Behavior Supports and Interventions) or RtII (Response to Instruction and Intervention) will recognize the benefits of using a three-tiered framework to support students with different behavior and learning needs. Research indicates that a tiered framework of care and support is an effective and efficient way to (1) promote pro-social behaviors, (2) prevent misbehaviors from escalating or repeating, and (3) provide interventions for students who need a more intensive response to turn around their behavior.[13]

A tiered framework is essential because different groups of students need different amounts of time, attention, tasks, and supports to behave responsibly, achieve at high levels, and become college- and career-ready. For example, students who may require more flexible and individualized interventions are those with IEPs, BIPs (Behavioral Intervention Plan), and 504 Accommodation Plans, as well as those students experiencing a family or personal crisis or students exhibiting chronic aggressive behaviors.

- **Tier 1** focuses on promotion and prevention. It serves all students in the school by establishing universal expectations, common classroom practices, and schoolwide initiatives accessible to all. Promotion efforts foster the personal, social, and academic efficacy of all students through schoolwide and classroom practices and programs. They teach, practice, recognize, and assess the skills, habits, and mindsets to encourage self-discipline and responsible behavior. Prevention efforts in the classroom enable teachers to intervene early, help students to re-engage, and defuse behavioral challenges before they become unmanageable. Schoolwide prevention efforts are intended to avert disciplinary incidents in public spaces and reduce negative social behaviors and high-risk behaviors among all students.

A Three-Tiered System of Support

TIER 1 PROMOTION and PREVENTON for all students

TIER 2 INTERVENTIONS assigned to students who meet specific criteria or thresholds

TIER 3 INDIVIDUALIZED INTERVENTIONS

- **Tier 2** interventions are provided for students who need additional academic, behavioral, or emotional support. Students participate in accountable, restorative interventions when they have committed high impact behavior violations or when unwanted behaviors become persistent. Sometimes these interventions are carried out by the teacher, other times they are carried out by the teacher in cooperation with other school staff and administrators. Additionally, they are carried out by assistant principals, deans, student support staff members, and mental health professionals.

- **Tier 3** interventions are provided for students with the highest level of need who require even more intensive and individualized interventions that are likely to last for an extended period of time. Interventions for these students are usually provided by counselors, social workers, psychologists, case managers, youth development specialists, and other trained mental health professionals. A typical Tier 3 intervention would involve the development of a comprehensive student success plan for students who are experiencing multiple academic, attendance, and behavioral challenges that erode a student's capacity to function successfully at school.

Both Tier 2 and Tier 3 interventions, delivered within a coherent case management system, are discussed in detail in Chapter Eleven. See Figure 2.4, which lays out the principles behind a three-tiered framework.

Figure 2.4

Three-tiered Framework

Tier 1			Tier 2		Tier 3
Schoolwide norming through alignment of core beliefs, values, and practices with the school code of character, conduct, and student support.	Classroom management and discipline practices, procedures, and instructional supports that align with school-wide rules and expectations and foster student engagement. Students learn and practice habits of learning and self-discipline.	When unwanted behaviors occur, teachers use "real time" strategies and practices that enable most students to self-correct, re-engage and get back on track.	When students engage in chronic unwanted behaviors, teachers use restorative conferencing to engage students in reflection and planning that will help them right themselves, repair harm, restore their good standing, and make it right.	Restorative interventions beyond the classroom for students whose behavior problems persist, who experience serious emotional distress, or who commit serious behavior violations that require more intensive interventions.	Restorative interventions for the highest needs students who receive intensive, individualized interventions, on-going coaching, and close progress monitoring.
Promotion		Prevention	Intervention		

Families and Adult Allies as Partners, Chapter Twelve

Middle and high schools are working to become more proactive and more strategic in their efforts to engage families and adult allies in supporting students' academic progress, their health and well-being, and their aspirations for the future. Administrators, school staff, and even parents themselves vastly underestimate the power of parent and family influence on students' performance in school and their postsecondary aspirations.

The Critical Need for Shared Responsibility of Student Discipline

Efforts to improve discipline must be implemented at the whole school and classroom levels. A school's efforts to improve schoolwide discipline and student support are dependent on efforts to implement parallel policies and practices in classrooms. The alignment between what people see, hear, and do in the larger school community and what people see, hear, and do in the classroom needs to be transparent to all stakeholders (administrators, staff, students, and families/adult allies).

Too often, administrators and student support staff are charged with developing and implementing schoolwide discipline while issues of classroom discipline remain the private domain of each individual teacher.[14] This type of bifurcated thinking can easily lead to an adversarial mantra from faculty that "Discipline is not my job —you fix it," inappropriately pitting the interests of administrators and student support staff against the interests of classroom teachers.[15] Furthermore, an artificial division of disciplinary responsibilities results in inconsistent and incoherent messages to students about what matters and what is the right thing to do.

Ultimately, discipline and student support must be seen as everyone's job. At the heart of a healthy school culture is the commitment of all staff to take responsibility for the healthy development of students. They must model the skills, behaviors, and mindsets they seek to cultivate in young people. The word *discipline* has everything to do with instruction. Among its Latin origins are the words, *discipulus* which means "pupil or learner" and *disciplina* which means "teaching, training, and instruction" in the broadest sense. Supporting students to become more self-disciplined involves teaching and practicing the habits, skills, and mindsets that strengthen students' personal efficacy (their belief in their capacity to manage their emotions, self-regulate, set goals, plan ahead, problem solve, and persevere.) Multiple studies confirm the role that self-discipline plays in improving students' academic performance and preparing students to be college- and career-ready.[16] We owe it to students to make the development of self-discipline a primary outcome for every student in every class.

We hope that the descriptions of these essential features have both clarified and inspired your thinking. While this chapter is intended to serve as a thought-provoking introduction, Section Two of this book will provide further insight and details on ways to make these gears (components) a functioning system in your school.

---

[1] US Department of Education. (2014). Guiding Principles: A Resource Guide for Improving School Climate and Discipline. Washington, D.C.

[2] Bower, T.G.R. The visual world of infants. Scientific American. (1966) 215,80–92

[3] Deal, T.E, & Peterson, K.D. Shaping School Culture: Pitfalls, Paradoxes, and Promises (2009) Jossey-Bass.

[4] Perkins, B.K. Where We Learn: The CUBE Survey of Urban School Climate. https://www.nsba.org/sites/default/files/reports/Where-we-learn_1.pdf

[5] Adelman, H.S., & Taylor, L. (2005). Classroom climate. In S. W. Lee (Ed.), Encyclopedia of School Psychology, Thousand Oaks, CA: Sage.

[6] Noddings, Nel. (1992) The challenge to care in schools: an alternative approach to education, New York: Teachers College Press.

[7] ibid

[8] Tauber, R. (2007) Classroom Management, Sound Theory and Effective Practice. Santa Barbara, CA.

[9] Dewey, J. (1916) Democracy and Education: An introduction to the philosophy of education. New York: Macmillan

[10] Byrk, A. & Schneider, B. Trust in Schools: A Core Resource for School Reform. March 2003, Educational Leadership pp. 40 –45.

[11] Wheatley, M. Leadership and the New Science: Discovering Order in a Chaotic World (1999) Berrett-Koehler Publishers.

[12] Guiding Principles: A Resource Guide for Improving School Climate and Discipline. (2014) US Department of Education.

[13] Beezley Mrazek, P. & Haggerty, R.J. (1994) Reducing Risks for Mental Disorders:

[14] Lortie, D. (1975) School Teacher. Chicago: University of Chicago Press

[15] Payne, C.M. So Much Reform and So Little Change: The Persistence of Failure of Urban Schools (2008) Harvard Education Press.

[16] ACT, Inc. (2007). Impact of cognitive, psychosocial, and career factors on educational and workplace success. Iowa City, IA. Balfanz, R., Herzog, L., & MacIver, D. (2007). Preventing student disengagement and keeping Students on the graduation path in urban middle grades: Early identification and effective interventions. Educational Psychologist, 42(4), 223 –235.

3

Understanding the Theories Behind the Model

What informs how and why we discipline the way we do?

The Research Reality

In the last 15 years, the educational community has become fixated with the notion of making sure every practice it undertakes is "research-based." We have gotten to the place where administrators and teachers rarely consider implementing a practice without asking the critical question, "What is the research behind this?" Given this climate and the current popularity of ranking instructional practices based on their effect size, we would be remiss if we didn't make intentional efforts to explain the research and theories that inform all aspects of our model.

While we applaud the call for research-based best practices, we would like to offer some cautions about over reliance on the current array of research-based disciplinary practices in secondary schools. First, the existing formal research base on effective secondary discipline and student support systems and practices is very limited in scope. Second, evidence of promising practices emerges from more than the formal research base of universities, government grants, and outsourced evaluations. Given the relentless pressure to make educational inquiry more scientific, the power of other kinds of less formal evidence-based data has diminished. School-based empirical evidence collected through observation, experimentation, and action-research inquiry can also tell powerful stories of promising practices as well as clarify which practices are less effective.

For example, a multiple-year project involving five Chicago-area high schools that delivered a three session skill building intervention to students involved in physical fighting resulted in no additional aggressive incidents for over 80 percent of the students. Although the collection and analysis of the data was internal, it is no less of a promising practice. At another school their data revealed that over three-quarters of the students assigned to in-school suspension received more than three in-school suspensions within a two month period. The in-school suspension program was clearly not generating the desired results they had expected. Both of these cases illustrate the value of school-based empirical evidence.

In developing this book, we wanted to share what is currently working to improve school discipline, knowing that it might be ten or more years before formal research catches up. It is a fact that right now students, teachers, and administrators need innovative ideas for reducing the discipline problems that exist in too many of our schools. We hope this book serves as a call to action.

Developing an inclusive research base for secondary discipline models is necessary, and it will be challenging. This chapter begins by suggesting some possible reasons behind the current limitations of secondary school discipline research. Next we discuss where our model fits in a continuum of theories that explain learning and human behavior and outline why our model moves away from a behaviorist approach. At the end of the chapter we offer snapshots that provide a more detailed look at selected theories and thought leaders who have informed our work with schools and the practices we promote.

The Limitations of Secondary School Discipline Research

In favor of candor and disclosure, we have tried to take a clear-eyed look into the muddy depths of discipline research. Our search for robust evidence that supports our model (or any other model of schoolwide discipline in secondary schools) produced limited results. Unfortunately, we know far more about what is not effective with adolescents than what is. The limitations of the discipline research base prompt a cautious skepticism about conclusions and recommendations that emerge from the research, particularly as they relate to discipline and student support practices that specifically support adolescents.

First, a comprehensive meta-analysis and study of middle and high school systems of discipline and student support are non-existent. In their literature review of schoolwide discipline codes and policies, Loyola University researchers noted that "the study of schoolwide discipline policies is in its infancy" and has received surprisingly little attention in comparison to other aspects of discipline and student behavior.[1] Other facts reveal the dearth of research on schoolwide policies and practices in secondary schools. *The Handbook of Classroom Management,*[2] a 1,300 page compendium of disciplinary research and practice, focuses almost exclusively on classroom discipline and conditions that influence student behavior in the classroom. There is no such research handbook that focuses on schoolwide discipline and student support or its impact on both students and school climate and culture. In the same vein, a review of discipline books and articles available online revealed a ten-to-one ratio of publications focused primarily on classroom management and children with "difficult" behaviors compared to publications that examined system-wide models of discipline and student support.

Although Positive Behavioral Supports and Interventions (PBIS) is frequently cited as a promising strategy to improve discipline in secondary schools, much of the data on successful PBIS implementation are culled from schools where PBIS is implemented as a "value-added" program — not typically as part of a reimagined model that actually tackles the overhaul of discipline rules and the use of exclusionary practices that have proven to be both ineffective and harmful to young people. Although many PBIS schools report reductions in total numbers of office discipline referrals and suspensions, they do not report comparative reductions in disproportional referrals and suspensions among different student groups.

A second research limitation centers on the subjects of discipline research. If a primary goal is to seek out research-based practices that will better serve adolescents, a big roadblock stands in the way. The subjects of most disciplinary research are elementary school-age children. For example, the robust research base that reveals strong links between social and emotional learning and better behavior and higher academic performance draws heavily from elementary school programs. Moreover, it is surprising to learn how many "proven-effective" programs and practices emerge from research on very young children. Even classroom management models that serve K–12 students, often begin as K–5 or K–8 programs and rely heavily on research conducted with elementary students to keep their "proven effectiveness" status.[3]

The age-level bias in discipline research may exist for a number of reasons. Some researchers defend a "one size fits all" view of discipline and human behavior – what works for young children works for all children, including adolescents. Another factor, however, may explain why elementary age children are more likely to be the subjects of discipline research specifically and educational research in general. Elementary school settings are far more conducive research environments, especially if one is engaging in research that seeks out a causal relationship: application of Treatment A will result in Outcome A. There are fewer children, fewer teachers to train at any one grade level, and most importantly a stable learning environment in which one teacher usually has 25 to 30 students in her charge every day for a year. In contrast, secondary students are likely to have seven teachers at any one time, seven different learning environments, and may even change courses and teachers each semester. Given this many variables, sussing out clear conclusions is a dubious proposition at best.

Third, when adolescents are the subjects of behavior research, the research setting itself becomes a limitation. Much of the "gold standard" research on adolescent behavior takes place in hospitals, treatment centers, juvenile facilities and residential and day schools for students with special needs. Transferring and replicating adolescent behavior programs and treatment models to middle and high school settings successfully is fraught with challenges. For starters, schools are not clinical settings, students are not patients, and teachers are not clinicians. A resource rich infrastructure, a cadre of highly trained mental health specialists who work with young people in one-to-one and very small group settings, and saturated treatment dosage (in many cases daily therapeutic sessions) are critical factors that contribute to successful results in many behavior intervention programs. These conditions are seldom present in regular school settings. Only recently have mental health providers and youth development specialists begun to think collaboratively with educators about the best ways to transfer and deliver effective interventions inside a regular school environment.

A Continuum of Theories About Learning and Behavior

Not knowing the sources of what we do and why we do it can lead to an unconscious acceptance of what's already in place or prompt hasty decisions to commit time and resources to the "latest and greatest" discipline fix because it initially sounds like a good idea. Thus it is critical to pause and closely examine the key theories that have shaped current beliefs about human behavior. Keeping the educational practitioner in mind, and acknowledging some oversimplification in advance, the continuum presented in Figure 3.1 is intended to be a lay person's quick guide to the distinguishing features of three psychological paradigms that offer different explanations of learning and behavior.

Figure 3.1

Three Psychological Paradigms that Inform School Discipline and Student Support[4]

	Behaviorist Theory and Practice	Our model draws from these two psychological paradigms.	
		Social-Cognitive Theory and Practice	Cognitive-Humanist Theory and Practice
Fundamental Principles that Explain Learning and Behavior	All behavior is determined by the external environment. Personal agency (free will) is an illusion. All behaviors are accompanied by consequences, and these consequences determine whether these behaviors are repeated. With the right operant conditioning using rewards and punishments any person can be trained to perform any task. Only what is observable and measurable is what is valued.	Behavior is a result of continuous reciprocal interaction between cognitive, behavioral, and environmental influences. Most human behavior is learned observationally through modeling: from observing others one forms an idea of how new behaviors are performed, and on later occasions this coded information serves as a guide for action. Social-cognitive theory has been called a bridge between behaviorist and cognitive learning theories because it encompasses attention, memory, and motivation.	Human beings have agency to choose and act, aim at goals, are aware that they cause future events, and seek meaning, value, and creativity. Free will is a reality. Thoughts, feelings, and environmental stimuli interact with each other to drive growth and development. Cognitive learning theory emphasizes perception, thinking, and memory. Personal agency, personality, motivation, insight, and discovery influence learning and behavior.
Thought Leaders	Ivan Pavlov, B. F. Skinner, Edward Thorndike, John B, Watson	Albert Bandura, J. D. Hawkins and R. F. Catalano, Albert Ellis, and Roger Weissberg, Mark Greenberg, and Joseph Zins (pioneers of SEL, social and emotional learning)	(Cognitive) Kurt Lewin, Jerome Bruner, Lev Vygotsky, Jean Piaget (Humanist) Abraham Maslow, Carl Rogers, William Glasser, Rudolf Dreikers, Edward Deci and Richard Ryan
Beliefs about Children	General distrust in children's capacity to think, reflect, and solve problems.	Intentional observation, modeling, and practice support students' capacity to think, reflect, and solve problems.	Expectant trust in children's capacity to think, reflect, and solve problems.
Goal	Carefully prescribed skill development and a highly controlled environment enable a child to be successful in the desired environment adults have created.	Skill mastery and self-regulation produce personal efficacy.	Student-centered academic, social, emotional, and moral development produce personal efficacy and the capacity to choose and live a good life.
Use of Power	Coercive Power (punish by means of meting out discomfort, unpleasant action, undesirable activity, verbal threat, reprimand, or berating.) Reward Power (reward by distributing or withholding desired rewards such as concrete objects, food privileges, activities, social reinforcement such as attention.)	A combination of coercive, reward, referent, and expert power.	Referent Power (power through relationships and identification with authority figure.) Expert Power (power through special knowledge and skills that someone desires or respects.)

Dominant Communication Style	Authoritarian: Command language, more rigid demands and learning goals, correction through reprimand and punishment, more emphasis on compliance and direct instruction.	Often varies according to the design of the program.	Authoritative: Invitational language, assertive expectations but more flexible learning goals, correction through invitation and conferencing, more emphasis on engagement, cooperation, and collaborative learning.
Function of Undesired Behaviors	The function of all behavior is to (1) get the desired thing one wants; (2) get attention of peers or adults; or (3) avoid or escape undesired demands, people, or situations in which skill deficits are pronounced.	Undesired behaviors are caused, in part, by social skill deficits: (1) social acquisition deficit (I don't know how); (2) social performance deficit (I can do it, but choose not to do it in specific situations); (3) social fluency deficit (I can do it, but don't always know when or where to do it or to what extent to do it.)	Undesired behaviors are a response to unmet needs and wants related to survival, belonging, autonomy, respect, power, freedom, and fun.
Interventions to Change Behavior	A change in the external environment (A = antecedent or stimulus) will prompt a change in the student's behavior (B= behavior) by resulting in a different consequence shaped by rewards and punishment. (C = consequence) A+B=C	Interventions involve social skills training—a sequence of steps that include explicit instructions, modeling, discussion, role-playing and behavior rehearsal, and feedback and reinforcement.	Interventions are "client-centered" and involve internal mental processing of thinking and emotions that drive motivation to act and generate insight and transformation to learn and change.
The Role of Community	Community matters only insofar as the group serves as the vehicle for shaping good behavior of individuals. Social control is attained through individual and group reinforcement and individual punishment.	Development of a cohesive group is an important condition for many social skills programs. Social control is attained through individual and group reinforcement, feedback, and individual punishment.	Belonging and reciprocal affiliation are basic needs. Social control is attained through accountability within a democratic learning community and shared responsibility to live up to social expectations and obligations, to respect the rights of others, and to practice the skills needed for public participation and good citizenship. The idea of community is informed by an ethos of care, justice, and empathy.
Notable Discipline and Skill Development Programs	BEP: Behavior Education Program, PBIS: Positive Behavior Supports and Interventions, Good Behavior Game, No Nonsense Nurturer (also known as Assertive Discipline), Tools for Teaching, Safe and Civil Schools	Boys Town Safe and Healthy Secondary Schools, Aggression Replacement Training, Skillstreaming for Adolescents, EQUIP: Teaching Adolescents to Think and Act Responsibly	Judicious Discipline, Social Discipline, Cooperative Discipline, Positive Discipline, Discipline with Dignity, Choice Theory, Authoritative Communities: The Scientific Case for Nurturing the Whole Child

Moving From a Behaviorist Paradigm to an Accountable and Restorative Approach

Our approach to schoolwide discipline and student support moves away from reliance on a behaviorist paradigm for many reasons. First, a behaviorist approach assumes that humans have no personal agency and that external factors (whether environmental conditions or the actions of other human beings) entirely determine who we are and what we do. As B. F. Skinner, behaviorism's most famous champion said, "I did not direct my life. I didn't design it. I never made decisions. Things always came up and made them for me. That's what life is."[5] We reject this view of the human condition and see behavior as the result of internal and external conditions: an individual's cognitive processing; her social and emotional development and moral reasoning; and an individual's complex interactions in the external environment. Behaviorism tends to ignore the role that motivation, choice, reflection, and empathy play in choosing how to behave.

Second, while many behaviorists emphasize the reward side of conditioning and shaping behavior more than the punishment side, fidelity to the theory requires both, and both punishments and rewards come with a catalogue of cautions and caveats. Although punishment may result in a quick fix, it may never address underlying problems that lie beneath an observable behavior. If we assume that the intention of punishment is to reduce the occurrence of unwanted behaviors, the data show, convincingly, that punishing adolescents rarely produces improvements in behavior.[6] Moreover, punishments appear to be least effective with students who are emotionally charged or who exhibit the most problematic behaviors.[7]

The downside of rewards has been chronicled in popular and research literature. Deci and Ryan call rewards "control by seduction."[8] Although "if-then" rewards may work for low-level tasks with a simple set of rules and a very clear predetermined end product or performance, rewards tend to worsen performance of more complex tasks that require some element of critical analysis, problem solving or creativity. Alfie Kohn asserts that "one of the most thoroughly researched findings in social psychology is that the more you reward someone for doing something, the less interest that person will tend to have in whatever he or she was rewarded to do."[9] Daniel Pink adds that, "Better performance is built more around intrinsic motivation, around the desire to do things because they matter, because they're interesting, because they're part of something important."[10] For children, the novelty of rewards may be motivating at first, but may also create situations in which students behave in order to receive a reward rather than experiencing internal satisfaction accrued from doing the right thing. When the rewards go away, the desired behavior may go away as well.

Behaviorism's overreliance on external control and compliance prompts another caution. Too much teacher-centered instruction that emphasizes compliance more than engagement may, in fact, impede the development and mastery of habits of learning and self-discipline that cultivate self-regulation, self-management, and perseverance — skills that are positively correlated with good grades, college- and career-readiness, and degree completion. Students who are constantly "managed" and told explicitly what to do, when to do it, and how to do it are likely to have a much tougher time internalizing self-regulation skills that enable students to take responsibility for their learning and behavior.

Alternatively, an accountable and restorative approach embraces the notion that behaviors are best influenced by modeling and teaching preferred behaviors and providing opportunities for students to practice, self-reflect, and get corrective feedback on skillful and respectful ways of behaving. Taking elements from both the social-cognitive theory and social-humanist theory, we believe that students learn behaviors from their social and educational contexts and that their actions are also the results of their choices. We contend that students need to be able to independently assess their options, foresee potential consequences, and ultimately make good choices about how to behave in any given situation. When we understand the developmental learning process and accept that students have agency, rewards and punishments can seem like a simplistic solution to complex and nuanced behavior challenges.

When students require Tier 3 interventions, functional behavior assessment (FBA) and applied behavioral analysis (ABA) are always identified in behaviorist literature as the "go-to" protocols of choice, yet they are rarely used in school-based settings outside of special education, and show little effectiveness with adolescents outside of more sheltered learning environments and treatment programs where so much of behavior research actually takes place. Completion of an FBA or ABA demands enormous amounts of time over many weeks, involves multiple interactions with large numbers of adults, and requires a high degree of expertise. These factors may inhibit both their use and effectiveness in schools.

On the other hand, both social-cognitive theory and cognitive-humanist theory inform a variety of strategies for preventing serious behavior infractions and providing effective Tier 3 interventions. For example, the one-to-one conferencing protocols we promote in this book help students mediate their own thinking resulting in increased self-awareness and better problem solving abilities.

Finally, though behaviorism, on its face value is politically neutral, no theory comes without values that influence its conceptualization and its practices. The deterministic underpinnings of behaviorism are undemocratic and in many ways contradict Americans' deeply felt values of freedom, self-determination, due process, respect for the rights of others, civility and civic-mindedness, and protection of minorities and the marginalized. Whether we acknowledge it or not, every school creates its own moral-political universe in which a school's specific discipline practices will mirror the values of the larger school culture. The last 30 years of public education have witnessed an inverse relationship between the growing reliance on behaviorist educational practices and the diminishing commitment to educate for democracy. The civic mission of schooling has all but disappeared.

Choices have consequences, and a school's choice of theories and models ultimately drives the end goals of schooling as well as the end goals of discipline. America's public schools have a long tradition of promoting the primary aims of education: a rich and balanced academic education and the transmission of democratic values, a civil culture, and civic dispositions from one generation to the next. A behaviorist model can surely support the acquisition of academic skills, higher standardized test scores, and perhaps even better behavior when the grown-ups are around to monitor and reward or punish it. In the end, however, it nurtures neither good character nor good citizenship. Alternatively, the approach we advocate is grounded in our belief that schools have the ability and the responsibility to nurture future generations of citizens who act in ways that are caring, accountable, and just towards others.

Theory and Thought Leaders That Inform the Model

For those of you looking for additional information about the big ideas that inform our model, we have provided snapshot summaries of select theories and their thought leaders in this section as well as a list of Recommended Resources for Further Reading in Appendix A.

Mental Health Levels of Prevention and Support

Thought Leaders: Howard Adelman, Linda Taylor, Robert J. Haggerty, Patricia Beezley Mrazek, David Osher, Kevin Dwyer, Jeffrey Sprague, and George Sugai.

Goals: Provide universal prevention, learning, and behavioral supports to inoculate everyone against risks. Make sure early interventions are provided to those who appear to be at some risk in order to reduce the numbers of students who are at severe risk and who require the most intensive interventions.

Assumptions and Core Principles: Children's behavior improves when schools provide the right tiers of supports and interventions that match students' specific learning and behavioral needs. Three tiers of learning and behavioral supports and interventions promote positive behavior, prevent inappropriate, unacceptable, and unskillful behaviors, help reduce and eliminate barriers to learning, and support students' acquisition of more positive mindsets and more skillful behaviors.

Social Support Theory and the Ethics of Care

Thought Leaders: Sidney Cobb, Carol Gilligan, Gloria Ladsen-Billings, Valerie Lee, Julia Smith and Nel Noddings.

Goals: Mediate stressors that may become barriers to learning and positive behavior by providing high social and emotional support and strong personal relationships.

Assumptions and Core Principles: Children thrive and do better in school when they feel supported, cared for, and feel positively attached to others.

Particularly for students of color; and for students who live in poverty are underserved and underperforming the quality of the student-adult relationship and the adult's commitment to know the student personally will often determine a student's willingness to learn and cooperate in school and in the classroom. Social support theory is based on the perception and actuality that one is cared for, "I expect to be helped and cared for," one has assistance available from other people, "I can count on _____ to be there," and one is part of a supportive social network, "I belong to a community of people who will respond to my needs." The ethics of care promotes a relational view of community, puts caring relationships front and center, and speaks of the ethical obligation to do what is right when we interact with others. Social support is conceptualized in terms of close relationships (companionship), enduring reciprocal communication, and positive emotional connections; it also includes access to tangible resources and information. High social support reduces stress, fosters personal agency, "I can do it," and increases focus and attention to the situation at hand.

Risk and Protection Theory, Psycho-Educational Prevention, and SEL (Social and Emotional Learning)

Thought Leaders: Albert Bandura, R. F. Catalano, John C. Gibbs, Arnold Goldstein, Ross Greene, J. D Hawkins, Roger Weissberg.

Goals: Teach the knowledge and skills needed for competent daily living that help young people develop more mature and accurate cognitive habits and behavioral skills that support more responsible thought and behavior.

Assumptions and Core Principles: Direct modeling, teaching, practice, and assessment of social and emotional competencies increases students' capacity to self-regulate and function effectively as individuals and within a group in the classroom. Adolescents' mindsets and skill sets are not fixed; young people have the capacity to restructure cognitive habits that have become barriers to responsible behavior. Early identification of risk factors (that predict increased likelihood of anti-social/high risk behaviors) is an essential first step to enhancing and expanding the right protective factors that exert a positive buffer against negative influences of risk factors and also promote positive youth development. Strong bonding to families, schools, communities, and peer groups (including attachment→positive emotional connections and commitment→personal investment in the group), forms the foundation of protection. Children's bonding is affected by (1) the quality and frequency of opportunities for active involvement in pro-social/youth development activities in the family and classroom; (2) the skills that children learn and apply in these social groups; and (3) the reinforcements and recognition provided to children in response to their behavior in these groups. Social and emotional learning (SEL) involves the processes through which children and adults acquire and effectively apply the knowledge, attitudes, and skills necessary to understand and manage emotions, set and achieve positive goals, feel and show empathy toward others, establish and maintain positive relationships, and make responsible decisions.

Challenging behaviors are best understood as a byproduct of lagging cognitive skills (rather than a result of attention-seeking or avoidance-seeking behaviors). Students who get in the most trouble at school often experience (1) developmental delays in moral judgment; (2) self-serving cognitive distortions; and (3) social and self-management skill deficits. Successful interventions address all three of these issues.

Choice Theory, Client Centered Communication, Self-Determination Theory

Thought Leaders: Edward Deci and Richard Ryan, William Glasser, Carl Rogers and Jerome Freiberg.

Goals: In a supportive environment that fosters autonomy and competence, adolescents become more responsible through awareness that they choose their behavior, that choices have consequences, and that collaborative problem solving will lead to better choices and better behavior.

Assumptions and Core Principles: Humans control their behavior to fulfill their need for satisfaction in one or more of these five areas: survival, to belong and be loved by others, to have power and importance, to experience freedom and independence, and to have fun. These needs shape our choices, and thus our behavior. Although we cannot control our feelings and physiological reactions directly, we can control how we think about, and act on our feelings. When people experience autonomy, competence, and relatedness, their commitment to learn and use more successful strategies and behaviors increases, and they are more likely to maintain new behaviors over time. Many behavioral problems are "relationship problems," thus relationship building in a democratic, caring environment is a critical component in quality schools and classrooms. Maintaining a change in behavior over time depends on a person's internal motivation and requires a person to internalize value for the skill and develop a sense of autonomy and competence in using the skill. For adolescents, interventions need to help develop a student's skill, "I can do it," but also need to develop a student's will, "I want to do it," for new behaviors to be maintained. Communication that is supportive, responsive, encouraging, accepting, respectful, and non-judgmental (versus communication that is critical, blaming, threatening, and judgmental) supports positive relationships and encourages students to be open to taking responsibility for their behavior. When students experience a sense of being respected, understood, and cared for by adults, providing behavioral interventions, they are more likely to engage in the hard work (reflection, correction, and practice) of changing behavior.

Restorative Justice

Thought Leaders: John Braithwaite, Paul McCold, Belinda Hopkins, Margaret Thorsborne, Ted Wachtel, Howard Zehr.

Goals: According to restorative justice pioneers McCold and Wachtel, the aim of socially restorative practices is developing a relational community that manages conflict and tensions by repairing harm and restoring relationships.[11] All parties affected by an incident, in which someone has harmed other people or the community, come together in a conference or circle in order to express their thoughts and feelings about the incident, share how the incident impacted those who were harmed, and reach agreement about what the offender will do to repair the harm done to the relationship and the community.

Assumptions and Core Principles: Restorative practices are rooted in the concept of "restorative justice," a new way of looking at criminal justice that focuses on repairing the harm done to people and relationships."[12] In the context of schools, most disciplinary incidents are about more than rule violations – they involve people who have been harmed or adversely impacted by the incident. Unless there is some resolution involving all parties, the people involved and the community are not able to move on to restore the community and the relationships. Human beings are more cooperative, responsive, and more likely to make positive changes in behavior when others do things with them, not to them or for them. The process of accounting for one's behavior, listening to those harmed who share the impact of the offender's behavior, and reaching a collaborative agreement for making things right, encourages those harmed to accept a "change of heart" and motivates the offender to change her behavior.

Restorative processes involve three primary stakeholders – the harmed person who seeks reparation, the person who has committed the harmful act and takes responsibility for her actions, and their communities of care who support reconciliation between the two parties. Those who are most directly involved and affected by the incident should have the opportunity to participate fully in a process that feels safe and supportive and builds relational trust. The degree to which all stakeholders are involved in meaningful emotional exchange and decision-making is the degree to which the outcome is fully restorative. Justice requires that we work to restore those who have been injured or mend relationships that have been harmed in order to restore order, safety, and calm to the community.

From a social discipline perspective, students are accountable for their behavior and must take some action with the support of a caring adult to make things right.[13] Restorative inquiry, conferences, and circles, the vehicles for engaging in a restorative practice, are informed by "fair process,"[14] that incorporates (1) engagement – involving individuals in decisions that affect them by listening to their views and genuinely taking their opinions into account; (2) explanation –

explaining the reasoning behind a decision to everyone who has been involved or who is affected by it; and (3) clarity of expectations – making sure that everyone clearly understands a decision and what is expected of them in the future. Through deep listening and dialogue, a restorative approach builds the capacity to empathize[15] by taking in the perspective of the others and supporting the development of moral reasoning about what is right and just.[16]

Restorative inquiry is grounded in a few basic questions:

1. What happened? (What was your role in what happened?)
2. What were you thinking and feeling at the time?
3. Who else was affected by this? How?
4. What have been your thoughts/feelings since then? What are you thinking/ feeling now?
5. What do you want to do to make things right?
6. What can I (others) do to support you?
7. When a situation like this comes up again, what actions might you take next time?

The mindsets we bring to a conflictual situation will determine the successful use of restorative inquiry. As important as it is to train staff and students to use a restorative inquiry protocol, it is the mindsets that we bring to the protocol that shift our thinking and our actions from a punitive to a restorative approach.

- *I have chosen to be a responsive listener in this situation.*
- *I value the speaker who has the right to be listened to and taken seriously.*
- *I bring my interest and curiosity about the speaker's thinking with me. I'm leaving my assumptions and pre-judgments about the situation behind.*
- *I seek to understand the situation from the speaker's point of view, even though I may see it differently. I want to know what you're thinking, what you're feeling, and what you need.*
- *I can and will validate the speaker's feelings.*
- *I care more about the future than the past. I want to move forward.*
- *I believe that a Win-Win outcome is possible—one that satisfies some important needs of people involved and seeks to maintain or mend the relationship.*

Ecological Approach to Classroom Management

Thought Leaders: Walter Doyle, P. V. Gump, Jacob Kounin, Gregory Schraw.

Goals: An ecological approach to classroom management utilizes the physical environment, high structure routines and procedures, immediate cues and prompts, and high levels of student involvement to capture, hold, and sustain students' engagement while minimizing classroom disruptions.

Assumptions and Core Principles: This approach enables students to become a high functioning group that is part of a dynamic classroom system by cultivating students' cooperation, engagement, and motivation, rather than relying on compliance, control, and coercion.[17] From an ecological perspective, activity management is as important as student management. Thus, instructional pacing, situational interest (external strategies and environmental stimuli capture and hold students' engagement) and personal interest (internal value placed on the content, activity, or goal) are critical tools for effective instruction.[18] Teachers who manage students effectively are acutely attuned to the environment and the ebb and flow of students' focus and energy. They demonstrate what Kounin calls "with-it-ness," the capacity "to scan the room while attending to other tasks; anticipate potential problems and learning gaps; sense a potential problem immediately and identify it accurately; and intervene promptly and unobtrusively before minor off-task behaviors become major disciplinary incidents."[19] Classroom order is established and maintained when students are engaged in the flow of the academic work task at hand, whether they are active or passive participants in the moment.[20]

Conflict Resolution Theory

Thought Leaders: Morton Deutsch, Ralph Kilmann, Kenneth Thomas.

Goals: Teach adolescents how to problem solve and resolve conflicts constructively in ways that solve the problem and maintain or restore relationships.

Assumptions and Core Principles: Adolescents have the capacity to resolve conflict. They learn how to handle conflict from the adults they observe. Conflict is viewed as a normal and natural part of life; it arises from unmet human needs or disagreements over resources, goals, values, or beliefs. Conflict can be positive and offers opportunities to learn and grow. How a person navigates the tensions between concern for oneself and concern for others will shape the conflict style that one chooses to use: force, accommodate, avoid or exit, postpone, compromise, or problem solve and negotiate a win-win solution. Win-Win solutions are non-violent, meet important needs and interests of both parties, and feel positive and satisfying to both parties. The concept of Win-Win is both a belief and a process. If parties do not think a Win-Win solution is possible, they are unlikely to use a Win-Win process. With students, everything adults do or say will either escalate or de-escalate the situation. Adults' physical stance and movement, tone of voice, emotional intensity, and choice of words will move the situation a step up toward a major confrontation or a step down to a place where the adult and student respond to the situation while keeping each other's respect and dignity intact.

Moral Development and Character Education

Thought Leaders: Mary Belenky, John C. Gibbs, Carol Gilligan, M.L. Hoffman, Lawrence Kolhberg, Thomas Lakona, Jean Piaget.

Goals: To develop moral convictions and qualities of character that lead to living good lives, exercising good citizenship, and engaging in right action.

Assumptions and Core Principles: Our moral selves evolve with time and experience. The development of "character" involves an individual's thinking, feelings, and behavior. Moral development and character education promote the individual's construction and commitment to a set of core ethnical values: justice, fairness, civility, courtesy, honesty, respect, rights and responsibility, tolerance rights, and concern for the welfare of others. It also promotes the development of character attributes like generosity, empathy, trustworthiness, and honesty. The development of moral judgment moves from exclusive dependence on external authority (parents, schools, civil law, religious doctrine) as the source of moral decision making to exercising one's independent judgment based on the sum of experiences that influence one's moral reasoning and one's principled convictions of what is right (justice) and what is good (empathy). Empathy is "the spark of human concern for others, the glue that makes social life possible,"[21] and thus the "bedrock of prosocial morality in which cooperation and the capacity to feel what others feel (empathy/perspective taking) are adaptive traits that are essential for human survival."[22]

Democratic Schools, Authoritative Communities, and Judicious Discipline

Thought Leaders: John Dewey, Forrest Gathercoal, Commission on Children At-Risk.

Goals: A primary aim of schooling is to prepare students to live in a democracy.

Assumptions and Core Principles: Students' first experience in civic (public) culture is likely to be their attendance in public schools. Students are viewed as citizens with rights and responsibilities within the school community. Discipline policies and practices serve as a platform for learning about one's rights and responsibilities and learning to regulate one's personal behavior in ways that do not violate interests of the school community or interfere with the interests and rights of others. Students' rights (freedom, justice, and equality) are informed by the Constitution and Bill of Rights and practiced within civil society. These rights must be balanced with responsibilities to behave in ways that support the school community's interests and needs for order, safety, and maintenance of a learning-focused environment in which all students can achieve their educational goals. "Children are hardwired for enduring connections to others and for moral and spiritual meaning." In a democratic society, children and youth are most likely to thrive when they experience institutions offering both warmth and structure that are created and sustained by dedicated individuals with a shared vision of building a good life for the next generation. It's about the power of building meaningful relationships within a community that champions decency, fairness, and goodness."[23]

---

[1] Bohanon, H., Fenning, P., Carney, K. L., Minnis-Kim, M., Anderson-Harriss, S., Moroz, K. B., & Pigott, T. D. (2006). Schoolwide Application of Positive Behavior Support in an Urban High School: Journal Of Positive Behavior Interventions, 8(3), 131–145.

[2] Evertson, C. M., & Weinstein, C. S. (2006). Handbook of classroom management: Research, practice, and contemporary issues.

[3] "An Overview and Comparison of School Discipline Models and Approaches," 2013.

[4] Lieber, C. (2013) Unpublished manuscript. Cambridge, MA. Engaging Schools.

[5] Skinner, B. F. (1953). *Science and human behavior*. Simon and Schuster.

[6] Lewis, T.J, Sugai, G. (1999) Effective Behavior Support: A Systems Approach to Proactive Schoolwide Management. Focus on Exceptional Children, ERIC.

[7] Bear, George G. (2010) School Discipline and Self-Discipline: A Practical Guide to Promoting Prosocial Student. The Guilford Press.

[8] Deci, E., & Ryan, R. (1985). Intrinsic Motivation and Self-Determination in Human Behavior. Springer Science & Business Media.

[9] Kohn, A. (1993). Punished by rewards: The trouble with gold stars, incentive plans, A's, praise, and other bribes. Boston: Houghton Mifflin.

[10] Pink, D. (2009, July). The puzzle of motivation. TED Conference. Lecture conducted from TED Global.

[11] Wachtel, T. and McCold, P. (2003, September 10). In Pursuit of Paradigm: A Theory of Restorative Justice. XIII World Congress of Criminology. Lecture conducted from International Institute for Restorative Practices, Rio de Janeiro.

[12] Wachtel , T. Defining Restorative. (2012) International Institute of Restorative Practice.

[13] Zehr, H. (1990). Changing lenses: a new focus for crime and justice. Scottdale, PA.: Herald Press.

[14] Kim, W., & Mauborgne, R. (1997). Fair process. *Harvard Business Review*, 65–75.

[15] Hoffman, M. (2000). Empathy and moral development: Implications for caring and justice. Cambridge, U.K.: Cambridge University Press.

[16] Kohlberg, L. (1984). The psychology of moral development: The nature and validity of moral stages. San Francisco: Harper & Row.

[17] How can we improve school discipline? Osher, Bear, Sprague, Dole. Educational Researcher. Vol 39, No. 1, pp. 48–58. 2010 AERA.

[18] Schraw and Lehman (2001) Situational interest: a review of the literature and directions for future research. Review of Educational Research, 51, 23–52.

[19] Kounin, J. (1977). Discipline and group management in classrooms. Huntington, N.Y.: R.E. Krieger Pub.

[20] Evertson, C. M., & Weinstein, C. S. (2006). Handbook of classroom management: Research, practice, and contemporary issues. Chapter 5.

[21] Eisenberg, N., & Morris, A. S. (2001). The origins and social significance of empathy-related responding. A review of empathy and moral development: implications for caring and justice by ML Hoffman. *Social Justice Research*, 14(1), 95–120.

[22] ibid

[23] Hardwired to connect: The new scientific case for authoritative communities. (2003). New York: Institute for American Values.

Adolescents and Discipline

In what ways do the cultural and developmental needs of adolescents drive the goals of our schoolwide discipline and student support approach?

CHAPTER OUTLINE

Introduction
The Collision Between Adolescent Development and Disciplinary Practices
Adolescent Development and Identity
Understanding Students Who Are At-Risk
Our Most Challenged and Challenging Students
School Discipline - What Students Want and Need

Introduction

In our work with districts and schools, we often discover that schoolwide discipline policies and practices do not align with the cultural and developmental needs of adolescents. School discipline can be unforgiving, and at times, shaming of students for mistakes and misbehaviors that are developmentally normal during adolescence. A punitive school discipline approach absent of strategic interventions to help students become more skillful and self-disciplined, can leave them feeling confused, angry, embarrassed, and distrustful of the adults who care for them. For students who enter school with complex social, emotional, and behavioral profiles these feelings are exacerbated and have the potential to be long-lasting.

Adolescents are at the heart of our work in secondary schools. Understanding them, with their myriad complexities, is essential to supporting their healthy growth and development. Our students come to school influenced by social, cultural, and environmental factors, whether positive or negative, which impact their engagement in school, their academic success, and their relationships with their peers and adults. Moreover, from a discipline perspective, adults' understanding of adolescents' developmental and cultural needs has a profound impact on students' perception of discipline and their responses to the adults they encounter during day-to-day disciplinary interactions.

The Collision Between Adolescent Development and Disciplinary Practices

We have all encountered teenagers who can misread situations, make impulsive decisions, react to a perceived tone of voice, are physically and cognitively disorganized, and who have difficulty focusing and sustaining attention. When analyzing office disciplinary referral data, we learn that students are being referred for irrational emotional outbursts, issues with impulse control, and the need for immediate satisfaction and attention—all of which are part of the adolescent experience. School staff members often appear to have gaps in their knowledge about their students' developmental needs and identities, and they have expressed an interest in learning more about the students with whom they work.

It is in an adolescent's job description to test us, and it is our job to analyze the range of behaviors that make appearances every day in our classrooms and schools. It is our job to be relentless about looking for as many interpretations of what might be happening to and within the adolescent that result in the behaviors we see. Often, the discipline policies and practices in schools focus on students' end behaviors and are about punishment with very little time devoted to engaging students in a reflective process about what led to their behavior and the harm they have done to themselves, others and/or the community.

Neuroscientists over the last decade have discovered that the teen years are crucial to cognitive development. The brain undergoes a significant growth spurt during this period leading to a surprising degree of malleability. In other words, adolescents' habits and behaviors are not yet hard-wired; they are absolutely capable of changing their life trajectories. The prefrontal cortex, often referred to as the CEO of the human brain, is in a constant "cycle of growth and reorganization"[1] throughout adolescence. Research indicates that the prefrontal cortex "may not be completely wired until adolescents hit their early 20s.[2] Coupling brain development with social, cultural, and environmental influences creates the potential for many students to walk through their day-to-day experiences at school with some degree of vulnerability. In response, savvy teachers are in tune with students' developmental considerations in order to preserve their own focus, sanity, sense of humor, and investment in their students and their craft as teachers.

The research on teenage brain development is welcome news to all of us working with adolescents. The notion of looking through a developmental lens is a paradigm shift and an opportunity for educators to engage in a collective dialogue about establishing discipline practices that will support students to strengthen their self-discipline, resiliency, and efficacy when they have failed to meet behavioral expectations.

Adolescent Development and Identity

Every adolescent is on a developmental journey, a personal and public journey to young adulthood. The period we define as adolescence (ages 11-19) is one where students are grappling with who they are. They are experimenting, challenging, and questioning the world around them in order to make meaning of the variety of experiences and interactions they have throughout the school day. Adolescents enter our schools with a wide range of emotions: excitement and curiosity, fear and anger, and a driving need to be in control and make choices. They need to belong and "to feel liked and likeable, if not even lovable."[3] As educators, we are responsible for understanding, embracing, and influencing the young people in our care. Our charge is to ensure that every student has a safe and supportive school and classroom environment both physically and psychologically; a school where they have a variety of opportunities to experiment in healthy and productive ways and try on new behaviors, beliefs, and values. Figure 4.1 identifies key developmental benchmarks during adolescence.

Figure 4.1

Developmental Benchmarks for All Adolescent Students

1. **Maturation:** Adolescents establish their own identities; become more intimate with peers, seek acceptance from peers, and attain a sense of belonging within peer groups; develop mature relationships with family; achieve a growing sense of autonomy, control, and mastery in the world.

2. **Learning and Cognition:** Adolescents become more critical and abstract in their thinking; develop greater self-awareness, reflection, and decision making skills; thrive on controversy, and problem solving; prefer active learning experiences and social interactions with their peers; and desire a voice in their choices of courses, what they learn, how they learn it, and how they demonstrate what they have learned.

3. **Learner Needs:** Adolescents' experience of schooling and their attitudes toward learning are varied and influenced by their learning readiness, preferences, and prior knowledge; their personal interest, effort, and motivation; their racial and cultural identity, gender, and class; their family background; and their developmental needs; adolescents need different amounts and kinds of time, attention, tasks, and supports to learn successfully, achieve at high levels, and behave responsibly.

4. **The Adolescent Experience:** Adolescents need reassurance that what they are experiencing, doing, thinking, and feeling is normal. It is absolutely normal for adolescents to experience and express intense emotions, challenge authority and critique adults' beliefs and positions; experiment and take risks; sleep at odd hours, and spend considerable time "goofing around and hanging out."

Understanding that a student's intellectual, social, emotional, ethical, and identity development are inextricably linked deepens our awareness of how these factors influence their development, and needs to be at the center of the conversation of what adolescents want, need, and deserve from school discipline policies and practices. Understanding how our own ethnicity, family background, and experiences influences our values and beliefs about adolescents, learning, and discipline will help us develop our capacities to deepen our empathy and compassion for the inner lives of our adolescents. This includes the worlds that adolescents navigate outside of school and the vast range of thinking, learning and feelings they grapple with on a day-to-day basis.

Schools need to consider how goals for discipline are responsive to the identities and developmental needs of our students. At the outset, we would like to note that all adolescents are trying on multiple identities as they mature into young adulthood. Some aspects of their identity will remain permanent while others will shift over time and with experience. Given the role of identity development during the adolescent journey, an awareness of racial identity development among students of color is of particular importance. Racial identity development refers to how students' racial self-identification influences perceptions, emotions, and behaviors of themselves and people in other groups.

Students who enter our school communities are accompanied by layers of cultural and historical experiences that contribute to their racial identity. As students move from one setting to the next their attitudes, mindsets, and behaviors may vary from one class to the next period. There are many variables that contribute to these shifts: the adult, the subject matter, the particular composition of peer groups, and/or the activity in which they are asked to participate. At times, the context of the learning environment can feel threatening to the student's identity, marginalizing a student's sense of opportunity. If we work with adolescents and wish to meet them where they are, we must "go there," to where they live racially – even when, and perhaps particularly when – "going there" takes us beyond our educational comfort zones."[4] Figure 4.2 captures some key aspects of adolescent racial/ethnic identity development attributed to students of color.

Figure 4.1

Key Aspects of Adolescent Identity Development and Racial/Ethnic Identity*

1. **Increased Awareness of Racial/Ethnic Identity:** All adolescents become increasingly aware of themselves as social beings, and their perception of self tends to be highly dependent on acceptance and affirmation by others. Students of color become increasingly aware of their racial/ethnic identity during adolescence and their identification with, and attachment to, peer groups can sometimes override other attachments to family, parents, and teachers in importance. As students of color get older, they also become more aware of the politics associated with race, becoming more cognizant of racial hierarchies and prejudice, even if they cannot articulate what it all means.[5]

2. **The Negative Impact of Stereotype Threat:** The work of Claude Steele and others has shown that students of color "are highly susceptible to prevailing stereotypes related to intellectual ability. When 'stereotype threats' are operative, they lower the confidence of vulnerable students and negatively affect their academic performance."[6]

3. **Distancing from Dominant White Culture and White Adults and Peers:** For many students of color, a common and absolutely natural reaction to the prejudices and biases that they witness, read about, or experience in school and the larger community, is a distancing from cultural values or institutions that may be perceived as "White." For some students of color, concerns about "acting White" (vs. "acting cool" in front of their peers), can lead to a temporary or even a permanent rejection of education as a direct pathway to their future aspirations. Research suggests that students' association of educational achievement with the dominant White culture is more likely to occur when students feel excluded from a school's academic culture and opportunities.[7] Overt patterns of bias displayed by some White educators (i.e. lower expectations, harsher punishments and more excessive use of suspension, and teacher talk that communicates dislike for and frustration with students of color) can sometimes trigger growing distrust and anger toward White people in positions of authority.

4. **Pathways to a Strong Racial/Ethnic Identity:** There is no single pathway to adolescent individuation and development of one's racial/ethnic identity. However, researchers of adolescent racial identity note that students of color who experience success in school and life engage in many of the following behaviors:

   - Adopt multiple identities to successfully navigate the worlds of adults, family, and peers in school and in the neighborhood[8]
   - Engage in an on-going investigation of one's ethnic and family heritage
   - Participate in groups, events, and movements organized by people within their own ethnic/racial group that foster positive racial identity and ethnic pride
   - Actively challenge racial stereotypes, stand up to discrimination and harassment, and reject the "rejecter"
   - Actively pursue and excel in some activity that counters common stereotypes of what people in different ethnic groups "do" or "do not do"
   - Seek out mentors who look like them

*Racial identity "refers to a sense of group or collective identity based on one's perception that he or she shares a common heritage with a particular racial group."[9]

Understanding Students Who Are At-Risk

"Risk and well-being are socially constructed, and schools play a key role in the dynamic processes that contribute to school failure and success."[10] As we take a look at some typical profiles of students at-risk who often need more intensive interventions, it is important to note that being at-risk is not a permanent condition. All students have the capacity to turn around their life trajectory, especially when schools provide a strength-based model of supports and interventions.

Students who are at-risk can experience a range of personal and environmental circumstances (e.g., homelessness, high mobility, poverty) that can increase the likelihood of encountering challenges in attending, succeeding, and remaining in school, particularly when students lack the supports that promote resiliency.[11] Risk factors are elements that raise the odds of poor outcomes and diminish the likelihood of successful development. While they do not predict or guarantee a particular outcome, risk factors can become long-term stressors that threaten students' health and well-being. Protective/resiliency factors have a positive influence and create a buffer against stressors. They do not eliminate risk, but they do moderate it. Figure 4.3 shows how a student's healthy development and success in school can be affected by both risk and protective resiliency factors and the complex balance and interplay among them.[12]

Figure 4.3

Spheres of Influence	Risk Factors	Protective/Resiliency Factors
INDIVIDUAL	Early aggressive behavior; Developmental delays associated with impulsiveness, poor judgment, and poor social skills	Self-Control; Personal and social efficacy; Positive sense of identity and future aspirations
FAMILY	Lack of parental supervision; Substance abuse; Serial crises; Family conflict; Abuse	Parental monitoring; Positive attachment to family; High expectations; Clear boundaries
PEERS	Negative peer group; Drug availability	Positive peer group; Pro-social bonding
COMMUNITY	Poverty; Drug availability; Violence	Strong neighborhood institutions and attachment; Anti-drug use policies; Violence prevention; Youth development opportunities
SCHOOL	Alienation from school; Poor grades; Suspension; Truancy; Lack of supportive school environment; Feeling disliked and disrespected	Strong attachment to school; Academic competence; Positive relationships w/ adults; Personalized caring and support; High academic and behavioral expectations; Clear boundaries; Youth development opportunities

A few words about aggression and aggressive students: the tendency to behave aggressively increases as students move from childhood to early adolescence.[13] Although the incidence of bullying behaviors is highest among 8th and 9th grade students, elementary school students tend to have more conflicts with peers while adolescents tend to have more conflicts with adults. Students' social skills and interpersonal effectiveness actually *decline* in early and middle adolescence before young people become increasingly competent at navigating new social settings, new kinds of relationships, and new social expectations during older adolescence. Thus, modeling, teaching, practicing, and assessing social skills is essential for 12 to 15 year olds, to ensure that students do not lose so much ground. Students who behave aggressively over a long period of time share four things in common:

1. They are unable to identify their own emotions, "read" the feelings of others, or empathize with the target of their aggression.

2. They have difficulty predicting the consequences of their actions.

3. They do not have constructive strategies for getting what they want; aggression, whether verbal, psychological, or physical, is often the only tool in their conflict tool box.

4. They present a "hostile attribution bias" in ambiguous conflict situations, immediately attributing hostile or aggressive intentions to others before they appraise what is actually happening.[14]

Having a better understanding of students who are at-risk is one thing; understanding these adolescents with compassion and empathy is quite another. These are often tough kids because they have had difficult lives and have a hard time "doing" school. They often feel disliked by teachers and peers. They often lack the skills, confidence, and motivation to take on the identity of a learner and a cooperative classmate. Their aggressiveness toward adults and resistance to authority may look and sound like a personal attack, but more often this stance serves the purpose of self-protection.

Dr. Ross Greene, who wrote *The Explosive Child* and *Lost at School* has written extensively about explosive and behaviorally challenged children and adolescents. Dr. Greene reminds us that this group of students needs a kind of deep understanding from those who care for them and teach them. Students with seriously challenging behaviors:[15]

- Are often responding to specific, unresolved problems that are usually highly predictable and can, therefore, be resolved proactively.

- Do not respond positively to punitive consequences like detention, suspension, expulsion, and isolation. In fact the "get tough" approach to building character often backfires and makes things worse.

- Experience genuine delays in developing flexibility and adaptability; tolerating frustration; expressing emotions appropriately; strengthening self-regulation, and engaging in constructive problem solving.

- Require the same care, attention, and guided instruction that we readily provide for students with reading and math problems.
- Want to be respected; have their concerns heard and their perspectives viewed as legitimate and important.
- Deserve an analysis of root causes that moves beyond simplistic labels like "attention-seeking" and "avoidance of unpleasant tasks."
- Experience improvement when the primary goal of intervention is to collaboratively solve these problems in a realistic and mutually satisfactory way that no longer triggers the challenging behavior.
- Need to learn and practice social skills and mindsets that will help them navigate in multiple settings with all kinds of people.

Our Most Challenged and Challenging Students

It has been our experience that the number of students with the most challenges can reach up to 50 students in a building of 1,000 students. What separates this group from other students at-risk is their disproportionately adverse impact on teacher and student morale and on the learning environment as a whole. Put simply, these are students who have great difficulty complying with social norms and navigating through the school day without causing constant disturbances in classrooms and public spaces. And, although they usually make up no more than two to five percent of the student population, this group will include a few students who actually do suffer from conduct disorders, and a few students whose explosive and dangerous behaviors persistently threaten others' safety.

The behaviors of this select group are familiar to anyone who has worked in a secondary school. These students accumulate significant numbers of behavior violations that typically include: leaving class and school without permission; arriving late and leaving early; walking the halls during class time; having physical altercations with peers; exhibiting argumentative and refusal behaviors with adults; and displaying abusive, hostile, and aggressive communication with peers and adults. They often avoid schoolwork and express their anger, frustration, distrust, and need for respect and attention through end-behaviors of non-completion, non-compliance, non-cooperation, and outward defiance of authority. However, it is their relentless involvement in one conflict after another inside and outside the classroom which draws everyone's attention to them, wearing both them and the adults around them down.

To say that these are adolescents with significant and complex issues is an understatement. Although their end-behaviors may look and sound similar, root causes of these behaviors are all over the map. Some students may "use their agency to resist—both actively and passively—the imposition of alienating demands. In their attempts to create and maintain their own sense of autonomy, dignity, and safety they often act tough and demonstrate little respect for school norms and adult authority. Although this resistance may feel good to youth in the short term, it further alienates them from learning, reinforces the oppositional behavior of their peers, and evokes counter-aggressive behavior of adults."[16] Regardless of the combination of personal and family crises, and serious academic, behavioral, and mental health problems, the overload of risk factors without the benefit of sufficient protective factors can make healthy choices and a healthy life feel like unreachable aspirations.

It is also important to note that many of these students have experienced repeated school failure that spans years if not their entire school career. Severe academic skill gaps can exacerbate students' disconnection from school. Unfortunately, the result is feeling "less safe, less supported, and less academically challenged than most of their peers."[17] They often experience school as aversive, particularly when they (along with others who look like them) experience academic tracking, demoralized and disempowered teachers, and punitive and exclusionary discipline.[18] Changing the projection of deeply rooted school-based behaviors for our most challenging students demands creative solutions beyond exclusion. Increasingly, schools are developing in-school opportunities that provide modified schedules, alternative academic programs, and more therapeutic learning environments that carefully scaffold academic successes and strengthen personal and social efficacy in ways that support a student's transition back to a regular school program. It would be naïve not to expect that the road back for some will be long and hard. This is exactly why these adolescents need the care and attention of our most skillful educational practitioners.

School Discipline – What Students Want and Need

An accountable and restorative approach to discipline that is developmentally aligned and supportive of adolescents fosters a school culture where students' identity, social, emotional, and learning needs are front and center and where their emerging capabilities are respected and cultivated. From an adolescent's perspective, the qualities of respect and fairness are the "must haves" that inform developmentally aligned discipline. These two qualities, more than any others, help create relational trust among students and staff. They cultivate a culture in which students are willing and able to right themselves and turn failure to thrive into a commitment to succeed.

---

[1] Lamke, S., Pratt, D., & Graeve, S. Safe and Healthy Secondary Schools (2009) Boys Town Press.

[2] Giedd, J. (1999). Brain development during childhood and adolescence: A longitudinal MRI study. Nature Neuroscience, 2(10).; Strauch, B. (2003). The primal teen: What the new discoveries about the teenage brain tell us about our kids. New York: Doubleday; Casey, B., Tottenham, N., Liston, C., & Durston, S. (2005). Imaging The Developing Brain: What Have We Learned About Cognitive Development? Trends in Cognitive Sciences, 9(3), 104-110.

[3] ibid, pg. 91

[4] Nakkula, M. J., & Toshalis, E. (2006). Understanding youth: Adolescent development for educators. Harvard Educational Publishing Group.

[5] Fergus, E., Noguera, P., & Martin, M. (2014). Schooling for resilience: Improving the life trajectory of Black and Latino Boys. Harvard Education Press.

[6] ibid

[7] Carter, P., (2005) Keeping It Real. New York: Oxford University Press.

[8] Phelan, P., & Davidson, A. (1998). Adolescents' worlds: Negotiating family, peers, and school. New York: Teachers College Press.

[9] Helms, J.E., I also Said, "White Racial Identity Influences White Researchers" The Counseling Psychologist April 1993 21: 240-243.

[10] Osher, D. (2015). The Pedagogy of Real Talk and the Promotion of Student Well-being and Success: Forward to Paul Hernandez, The pedagogy of real talk: Engaging, teaching, and connecting with students at risk (viii-ix). New York: Corwin.

[11] Haggerty, R.J., Sherrod, L.R., Garmezy, N. & Rutter, M. Stress, Risk and Resilience in Children and Adolescents; Processes, Mechanisms, and Interventions. Journal of Child Psychology and Psychiatry, Volume 37, Issue 2, page 237, February 1996)

[12] Catalano R, Hawkins J. The social development model: a theory of antisocial behavior. In: Hawkins JD, ed. Delinquency and Crime: Current Theories. New York, NY: Cambridge University Press; 1996:149-197.

[13] Aber, J. L., Pedersen, S., Brown, J.L., Jones, S.M., Gershoff, E.T. (2003) Changing Children's Trajectories of Development Two-Year Evidence for the Effectiveness of a School-Based Approach to Violence Prevention.

[14] Brown, J., Jones, S., LaRusso, M., Aber, L. Journal of Educational Psychology 2010, Vol. 102, No. 1, 153–167 Improving Classroom Quality: Teacher Influences and Experimental Impacts of the 4Rs Program.

[15] Adapted from Bill of Rights for Behaviorally Challenging Kids, Lives in the Balance website. http://www.livesinthebalance.org/bill-rights-behaviorally-challenging-kids.

[16] Osher, D. (2015). The Pedagogy of Real Talk and the Promotion of Student Well-being and Success: Forward to Paul Hernandez, The pedagogy of real talk: Engaging, teaching, and connecting with students at risk (viii-ix). New York: Corwin.

[17] Osher, D. & Kendziora, K. (2010). Building conditions for learning and healthy adolescent development: Strategic approaches. In B. Doll, W. Pfohl, & J. Yoon (Eds.) Handbook of youth prevention science. New York: Routledge. ; Spier, Garibaldi, & Osher (2012).

[18] Osher, D. (2015). The Pedagogy of Real Talk and the Promotion of Student Well-being and Success: Forward to Paul Hernandez, The pedagogy of real talk: Engaging, teaching, and connecting with students at risk (viii-ix). New York: Corwin.

Section 2

The Gears that Drive the Model

5

School Vision

To what extent does your school's mission, beliefs, and values provide direction for your schoolwide discipline and student support model?

Introduction

Without a coherent vision, a school lacks direction, which can result in a host of problems, including a disconnect between what a school says it believes and actual disciplinary policies that it carries out. What does our school value, believe in, and hope for? Holding a strong vision helps the school establish a common understanding of their desired destination for their staff, students, and families. A vision must inspire and announce to all stakeholders where the school is headed and why they should embark on the journey.

The School Vision gear enables a school to use its mission, core beliefs, and core values to inform its disciplinary policies, practices, and student support systems. If a school is in a place where the vision and mission are unclear, teams can begin with this process as all other school improvement efforts need to align with it.[1] We have included discussion questions and interactive exercises throughout this chapter that can assist school teams in examining their school vision.

Developing a Coherent School Vision

A school vision is an aspirational description of what the community would like to achieve or accomplish in the mid- or long-term future. A coherent vision "provides a compass to keep learning on course."[2] This vision influences the direction of the school's mission, core values, and core beliefs. The intentional alignment between these helps shape the goals for discipline and student support policies and practices. This, in turn, informs the school's message about discipline and student support that is communicated to students, families, and staff. Discipline and student support can be placed at the center or in the margins of a school's work, based on the choice of language that is used to communicate mission, beliefs, and values.

Mission

When a School Climate-Discipline team comes together to draft their goals, policies, practices, and protocols for their schoolwide discipline and student support model, the mission statement needs to be at the center of the conversation. The **mission,** to use Peter Drucker's words, "is broad and eternal."[3] It is "why" the organization exists.[4] Good mission statements are often comprised of just one pithy sentence that communicates: (1) who you are, (2) what you do, (3) your primary purpose, and (4) an expected outcome of your work or a key indicator of success. Mission statements matter because they drive what gets time and attention. Three mission statements in Figure 5.1 generate three different pictures of a high school student's experience.

Figure 5.1

Mission Statements

1	2	3
Through rigorous course work, character development, and leadership opportunities, X-High School will graduate young adults who are self-directed, intellectually engaged and possess a commitment to personal and civic responsibility.	The mission of X-High School is to facilitate and support all students to learn and demonstrate essential academic skills, personal and social efficacy, and qualities of character and citizenship that enable them to graduate college, career, and life ready.	The mission of X-High School is to ensure that all students can demonstrate mastery of common core standards through the challenges of a rigorous curriculum that will guide them to college entrance and success.

Discussion Questions about the Mission

1. What do these three mission statements communicate about these schools? What do they say about the role of personal, social, and learning development in the educational program?

2. What are the key ideas or phrases you already have or would like to see in your own mission statement?

3. In what ways does your mission statement inform or align with your goals for discipline?

Beliefs

Beliefs "represent the core understandings about student capacity"[5] and the ways an organization conducts itself and does its work. Beliefs serve as a guide for how adults view and carry out their roles and responsibilities within a school. Leaders that co-create beliefs with their staff will see the benefits of their efforts because their voice was being considered. When engaging in belief building it is important to have the mission statement available, sample belief statements, and a conversational structure that will help staff imagine what it would look like if these were living in the hearts and minds of the teachers, administrators, and staff as they move through their day.

We offer several belief statements about students, teachers, and administrators that inform our work when we partner with school staff members on school climate, culture, and discipline.

Beliefs about Students

- Students invest in school because of the presence of trusting and caring relationships with adults.
- Respecting student voice garners their cooperation and commitment; and providing student choice makes their voice central, and learning differentiated and relevant.
- Establishing routines creates safety through predictability, allowing students to engage their "thinking brain" to take intellectual risks.
- Establishing learning protocols fosters positive interdependence and develop students' ability to comprehend and make meaning of what they are learning, which results in students' self-direction.
- Different groups of students need different kinds and amounts of time, attention, tasks, and supports to behave responsibly and succeed academically.
- Each and every adolescent is capable of changing their behavior with guidance, instruction, support, and coaching.
- The ability to notice and step in quickly and discreetly to prevent or defuse unwanted behaviors helps students to self-reflect and self-regulate leading to shifts in their behaviors.
- Students who are respected and treated fairly understand and can anticipate consequences leading to self-discipline.
- Meaningful interventions help students to learn more skillful behaviors when encountering challenging situations.
- Restorative actions done by students, not to students, enable them to self-correct, problem solve, make amends, repair harm, and restore their good standing.

Beliefs about Teachers

- Personalized relationships between and among teachers, students, and their families must take into account the varied student characteristics in a classroom. "It's my responsibility to take strategic and intentional steps to know the developmental levels, race, ethnicities, cultural backgrounds, socio-economic status, and ability of my students; and to craft an educational program and create a classroom culture that maximizes the capacity of all students."
- Effective classroom management creates order. "It is my job to create rituals, routines, procedures, and academic and behavioral expectations to support a high-achieving, high-performing classroom."

- At the heart of a healthy school classroom is the teacher's commitment to model, teach, practice and assess the skills, behaviors, and qualities they seek to cultivate in their students. "It's my job to intentionally expose and train students on a set of academic behaviors, mindsets, and social emotional competences that support habits of participation, communication, and discipline."
- Academic achievement is linked to the coupling of high expectations with high levels of support for all students. "It is my job to help students do their best and be their best."
- Motivation is an internal quality driven by a person's feelings, thoughts, beliefs, and experiences. "It is my job to create hope by building each student's expectation of success and communicating my confidence in the student's ability to succeed."
- Responses to disciplinary problems restore order. "I know that students will make mistakes and will learn from their mistakes, and it is my job to help them self-correct, re-engage, and remain in the classroom."

Beliefs about Administrators

- School leaders have a vision (mission, core values and beliefs) that is transparent and ever-present in the ongoing dialogue and work of school.
- School leaders have a responsibility for creating a culture where students are to be inquisitive, resourceful, energetic, and responsible for their own learning and behavior; and hold the same expectation for every adult in the school, and most especially themselves.
- School leaders value the persistent questions presented to them. They have a responsibility to harness the dynamic energy of the school culture to promote problem solving, effective decision making, and healthy relationships.
- School leaders have a responsibility to co-create with staff the structures, policies, and procedures that will shape a safe, engaging, orderly, and positive school climate.
- School leaders promote and model supportive accountability based on relational trust among and between administration, staff, students, and families.
- School leaders strategically use resources to systematically monitor and assess the programs and people supporting the school improvement goals.

Discussion Questions about Beliefs

1. What beliefs from this sampling align with your mission? In what ways are they part of the ongoing dialogue to support students' social, emotional, and learning development?

2. What beliefs would you like to see as part of your vision alignment? How do they support the mission of your school?

Schools should consider selecting or composing belief statements to guide their vision.

Core Values

Core values "capture a deeper sense of a school's priorities"[6] and define the standards that schools hold. Core values underlie our work. They serve as a kind of shorthand for the big ideas associated with a good education; the qualities of character to which we aspire; how we present ourselves in the world; and how we treat each other in it. Schools that have developed critical core values see them as an unwavering and unchanging guide for students, staff, and families, as they work together to fulfill the mission of their school. Core values take the mystery out of how we will interact with each other. Core values will address how staff will conduct themselves in all aspects of communication with each other, and in interactions with students and their families. It will address, for example, how they communicate with others in the classroom, in the parking lot, and in the faculty room, as well as at a meeting and via email.

Core values provide direction for what we want to model and teach our students. For thirty years, we have asked the following question to educators and parents to elicit a quick snapshot of the values they hold. "If you could teach one thing to every student and every student would really learn it, and as a staff we could live by this one value in our day-to-day interactions, what would that one value be?" Over three decades and hundreds of opportunities, the list stays remarkably stable and usually includes most of the following words and phrases included in Figure 5.2.

Figure 5.2

Values

Respect	Self-Discipline	Accountability
Team Work	Efficacy	Effective
Work Ethic	Perseverance	Communication
Caring	Equity/Diversity	Personal Responsibility
Excellence	Critical Thinking	Academic Mastery
Empathy	Self-Direction	Cooperation
Engaged Learning	Literacy	Problem Solving

Discussion Questions about Core Values

1. When you look at these values, which ones align with your mission statement?

2. In what ways do these core values live in your schoolwide disciplinary policies and practices?

Consider identifying core values to guide your vision for your schoolwide discipline and student support system.

School Vision Alignment

When crafting a school's mission, beliefs, and core values, it is important to ensure that these critical documents are aligned in language, intention, and spirit. Being purposeful and identifying overarching themes to convey the vision helps the design team be intentional when crafting the mission, and core beliefs and values. One should see a repetition of words, phrases, and themes running through these documents that convey an overarching message about what the school believes and values. Looking through this lens of consistency and coherence when drafting and/or revising these documents will ensure alignment and result in a mission, and core beliefs and values that will be foundational to the development of an accountable and restorative schoolwide discipline and student support model. When the alignment is transparent, it provides steady direction, and there is no doubt about what a school champions within the classroom and the larger culture.

Another form of alignment is the congruence between the school vision (mission, beliefs, and values) and the expectations, policies, and practices defined in the school's code of character, conduct, and support. When there is a solid vision, a School Climate-Discipline Team (SCDT) can begin to analyze the expectations, policies, and practices and see how they stack up against the mission, beliefs, and core values. In our experience with districts and schools across the country, this exercise often reveals a mismatch between the language, intention, and spirit of the vision and their code of character, conduct and support.

When a SCDT gathers to examine the alignment between all of these documents, it can feel like walking through a labyrinth and getting lost along the way. We offer the metaphor of looking for the "red threads" of alignment as you navigate among your various documents. Identifying alignment will guide your process.

Interactive Exercise: Red Thread Alignment

On the facing page is an example of "red thread" alignment that begins in a mission statement and weaves its way through to discipline policies and practices.

As you read through the graphic, highlight repeated words and phrases ("red threads") that convey what this school stands for. What are the evidences of alignment?

Mission
The mission of X-High School is to facilitate and support all students to learn and demonstrate essential academic skills, personal and social efficacy, and qualities of character and citizenship that enable them to graduate college, career, and life ready.

Core Beliefs
All young people are capable of changing their behavior with guidance, instruction, support, and coaching.

At the heart of a healthy school culture is the adult commitment to model the skills, behaviors, and qualities they seek to cultivate in their students.

Core Values
Personal responsibility, cooperation, personal and social efficacy

Behavior Expectations
Manage yourself responsibly and be self-disciplined.

Treat others with a sense of respect, decency, and dignity

Accept responsibility for the consequences of your behavior and do something to make the situation right.

Goal for Discipline Policies and Practices
Increase every student's capacity to self-regulate and interact positively and responsibly with others.

The Role of Staff Members in Discipline and Student Support
All adults communicate to students, "It's my job to help you do your best and be your best."

School Rule
Use appropriate and respectful language with students and adults.

Violation
Inappropriate language including teasing, taunting, put-downs, racial slurs, profanity, name-calling, or verbal threats directed at any student or adult.

School Sanctions/Consequence:
Conference with administrator or dean; notification and conference with parent

Intervention:
Restorative conference with person who was targeted, an action of apology, session with Student Support Coach to discuss the impact of aggressive language and practice alternative ways of expressing oneself, and/or progress monitoring of student's use of language across classes.

Making Time and Building Commitment

When schools discover few intersects between one document and another, Peter Senge reminds us that "the gap between vision and current reality is also a source of energy."[iv] If there were no gaps, there would be no need for any action to move towards a more coherent vision. We anticipate when working with schools that misalignment between the vision and the code of conduct, character, and support will be there, and we see this as an opportunity. We are very sensitive to the time it takes to be thoughtful and thorough when engaging in a review and analysis of your school vision (mission, core beliefs, and values) and your code of character, conduct, and support. We are confident that you are asking some of the following questions: How do we carve out the time to make a space for this critical conversation? What are the ways to engage teachers, students, staff, and families in the conversation? How do we keep our vision alive? What might our first steps be when tackling the alignment opportunity? Whether you are reading this book in the summer, fall, early winter, or spring, it is never too late to start the process of keeping your vision in front of your work. A core part of your conversations stem from your vision. It is a strategy that informs your decisions with regard to school improvement plans and initiatives throughout the year. We offer a couple of entry points, considerations, and ideas for addressing these questions:

1. Keeping the vision (mission, core beliefs and values) alive: Find natural ways to embed the mission statement into existing structures/conversations:
    *   If you have a mission statement that has institutional memory and is working for the school, pull it out and bring it into staff meetings, key decision making meetings, and meetings with students and families. Reference it in authentic ways and link it to the outcomes of the meeting. This will add credibility to the dialogue at hand. It will also lend support to new and alternative perspectives as well as changes in behaviors.
    *   The mission can be an anchor for strategic conversations and activities at the start of a new year with all staff and in new staff orientation. Lead the staff through an interactive activity where they have to unpack the vision and name the values and beliefs of the school. They might identify practices in which they engage that link to the vision.

2. Aligning your vision (mission, core beliefs and values) initially takes a dedicated steering committee that has the time and interest to dive into this work. It is critical to have a senior administrator, a Student Support Team member, and teacher leaders as part of this effort. Ideally, choose strategic points in the process to invite students to participate in the discussion. Identifying and sharing the goals and outcome for this work with staff sets the stage for the conversations related to "how we have done things around here"[v] and "the changes we might need to make"[vi] in order to pull our programs, initiatives and our attitudes and mindsets into alignment with our vision. This committee needs to be deliberate about how to communicate their findings and design strategic experiences for the staff to build belief and commitment over time. These experiences need to be interactive and authentically engage the voice, perspectives, and opinions of the faculty.

1   Senge, P. M. (2014). The fifth discipline fieldbook: Strategies and tools for building a learning organization. Crown Business. Peterson, K. D., & Deal, T. E. (2011). The shaping school culture fieldbook. John Wiley & Sons.

2   Senge, P. (1990)

3   Drucker, P. (2010) The Five Most Important Questions. John Wiley & Sons.

4   Senge, P. (1990). The fifth discipline: The art and science of the learning organization. New York: Currency Doubleday.

5   Deal, T., & Peterson, K. (2009). Shaping school culture: Pitfalls, paradoxes, and promises (2nd ed.). San Francisco: Jossey-Bass.

6   ibid

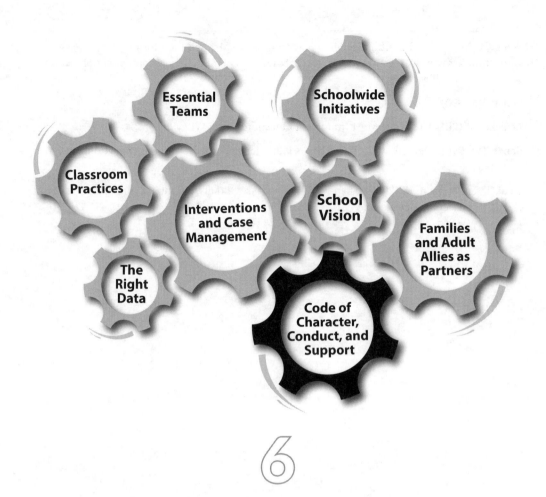

6

Code of Character, Conduct, and Support

How does a district's or school's code of disciplinary policies and practices directly support students' good conduct, character, and citizenship?

CHAPTER OUTLINE

Introduction
A More Inclusive Title: Code of Character, Conduct, and Support
Goals for a Revised Code
Critical Elements of District Codes and School Policy Handbooks
Potholes to Avoid and Remedies to Fix Them

Introduction

A Code of Character, Conduct, and Support is a critical resource that has the potential to bring stakeholders together to collaboratively align their efforts in support of each and every student in the district and school. Often the Codes we are asked to review have a multitude of problems and read as vague, confusing, and punitive in nature. As a result, schools can go down various paths resulting in codes that often lack the support and direction needed when working with secondary students and their families.

A thoughtfully crafted Code of Character, Conduct, and Support provides a "behavioral blueprint"[1] that communicates, "This is who we are here at school and 'this is how we do things around here.'"[2] This gear is critical for districts and schools to consider because an effective Code of Character, Conduct, and Support provides a framework for a district and school to continually revisit the decisions they make when students struggle academically, socially, behaviorally, and emotionally. Ideally, revisions to district Codes of conduct delineate district-wide policies and practices. They also lay out policies and practices that individual schools are responsible for developing. When existing district Codes contain language that is vague or confusing, individual schools need to consider how they incorporate more explicit policies and practices into their own school handbooks.

This chapter takes a look at the critical elements of an effective Code of Character, Conduct, and Support and provides an annotated outline for revising district and school codes of conduct. We have also identified Code Potholes that lead to ineffective and inequitable practices with suggested remedies to fix them. You will also find a Code of Character, Conduct, and Support Essentials checklist to use when reviewing your Code in Appendix B.

A More Inclusive Title:
Code of Character, Conduct, and Support

An effective Code communicates a district's commitment to support the development of every student's good character and conduct. As you revisit your current Code, consider the name you give to this document for your district and/or school. Nomenclature is critical when naming a Code. It provides clarity and direction for all of the stakeholders who interface with it, leaving the mystery out of each individual's responsibility for implementing the Code with fidelity and integrity. We suggest incorporating the words "character, conduct, and support" into a Code's title for several reasons. An effective Code communicates a district's commitment to support the development of every student's good character and conduct. An individual's character reflects his or her attitudes, attributes, values, moral convictions, and social and emotional learning competencies. The word *conduct* refers to the way a person behaves on a particular occasion and in a particular place or situation. The word *character* lives beside the word *conduct* because a student's character will shape her conduct. The development of good character is essential to healthy development and responsible behavior, academic success in school today, and future success in college, career, and life. Principals, administrators, teachers, school staff, parents and adult allies, and the larger community have an obligation to cultivate good character in students by enabling them to discern right from wrong; fostering in them the desire to do what is good; and encouraging them to take responsibility for their words and actions."[3]

Finally, placing the word "support" in the Code's title calls attention to the district and school's responsibility to provide students with equal access to a wide range of supports and interventions that promote positive behavior, help students develop personal and social efficacy, and enable students to correct and reduce inappropriate, unacceptable, and unskillful behaviors. In our work with a 50 member task force charged with rewriting the Code for an urban district, the task force recognized that including "support" in the title of the document set an expectation and accountability for all schools to:

- Promote positive social behaviors and prevent discipline problems through universal practices and procedures.
- Prevent most discipline problems by providing timely and effective responses in the classroom.
- Provide accountable and restorative interventions that would support students to improve their behavior and experience greater success at school.

Goals for a Revised Code

Consider how the goals of a Code might reflect the kind of school climate your district or school wants to promote. "School climate, the collective perceptions, mood, and morale of the staff members and students, is created through the interaction of human relationships, the physical setting, and the psychological atmosphere. Researchers and educators agree that school climate influences students, teachers, and staff members and affects student achievement."[4]

The overarching goal of the Code is to secure every student's right to an education in a safe, civil, and caring community. It is based upon the laws, rules, regulations, and policies that create access to education for all while protecting the due process rights of individuals. The Code recognizes that schools are public places where individual rights must be balanced with civic obligations and the responsibilities that make it possible to live in a free, open, and democratic society. A school's Code of Character, Conduct, and Support serves as a guide to good citizenship and provides the tools for helping students to understand, appreciate, and honor the articulated norms of behavior within the school culture.

In addition, revisions to a Code should make more specific goals transparent:

- Establish the schoolwide and classroom rules, policies, and expectations that all adults are committed to support and enforce.

- Ensure that classrooms and public spaces are physically and psychologically safe, civil, and orderly.
- Reduce the overuse and disproportional use of exclusionary punitive sanctions (student removal from class, suspension, and expulsion).
- Maximize every school's capacity to promote positive behaviors, prevent unskillful, inappropriate, and unacceptable behaviors, and support improved behavior for students with the highest incidents of unacceptable behavior.
- Develop aligned consequences and interventions that enable students to become more self-disciplined by increasing their capacities to self-regulate and interact positively and responsibly with others.
- Increase efficacy of administrators and Student Support Teams to intervene early and effectively with students with high needs.
- Increase capacity of teachers to address unacceptable behaviors effectively and respectfully.

Explicit and transparent goals enable schools to link measurable student and staff outcomes directly to goals put forth in the Code. In addition, concrete goals in a Code can galvanize support for shifting current school policies and practices. For example, when a goal advocates for strengthening students' self-regulation, adults might begin to see discipline incidents as an opportunity to support the student to develop the skills necessary to be self-disciplined, act appropriately, and take responsibility for their actions.

Critical Elements of District Codes and School Policy Handbooks

In addition to defining the goals for a Code of Character, Conduct, and Support, there are other elements that we would like to highlight when teams are drafting or revising district codes or school policy handbooks. At the district level, Codes should pay particular attention to student and parent rights and responsibilities, "due process" entitlements associated with disciplinary incidents, the alignment of assigned consequences to accountable and restorative interventions, and the role of administrators and staff in implementing discipline and student support practices. At the school level administrators need to pay particular attention to schoolwide expectations and schoolwide rules.

District Codes

Student and Parent Rights and Responsibilities

According to the state, students are citizens, and, as citizens of the United States, children are entitled to the same rights of due process, freedom of expression, and equal protection under the law as adults 21 and older.[5] Public school employees are guarantors of these rights. To ensure that students and parents understand their rights, it is important to articulate the freedoms of expression and non-discriminatory protections that public schools afford to students and parents; the type of access to information that the district provides; and most importantly, the specific actions parents, students, and their advocates can take as part of due process, particularly when students are involved in exclusionary punitive sanctions or a district disciplinary hearing.

The language of student responsibilities should describe expectations related to personal conduct, cooperation, the treatment of people and property, responsibilities as a learner, and responsibilities associated with maintaining a safe school community. Parent responsibilities outline specific ways to support their children's success at school and provide guidelines for sharing concerns and complaints, and for engaging in civil discourse with school personnel, other families, and students.

Alignment of School Sanctions/Consequences to Interventions

Assigned school sanctions/consequences need to be aligned to accountable and restorative interventions. In other words, when students commit Tier 2 and Tier 3 behavior violations, they are assigned a Tier 2 or Tier 3 School sanctions/consequence and a Tier 2 or Tier 3 intervention. The **consequence phase** begins when a staff member submits an office disciplinary referral. If it is an extremely aggressive, dangerous, or destructive act or an incident that seriously jeopardizes student and staff safety, the student is also likely to be removed from the classroom or other location. Submission of a referral and student removal serve as alarm bells that a student's behavior is unskillful, inappropriate, or unacceptable, and will warrant the assignment of a school sanction/consequence beyond what teachers do in their classrooms.

The consequence phase for serious behavior violations usually involves students' temporary assignment to an Intervention Center or other location where they have an opportunity to calm down, regain their equilibrium, and complete an Incident Reflection and Return Form. Typically, an administrator usually investigates the incident, confers with the student to discuss the incident, and determines what further school sanctions/consequences are warranted. School sanctions are likely to include any of the following responses:

- parent notification
- a parent conference with administrator, dean, or Student Support Coach
- a conference with administrator, student's teachers, the student, and parent
- a school hearing with the principal, student, and parent
- in-school suspension for one to three days

- out-of-school suspension for one to five days depending on the severity of the incident, or an official district hearing to determine further sanctions and interventions

The **intervention** phase involves some action carried out by the student with adult support and supervision. The ultimate aim is to help students acquire the mindsets and skills that strengthen their personal and social efficacy and enable them to function more successfully at school. Interventions enable students to learn replacement behaviors and habits, work through personal obstacles, resolve conflicts, and develop goals and plans to get back on track for school and life success. Lower tier interventions include teacher facilitated problem solving and planning conferences, close monitoring of student progress, mediation, behavior plans that emerge from consultation with a grade level team, or assignment of a Student Support Coach. Restorative group conferences are typically used when students engage in aggressive acts that harm others. More intensive interventions at a Tier 3 level involve a consultation with the school intervention team to determine the type of comprehensive student success plan and combination of interventions that will serve the student most effectively. In situations where students are experiencing multiple behavior, academic, and attendance challenges, students are likely to be involved in longer-term interventions.

Role of Administrators and Staff in Discipline and Student Support

All administrators and staff members play a critical role in helping students learn to be good citizens and lead productive lives. An effective Code of Character, Conduct, and Support deepens their understanding of the ways they can promote pro-social behaviors and prevent disciplinary problems through the use of effective procedures, practices, and strategies. Effective Codes also provide specific information about the roles that administrators, teachers, student support staff, and specific teams play in delivering effective school sanctions/consequences and interventions when students do not meet expected standards of behavior or violate school rules and policies.

The Code needs to be coupled with systematic professional learning to ensure that staff internalize the implications of major shifts in policies and practices and develop the skill sets necessary to implement changes with fidelity and integrity. In our experience, schools that roll-out implementation of revised Codes successfully, identify a small committed team who oversee all activities related to the launch and monitor the progress of implementation over time. See more detailed information about the work of essential discipline and Student Support Teams in Chapter Seven.

School Policy Handbooks

Expectations

Expectations and rules are often confused by staff and schools. Expectations are normative and aspirational. They communicate the beliefs we hold about what students are capable of doing and achieving; they convey adult's confidence in the students' capacity to succeed and thrive in school and life. Expectations provide reassurance that students can, and will be expected to right themselves when they make mistakes, academically or behaviorally. They provide enduring guidelines for how we present and express ourselves, how we should behave, how we learn, and what we are capable of achieving.

Most schools craft three to five schoolwide academic and behavioral expectations. Narrowing the selection to a few expectations provides the opportunity for conversations with staff, students, and families about the ways in which school expectations align with the school vision (mission, core beliefs and values) and how expectations will be taught, modeled, and practiced, at the beginning of the school year and re-visited at key moments throughout the year (e.g. at end of semester, after long vacations, when there are clear indications that expectations are not being met, etc.). The language of expectations should always be positive and the statements brief. Typical examples include "Be respectful; Be responsible; Work hard; Be safe; and Make your best effort." Because expectations are global, rather than specific, they are not enforceable. Some schools, however, use their global expectations as a basis for crafting very specific and enforceable rules.

School Rules

Many schools with whom we work come to the conversation about rules with a number of perspectives and confusions. We define rules as a set of explicit enforceable regulations, or directives, that govern conduct, which refers to the way a person behaves on a particular occasion in a particular context. A rule can be broken and violations of school rules are linked to tiered consequences and interventions. Even though district codes need to describe up to 40 or 50 explicit behavior violations, rolling out 40 or 50 schools rules at the building level does not work for anyone. Consequently, most schools review their data to identity the big six to eight rules that address the most frequent behavior violations that negatively impact safety, order, and a positive learning environment. Typical school rules provide direction for personal conduct in the classroom and public spaces; what students may and may not do in public spaces; what students may and may not wear; what students may and may not bring to school; where and when students can and cannot travel in the building. Naming something a rule comes with the obligation to enforce it consistently. When rules are clear, and have been explained, students might engage in a version of this internal thought: *"This is what I can do and this is what I cannot do. These rules are here for me to be my best self. These rules will help me feel safe at school. And, if I engage in behaviors that break the rules, I will receive a consequence and someone will help me, so I can avoid making a mistake the next time."*

Rules foster a sense of order, calm, and purposefulness. Even though adolescents are not likely to thank you for creating rules that support responsible behaviors, they are grateful for the high structure and clarity that effective rules provide when they understand the interests behind them.

When creating rules it is important to use language that is appropriate, civil, and courteous at all times. Positively stated rules are important because research has shown that recognizing students for complying with rules is even more important than catching them breaking the rules. When rules are stated positively, the school staff is more likely to acknowledge students for engaging in appropriate behavior. On the other hand, there are always a few students who have a clear need to know explicitly what they are not supposed to do. Figure 6.1 provides samples of typical schoolwide rules.

Figure 6.1

Sample Schoolwide Rules

Issue	Positively Stated Rule	The Rule Violation
Tardy during School Day	Be inside the classroom before the late bell/start of class.	Do not be late to class.
Hall Walking	Get a pass from an adult to travel in public spaces during class time or lunch.	Do not leave class without permission or a pass. Do not run away from an adult who is speaking to you.
Public Space Conduct	Walk calmly, talk in quiet voices, keep your hands to yourself, and keep moving as you travel from one place to the next.	No horseplay, yelling, throwing, or clustering in groups anywhere in the building.

It is important to make sure that staff members and students have an opportunity to discuss the rule, the interests behind the rule, and a reminder to follow the rule, consequences, and interventions when a rule is broken. In most situations, giving students a quick and respectful reminder results in immediate compliance, thus preventing any escalation of the incident or enforcement of further school sanctions/consequences. When students refuse to comply, the enforcement protocol must be very clear to all students and adults.

A school that we worked with in New York surveyed their staff and students to identify behaviors that made the school feel chaotic, unsafe, and disorganized. A Climate Discipline Team analyzed the survey results. They prioritized the six rules for the school, the interests behind each rule, and the consequence and an aligned intervention when the rule is broken. A scaffolded process for developing rules encourages commitment from students who are expected to follow them and for staff who are expected to support and enforce them. Clarity around a targeted number of rules also helps families understand what is expected of their children.

Potholes to Avoid
and Remedies to Fix Them

This section illustrates the potholes that surface from poorly written Codes. We use real examples from various Codes of Conduct, and provide suggestions for fixing the potholes. We recognize that many of you may find some of these potholes familiar. This is an opportunity to explore and assess your current Code and consider how some of these remedies might resonate for your district and school context.

POTHOLE #1

Too much discretion related to removal of students from the classroom

In many districts, student removal from the classroom is permitted for infractions simply identified as "disruptive" and teachers are not required to document strategies they have used to address the behavior prior to removal. In addition, students can often be removed for the lowest level of behavior concerns such as not following directions, not bringing materials to class, having difficulty getting along with others, etc. This removes the expectation that a teacher is responsible for engaging the student in interventions that will address the unskillful, inappropriate, or unacceptable behaviors. Remember, student removal from the classroom is directly connected to the vast majority of suspensions.

Example of Poor Code Language:

"**Removal of Disruptive Student:** *On occasion, a student's behavior may become disruptive. For purposes of this Code, a disruptive student is a student who is substantially disruptive of the educational process or substantially interferes with the teacher's authority over the classroom.*" (In many schools, the "disruptive" descriptor provides the unfortunate license to use student removal as a catch-all consequence when students are non-compliant.)

The Fix: Eliminate the use of student removal for Tier 1 behavior concerns (low impact behaviors), eliminate "disruptive" as a descriptor, insist that teachers identify exactly what the student said and did when Tier 2 or 3 behavior violations require a behavioral referral, and provide an Intervention Center referral slip that identifies specific behaviors that warrant student removal from the classroom.

POTHOLE #2

Use of vague, global language to describe behavior concerns and violations

The Codes in many districts include vague language to describe behavior violations. We encounter words like disruptive, disrespectful, disobedient, disorderly, and defiant to describe a range of behaviors. Vague words and phrases prompt multiple interpretations. As an example, one person's understanding of defiant may include a "student's refusal to complete assigned work" or a "student's refusal to follow directions," while a much more clinical understanding of "defiant" might refer to "student's repeated displays of relentless argumentativeness, aggressively hostile refusal to comply with adult requests and rules, and vindictive and spiteful responses to adults in authority."[6] In other words, low-level non-compliant behaviors are a long shot from more serious behaviors associated with defiance.

Example of Poor Code Language:

Behavior Violations	The Fix
Disorderly Behavior	Avoid using the "D" words (disruptive, disrespectful, disobedient, disorderly, defiant) and the word insubordination to describe rule violations or behaviors. As much as possible, use precise language that describes specific behavior concerns and violations. Precise language helps teachers to depersonalize students' inappropriate behavior, so they are less likely to perceive typical adolescent behaviors as a personal attack.
Defiance	
Disobedient	
Disrespect	
Insubordination	

Example of Specific Code Descriptors for Concerns and Violations

Tier 1 Behavior Concerns	Tier 2 Behavior Violations	Tier 3 Behavior Violations
Does not comply with classroom rules, norms, and procedures. Refuses to respond to school staff directives, questions, or requests. Makes excessive, distracting, or disruptive movements or noises. Does not work cooperatively in small and large groups. Initiates or joins in "side bar" conversations, interrupting, blurting out, and talking out of turn. Occasional incidents of arguing, refusal, or back talk.	Persistent confrontational and aggressive arguing, refusal, or back talk. Verbal aggression against school personnel: Name calling, profanity, insults, offensive language, or threatening gestures. Unsafe explosive outburst or rage. Leaves the classroom without permission.	Persistent verbal aggression against school personnel: Name calling, profanity, insults, offensive language, or threatening gestures.

POTHOLE #3

Behavior descriptors that do not differentiate similar behaviors

Often behavioral violations are described under broad labels like fighting or aggression without attaching qualifying words that pinpoint key differences among similar, but distinct behaviors. As a result, individual administrators are left to interpret what constitutes minor or major fighting or determine for themselves what distinguishes physical aggression from minor fighting.

Example of Poor Code Language:

Behavior Violations	The Fix
Physical aggression	Use precise and exacting language to differentiate similar, but distinct behavior violations. For example, consider calibrating the severity of violent incidents by using fuller explanations.
Minor fighting	
Major fighting	

- **Attack on Student with Serious Bodily Injury with No Provocation:** Hitting, kicking, or punching another student
- **Attack on Student with Serious Bodily Injury with Provocation:** Hitting, kicking, or punching another student
- **Fighting with Serious Bodily Injury:** All students involved engage in hitting, kicking, or punching the other person
- **Fighting with No Serious Bodily Injury:** All students involved engage in hitting, kicking, punching the other person
- **Minor Physical or Verbal Aggression or Threat without Injury:** Unwanted touching, poking, pushing, shoving, physical intimidation, verbal threats, persistent teasing, taunting, or name calling

POTHOLE #4

Too many levels of consequences

Most teachers and administrators are familiar with the PBIS / MTSS (Multi-tiered support system) of three tiers. Incorporating four to six tiers of consequences can become confusing, particularly when schools make attempts to align consequences to appropriate interventions, which are most often sub-divided into three tiers, not four to six tiers.

Example of Poor Code Language:

Offense/Violation	Level of Consequence					
	1	2	3	4	5	6

The Fix: Streamline school sanctions/consequences by using three tiers throughout the Code, even it if means subdividing Tier 3 into 3A and 3B school sanctions/consequences in order to accommodate the most serious tier of violent or dangerous incidents.

	Official District and School Sanctions/Consequences		
Tier 1	**Tier 2**	**Tier 3A**	**Tier 3B**
There are no official office disciplinary referrals, classroom student removals, official school consequences/ sanctions, or suspensions for Tier 1 behavior concerns Teachers observe the behavior, use a range of strategies to support the student and submit observation notes electronically describing the behavior and attempts to remedy it.	From submission of Behavior Referral, to removal of student with assignment to Intervention Center, to possible one or two day in-school suspension to possible one day out-of-school suspension.	One to three day out-of-school suspension.	From three day out-of-school suspension to possible five day out-of-school suspension with District hearing request for long-term suspension.

POTHOLE #5

Consequence levels that include too broad a range of options

A very broad range of options within one consequence level leads to inconsistent application from one administrator to another. This creates unnecessary confusion and frustration among students, parents, and teachers.

Example of Poor Code Language:

Behavior Violations	Consequence Levels			
	1	2	3	4

Level 1 consequences range from a warning to a teacher conference to parent-student conference with administrator to optional office referral, to detention, to removal of student from the classroom.

Level 2 consequences range from teacher conference to detention, to required office referral to a two-day suspension.

Level 3 consequences range from detention, to in-school intervention, to assignment to decision making room, to one to three day in-school suspension to one to five day out-of-school suspension.

Level 4 consequences range from five to ten day out-of-school suspension to adjustment transfer to expulsion.

The Fix: Narrow the range of consequences within each specific tier. This is the same fix as Pothole #4.

Tier 1	Official District and School Sanctions/Consequences		
	Tier 2	Tier 3A	Tier 3B
There are no official office disciplinary referrals, classroom student removals, official school consequences/sanctions, or suspensions for Tier 1 behavior concerns	From submission of Behavior Referral, to removal of student with assignment to Intervention Center, to possible one or two day in-school suspension to possible one day out-of-school suspension.	One to three day out-of-school suspension	From three day out-of-school suspension to possible five day out-of-school suspension with District hearing request for long-term suspension
Teachers observe the behavior, use a range of strategies to support the student and submit observation notes describing the behavior and attempts to remedy it.			

POTHOLE #6

Too many consequence levels attached to the same behavior violation

When consequences for a specific behavior violation spill across many levels, the assignment of consequences becomes muddied and, as a result, overuse and disproportional use of student removal and suspension are likely to continue. We have observed deans and assistant principals responsible for the oversight of discipline for different grade levels within the same building assign anywhere from detention to five days of out-of-school suspension for incidents committed by different students that are more or less identical.

Example of Poor Code Language:

Behavior Violations	Consequence Tiers				
	1	2	3	4	5
Behaviors that Disrupt Student Learning or Distract Students from Learning		•	•	•	
Physical fighting		•	•	•	•
Disrespectful Behavior	•	•	•		
Verbal aggression directed at an adult	•	•	•	•	

The Fix: As much as possible identify only one consequence tier that is associated with each behavior violation.

Behavior Violations	Consequence Tiers			
	1	2	3A	3B
Attack on Student with Serious Bodily Injury with Provocation: Hitting, kicking, or punching another student				•
Attack on Student with Serious Bodily Injury with No Provocation: Hitting, kicking, or punching another student				•
Fighting with Serious Bodily Injury: All students involved engage in hitting, kicking, or punching the other person			•	
Fighting with No Serious Bodily Injury: All students involved engage in hitting, kicking, punching the other person		•		
Verbal Aggression against School Personnel: Name calling, profanity, insults, offensive language, or gestures		•		

POTHOLE #7

No mention of more intensive responses for multiple violations or chronic violations for the same behavior

Teachers often share their frustrations when the list of behavior violations does not account for students who engage in multiple low-impact behaviors or commit chronic violations of the same or similar misbehaviors.

Example of Poor Code Language:

> *This box is empty because any language related to persistent misbehaviors is simply absent from violation descriptions.*

The Fix: The description of behavior violations in the Code needs to include a statement that reassures teachers that they are able to red flag situations in which students persistently engage in low-impact misbehaviors or engage in chronic violations of the same or similar behaviors.

Some district codes include this statement, "Multiple incidents or chronic violations of the same or similar behaviors (three to five incidents) will warrant more serious consequences and more intensive interventions." They also list "Persistent Tier 1 Misbehaviors" as a Tier 2 behavior violation. Submitting an office disciplinary referral under this coding is likely to prompt a conversation with the student's grade level team, an assistant principal, or someone on the School Intervention Team to assess the student's situation and explore the most appropriate Tier 2 interventions.

POTHOLE #8

Placing all interventions in a single list

Listing all interventions that the school offers in one big cluster can be very confusing for teachers, for students, and for parents who want to know "What will happen when..." In addition, guidelines need to be developed that help them to standardize interventions delivered at each Tier.

Example of Poor Code Language:

School Interventions	
Alternative school-based program	Counseling
Campus clean-up	Decision-making room
Check In-Check Out (progress monitoring)	Informal and/or preventative school-based mentoring
Community Conferencing	Modified school day
Community Service (Volunteer work for any non-profit organization, public or private, as a form of restitution)	Referral to Student Support Team
	Restitution
	Restorative Group Conference
Conflict resolution	Small group skill-building sessions
	Student re-entry or success plan

The Fix: For serious incidents that jeopardize student and staff physical and psychological safety, try to align specific interventions to the behavior violation and the assigned school sanction/consequence.

Behavior Violation	Assigned School Sanctions / Consequence	Intervention
Attack on Student with Serious Bodily Injury with No Provocation: Hitting, kicking, or punching another student with no provocation	**Tier 3B**→5 day out-of-school suspension and District hearing	Anti-violence treatment program delivered by community agency Highly recommended "Restorative Group Conference" if both the aggressor and the target agree to participate. School re-entry protocol when student returns to school
Bullying: Persistent and repeated incidents targeted at same person or group	**Tier 2**→One day in-school suspension for first time incident Student-administrator conference Administrator-parent conference	Three anti-bullying sessions with bullying-harassment facilitator Close monitoring of student through staff feedback and student support coaching for one month
Verbal Aggression: Persistent confrontational arguing, refusal, and backtalk	**Tier 2**→One day in-school suspension during which student receives the appropriate intervention	Student-teacher conference facilitated by Student Support Team member Behavior replacement intervention Monitoring and feedback of student progress for one month

For each tier of behavior violations, cluster the array of interventions that are most likely to be used in conjunction with assigned school sanctions/consequences for that tier. Remember, assigned school sanctions/ consequences involve other school staff beyond the classroom teacher. The interventions involve some action carried out by the student, accompanied by adult support and supervision with the ultimate aim of helping students acquire skills and mindsets that strengthen their personal and social efficacy and enable them to function more successfully at school.

Tier 2 Behavior Violations	
Tier 2 School Sanctions / Consequence	Submission of office disciplinary referral.
	Student removal from classroom or other location and temporary assignment to Intervention Center.
	Assignment to Intervention Center.
	Student conference with administrator or dean.
	Student conference with grade level team.
	Parent conference with administrator, dean, or Student Support Coach.
	One to two day in-school suspension.
	One to two day out-of-school suspension.
Options for Tier 2 Aligned Interventions	Teacher facilitated problem solving and planning conference, coaching, and support to close behavior and/or academic learning gaps.
	Restorative practices that may include an act of apology, restitution, mediation, or Restorative Group Conference.
	Student-teacher restorative conference (without or with a facilitator) when student returns to class after being removed.
	Assignment of Student Support Coach who engages student in restorative conferencing, coaching, behavior replacement skill building, development of positive mindsets, strengthening of personal and social efficacy, and progress monitoring.
	Grade level team consultation to determine a common set of strategies across classes to implement with the student.
	Small group social skill building sessions.

POTHOLE #9

No timelines for expected delivery of disciplinary protocols and interventions

Although newly revised Codes often outline disciplinary protocols and interventions, they may not be accompanied by timelines for their expected delivery. As a result, the loop between the initial incident, the processing during the consequence phase, and the determination and delivery of interventions might take days or even weeks. Staff members feel frustrated when the loop is not closed quickly and parents become concerned or frustrated when they have not received timely notification or when interventions are not delivered close to the incident. Most importantly, students are left either wondering why they are not getting the help they need or assuming that nothing much will really happen after the incident.

Example of Poor Code Language:

"In instances where a student receives an out-of-school suspension, the student must receive their due process and parents must be informed in writing of the suspension and any follow-up interventions. Parents may request conference with an administrator." Notice that there are no specific time windows within which the due process investigation must occur, an administrator must inform the parent, a parent can request a conference, or start time for the intervention.

The Fix: Disciplinary protocols and interventions that are time-sensitive or require consistent delivery should be described in some detail in the Code, so administrators, teachers, or student support staff who are responsible for delivering them have a clear pathway to follow.

Examples

Intake Conference when Student Has Been Removed from Class or Another Location: Students who have committed behavior violations serious enough to warrant immediate removal from the classroom or other location will be escorted to the Intervention Center for the remainder of the class period (for more information about the Intervention Center, see Chapter Eleven). The Intervention Center coordinator or a Student Support Team member will facilitate an intake conference to defuse emotional upset, reflect on the incident, and discuss what the student will need to do to repair the harm, right oneself, and restore one's good standing. An administrator will determine whether the student returns to regular classes or remains in the Intervention Center for the remainder of the day while a parent is being contacted.

Restorative Conference After Student Has Been Removed from Class: Within 48 hours of the student's return to class, the teacher must facilitate a one-to-one conference with the student or arrange for a Student Support Team member to facilitate a conference between the student and teacher to discuss reasons for removal and make a plan to improve the student's behavior and engagement in the classroom.

Comprehensive, Longer Term Interventions: The Case Management Team will identify students who are experiencing multiple problems (social, emotional, and academic challenges; personal distress and/or family crisis) that have become barriers to functioning successfully at school. Within a week of a student's identification, the Case Management Team will consult with the student's teachers, parent/guardian, and others to determine components of a long-term intervention that will include a Comprehensive Student Success Plan as well as other interventions that are facilitated by Student Support Team members within the school as well as referral for services provided by the District or external partner agencies.

Return from Suspension: Upon a student's return from out-of-school suspension, the student can expect six things to happen:

1. On the day of a student's return→ Student and parent will conference with an administrator or designated Student Support Team member.

2. On the day of a student's return→ A learning and behavior plan will be signed.

3. Within 24 hours of a student's return→ The plan will be distributed to the student's teachers.

4. Within 24 hours of a student's return→ A Student Support Coach will be assigned to the student and will check-in with the student on a regular basis during the two weeks following the student's return.

5. At the end of the first and second week following a student's return→ The student's teachers will provide written or verbal feedback to the student's support coach in order to assess the student's progress.

6. Within the first week of a student's return→ An administrator will check-in with the student to discuss the student's learning and behavior plan.

The beauty of identifying potholes is that you can fill them in once you have a team to evaluate the current Code against criteria for an effective one. Getting the right people at the table to draft a scaffolded work plan with key deliverables and a timeline will enable you to confidently move forward to tackle each pothole. We understand the complexity of this work, and the time it takes. It is time well spent, as the Code, when effectively written, becomes a strategic resource for multiple stakeholders to responsibly do their jobs in service of their students and the community at large.

---

[1] Deal, T., & Peterson, K. (2009). Shaping school culture: Pitfalls, paradoxes, and promises (2nd ed.). San Francisco: Jossey-Bass.

[2] Bower, M. (1966). The will to manage; corporate success through programmed management. New York: McGraw-Hill.

[3] Center for Character and Social Responsibility http://www.bu.edu/ccsr/resources/publications/

[4] Perkins, B. (2006). Where We Learn: The CUBE Survey of Urban School Climate. The Urban Student Achievement Task Force.

[5] Tauber, R. (2007) Classroom Management, Sound Theory and Effective Practice. Praeger.

[6] Mayo Clinic, Patient Care and Health Information: oppositional defiant disorder. http://www.mayoclinic.org/diseases-conditions/oppositional-defiant-disorder/basics/definition/con-20024559

7

Essential Teams

What are the ways we can harness the energy of well-appointed teams to engage in the complex work of creating and sustaining an effective schoolwide discipline and student support model?

CHAPTER OUTLINE

Introduction
Four Essential Teams
    1. Administrative Team
    2. School Climate-Discipline Team
    3. Student Support Team
    4. School Intervention Team
Collaborating With External Support Partners

Introduction

Bringing strategic teams together to work collaboratively to design and/or refine an effective schoolwide discipline and student support model is a formidable challenge and an opportunity. Schools struggling with their discipline and student support model often encounter administrators and student support staff who feel overwhelmed, defeated, and stressed. This is largely due to social workers, counselors, psychologists, coaches, and special educators being unclear about their roles and responsibilities. They may not realize the increased ease, fidelity, and integrity accrued from working interdependently. These staff members often work in isolation or in small teams that do not have a specific charge, or focus, because there has not been a dialogue about how to harness everyone's collective energy.

This chapter identifies four interconnected teams that help to establish and maintain an effective model. It also describes the roles within teams that are essential to building a high functioning student support system with the appreciation that titles and roles will vary from school to school. We recognize that some staff will have many responsibilities outside of those associated with discipline and student support, and some staff may "double up" taking on several roles within or across teams. We also know that the size of these teams in any school will vary, depending on three things: (1) the district's formula for allocating and assigning student support staff to individual schools; (2) the school leader's efforts to increase the number of student support staff by reconfiguring current staff positions and roles or allocating discretionary funds to "buy" additional staff or staff time; and (3) the district or school's efforts to partner with community-based organizations that provide case managers or youth advocates who work full-time or part-time within the school. No matter the size or configuration of the teams, it is critical for colleagues and teams to work together to eliminate the silos in which disciplinary, academic, and counseling support staff create their own cultures, systems, databases, and interventions. All too often, these result in inefficiencies such as:

- Adult-to-student communication is driven by different goals and beliefs; thus, students receive contradictory messages from different adults.

- Information is not shared among key keepers of the data; as a result, holistic interventions are rarely in place. This has a particularly adverse impact on students who experience multiple academic, behavior, and mental health challenges.

- Traditional consequences and interventions are carried out in isolation from each other and are completely separate from academic interventions. Students then have difficulty making connections among their academic, behavioral, social, and emotional performance/skills.

- Shared adult accountability for engaging students in interventions that actually support improved academic and behavioral performance is absent; thus, students are rarely held accountable to right themselves or make things right with others.

- School staff members who have responsibility for providing specific support to students are rarely expected to assess and monitor the effectiveness of their interventions; thus, students are not getting timely and real-time feedback to support their growth and development.

Four Essential Teams

While other gears focus on policies, processes, and practices that support a restorative and accountable model of schoolwide discipline and student support, this gear focuses on the teams that make the model work. In Figure 7.1, we offer four teams to consider establishing, and trust as a reader that you will discover ideas and concepts that might transfer to your unique setting: (1) Administrative Team, (2) School Climate-Discipline Team, (3) Student Support Team, and (4) School or Grade Level Intervention Team.

Figure 7.1

Four Essential Teams

1. Administrative	2. School Climate-Discipline	3. Student Support	4. School Intervention
This team's primary purpose is to serve as visible champions of schoolwide discipline and student support; supervise the work of the other three teams; complete all transactions with students, staff, and parents related to due process investigations and determine consequences.	This team's primary purpose is to coordinate activities, events, and strategies to promote a positive school climate; review and use comprehensive school data (behavior, attendance, and grades) to inform their school discipline plan; and implement, assess, and refine the schoolwide discipline and student support plan.	This team's primary purpose is to build a shared commitment to a holistic view of student support; create common goals to provide direction for the program; and manage, organize, schedule, and discuss the efficacy of their work with young people.	This team's primary purpose is to review data to determine specific interventions; discuss high needs students; and arrange and facilitate some Tier 2 and all Tier 3 interventions.

Administrative Team

Team Purpose and Tasks

The Administrative Team drives the schoolwide discipline and student support vision and its implementation. Everyone – staff, students, and parents – looks to administrators to set a tone of decency, fairness, and attentiveness in all disciplinary interactions. That tone is demonstrated by their friendly and alert presence throughout the school and through their responsive communication with staff, students, and parents when safety and disciplinary issues arise.

An administrator's capacity to do the following three tasks with agility, authority, calm, and care will cement perceptions of trust, good will, and dependability with staff, families, and students. When administrators do not make these tasks part of their daily repertoire, trust in their leadership can be jeopardized.

- Mediate student-teacher and school-parent conflicts sensitively and effectively.
- Respond to the most serious disciplinary incidents immediately and "close the communication loop" with staff, students, and parents.
- Take charge and handle extremely violent and explosive situations in ways that restore safety, calm, and order within 24 hours of the incident.

In addition, at least one person on the Administrative Team should be skilled and comfortable facilitating restorative group conferences when students are involved in high impact incidents that broadly affect the school community. For more information about administrator responsibilities in Tier 2 and Tier 3 incidents, please see Chapter 11.

From the purview of federal, state, and local district laws and policies, school administrators are charged with some tasks that only administrators can execute: due process investigations of disciplinary incidents; determination of school sanctions/consequences for incidents officially reported through the school's referral system; assignment of in-school, out-of-school, and long-term suspensions or modifications to a student's program; representing the school in district disciplinary hearings; processing all disciplinary paperwork in a timely manner; and verifying the accuracy of all submitted disciplinary data. These administrative expectations are significant requiring that the Administrative Team create an explicit roadmap to determine and define who is responsible for these critical tasks.

Team Composition

All administrators are members of this team. Other team members might also include disciplinary deans, whom the principal can designate to carry out some administrative responsibilities, and clerical staff members who have responsibilities to input and organize disciplinary data and process paper work related to suspensions, hearings, and expulsions.

Frequency of Meetings

Weekly meetings scheduled at a strategic time where all members are present are imperative in order to review data, assess the status of individual students, determine follow-up responses for situations that impact the entire community, and engage in collaborative problem solving and case study discussions in order to improve the Administrative Teams' collective efficacy.

Important Team Roles

Based on our experience we know that in many districts a senior administrator is holding the vision for this work and monitoring implementation. Even if multiple administrators are assigned disciplinary responsibilities, one administrator typically serves as the administrative coordinator of schoolwide discipline and student support and ensures appropriate distribution of tasks among the team members. In many middle and high schools, each administrator is assigned to a grade level that frames their primary responsibilities: investigating and processing serious disciplinary incidents, conferencing with students, assigning consequences, and delivering some interventions to students in their grade level. When administrators follow the same cohort of students for all three years of middle school or all four years of high school, they get a fuller picture of their students. This, in turn, creates an atmosphere where students are more likely to trust that the administrator has their best interests at heart and parents appreciate having one administrator who is their primary contact over multiple years.

Ideally, the grade level administrator also evaluates and supports teachers whose primary teaching responsibilities are with students in that grade level. Since the vast majority of disciplinary incidents begin in the classroom, this organizational structure is ideal for identifying and providing support for teachers who experience the greatest challenges with the students who receive the most referrals.

Resources for the Administrative Team

We refer you to Chapter 11: Interventions and Case Management, and Chapter 12: Families and Adult Allies as Partners.

School Climate-Discipline Team

Team Purpose and Tasks

The School Climate-Discipline Teams (SCDT team, and also called the PBIS team in some schools and districts) holds the vision for a safe, civil, and respectful school climate and culture. The team develops, discusses and approves the schoolwide discipline and student support plan, makes adjustments to the plan as needed, reviews discipline data regularly in order to trouble-shoot specific school climate concerns, presents data and recommendations to the entire staff, and assesses the status and progress of major school climate initiatives. The team has a major role in coordinating and organizing activities and events that promote a safe, positive school climate, promote pro-social student behaviors, and prevent violent and anti-social behaviors like fighting, bullying, and harassment. The team also plays an important role in the maintenance of general school safety through annual review and presentation of school safety and emergency plans and district, municipal, and state policies and laws related to serious acts of violence and possible criminal acts. Ideally, the School Climate-Discipline Team meets periodically with all school safety staff to elicit their perspectives on school climate and takes responsibility for delivering professional learning modules to all school safety staff. Descriptions of schoolwide promotion and prevention activities and events are included in Chapter 9, Schoolwide Initiatives.

Team Composition

The size of this team will vary from school to school based on the school's unique setting and staffing configuration. The following staff work collaboratively on this team: lead discipline assistant principal, key teacher leaders, select student support staff, and at least one parent and non-certified staff member. In addition, schools might have a group of representative students who are invited to participate in parts of meetings to strategically partner and think with staff to problem-solve and generate ideas to support the interests and needs of all students.

Frequency of Meetings

We recommend that the team meet weekly during the first month of school and at least monthly during the remainder of the school year. It is not uncommon for these meetings to last two or more hours.

Important Team Roles

We are very aware that different schools have different resources, and in some schools, staff members play multiple roles.

- Co-chairs (assistant principal and faculty member): facilitate meetings, solicit agenda items, develop agendas, ensure all materials are provided for team members before meeting to review, prepare data reports to submit to school leadership team or Administrative Team and communicate with regularly with the staff.
- Data Coordinator: gathers all data to present at meetings.
- Professional Learning Coordinator: Develops, coordinates, and schedules all professional learning related to the opening of school; schoolwide discipline and student support; and classroom management.
- First Month of School Coordinator: Coordinates the delivery of lessons that focus on school culture and the code of conduct during the first month of school, as well as other culture-building activities, events, and strategies for students, staff, and parents/families/adult allies.
- Recognition and Events Coordinator: Coordinates events, and recognitions that foster positive behavior, good citizenship, and school pride.
- Welcome Coordinator: Coordinates activities for parents and students who enroll in the school after mid-September; may also be responsible for language translation for parents/families/adult allies.
- Youth Leadership Coordinator: Coordinates youth leadership and peer education opportunities during regular school hours, after school, on weekends, and in the summer months, including summer bridge/transition programs and student orientation programs for all students before the school year begins.

Resources for the SCDT

We refer you to Chapter 9: Schoolwide Initiatives for a variety of activities, events, and strategies to support the SCDT.

Student Support Team

Team Purpose and Tasks

The Student Support Team (SST), comprised of all student support staff, comes together to set goals, reflect on their work, and make adjustments along the way to meet the demands of the context in which they work. This team builds a shared commitment to a holistic view of student support informed by the belief that students' school success is influenced by their academic profile and performance, their personal and social efficacy, their family conditions, and other risk and protection factors. SST meetings are about discussing the management, organization, scheduling, and efficacy of their work with young people. Ideally, one administrator manages and supervises all student support staff to ensure clarity about their specific staff roles and responsibilities, and oversees how various student support staff work together in smaller groups. In some schools, the entire Student Support Team also functions as the School Intervention Team, the fourth team described in this section.

Meetings of the whole SST offer an opportunity to review and share common goals and language that foster a restorative and accountable approach to discipline and student support. They share expertise across the team and refine and assess the effectiveness of common practices, protocols, interventions, and major initiatives to ensure fidelity of implementation. It is important for this team to systematically discuss their roles and responsibilities to maximize everyone's time and efficiencies. In times of crisis and when there are significant problems affecting the health and well-being of students, this team thinks together about viable solutions. Finally, the work of this team needs to be nuanced, creative, and on point to meet the complex problems of students and their families. Thus, discussing professional learning opportunities to support their efficacy and craftsmanship is critical to their own health and well-being as they hold an essential role in helping all young people in their care.

Team Composition

The SST team is comprised of all internal and external student support staff whose responsibilities include addressing students' disciplinary and attendance problems, and/or providing direct academic, behavior, and physical and mental health interventions and services to students. The group size will vary from school to school but team members might include: discipline-student support assistant principal, lead social worker, Intervention Center coordinator, behavior intervention specialist, restorative practices specialist, case managers, graduation coaches, dignity coordinator, transition coordinator, and academic intervention specialists.

Regardless of the size and composition of the whole SST, every team member needs to devote some percentage of time to activities that support restorative interventions involving individual students at risk. For the most part, members of the SST carry out their work with students individually during the school day.

In our experience there are often tensions around roles and responsibilities between guidance/counseling staff and other members of Student Support Teams that may complicate the capacity problem in many schools. Given the current press for providing "college- and career-ready" preparation to all secondary students, many school counselors do not see initiatives to support at-risk students or delivering interventions to improve students' academic and behavior outcomes as one of their responsibilities. In schools that have limited resources, it is critical to address this issue and engage in a conversation with the counseling staff members about ways they might reimagine their roles to support high needs students. A final note: schools that employ school counselors but do not employ at least one social worker must rethink the composition of their SST before committing to an accountable and restorative model of discipline and student support.

Frequency of Meetings

We recommend that the SST meet weekly during the first month of school and at least monthly during the remainder of the school year. Team members are also likely to meet in smaller subgroups for professional learning related to specific roles (i.e. counselors, special education case managers, behavior specialists, etc.).

Important Team Roles

- Assistant Principal: Oversees the interactions of this team, monitors their progress and communicates regularly with the principal and other senior administrators about the work of this team.
- Co-chairs: Develops agenda, facilitates weekly meetings, and manages and organizes the tasks and the professional learning for the SST.
- Note Taker / Record Keeper: Takes notes at meetings and keeps a record of decisions made by the whole team and action steps to be carried out.
- Turn-Key Training Coordinator: Ensures that embedded trainings are scheduled in the building so that individual Student Support Team members who receive special training outside of the school are prepared to "turn-key" what they have learned to their colleagues back at their home school.
- Special Education Director / Coordinator: A student support player who needs to ensure that all special education liaisons, case managers, and teaching assistants develop the skill sets to serve as Student Support Coaches to students in their charge and assist students' teachers in implementing students' academic and behavior plans with fidelity. In addition, the special education director needs to be available to consult with the School Intervention Team, particularly in situations when special education students need additional Tier 2 and Tier 3 services and interventions.
- Transition Coordinator: The transition coordinator coordinates re-entry of all students returning from a long-term suspension, alternative educational programs, homebound instruction, hospitalization or residential treatment, juvenile detention facilities, or incarceration.

- Student Support Coaches: Every SST member serves as a Student Support Coach for some students with high needs to ensure that the school has the capacity to deliver support throughout the year regardless of when students are referred. These students require ongoing support to stay connected to school, turn around their behavior, and experience greater academic success. These are often students who do not know how to "do school" and have a complex array of academic, social and emotional difficulties, which impacts their ability to move through an entire school day without major incidents. They need what we call a "high touch" approach where one person consistently checks in with them throughout the week to improve student outcomes. Students may be assigned a coach for a grading period or for the entire school year. We refer you to Appendix C: Guidelines for Student Support Coaches to provide guidance for Student Support Coaches in their important role.

Resources for the SST

We refer you to Chapter 11: Interventions and Case Management. Appendix D: Memorandum of Understanding Checklist for Student Support Team and Partners provides greater detail about the goals, roles, and responsibilities of SST members, and Appendix C: Guidelines for Student Support Coaches.

School Intervention Team

Team Purpose and Tasks

The meetings of the School Intervention Team (SIT) are action-focused. Put simply, the SIT is the organizing structure for establishing and overseeing a comprehensive case management system within the school. The team uses data to identify students who experience the most serious behavioral and academic challenges in the classroom in order to determine targeted academic, behavioral, and mental health interventions that are timely and predictable. Distribution of specific data to those providing interventions is a weekly routine, as is updating each student's cumulative/electronic file. This type of "high touch" support and supervision is the cornerstone for helping young people increase their personal and social efficacy.

Establishing the weekly ritual of reviewing student cases using a "kid talk" protocol ensures that all students have equitable access to the services and interventions they need. See Appendix E: Kid Talk Consultancy Protocol for step-by-step directions. For students with extremely complex profiles, the SIT determines interventions; creates comprehensive student success plans (behavioral, academic, attendance, mental health issues) or more intensive behavioral plans; facilitates Tier 3 consultations that can involve other staff members, parents, students, and a student's coach or advocate; and monitors student progress. Typically, the SIT will assign students with high needs to a Student Support Coach who monitors and assesses the status and progress of their students, communicates directly with students' teachers and families, and ensures that follow-up and follow-through take place. For specialized situations, the SIT team schedules and coordinates the delivery of small group interventions.

In schools that have developed an advisory program, a SIT team member is likely to serve as a conduit to inform every student's advisor/graduation coach of any issues or events that have become barriers to a student's personal wellness and success at school. This back and forth communication includes providing a "heads-up" to a student's advisor/graduation coach about action plans, interventions, or special programs that are being put in place for a student and sharing updates about a student's progress.

Timely access to key data maximizes the capacity for SIT team members to do their job (ideas for creating a comprehensive and strategic data plan are explored in Chapter Eight). Turning around students who are at risk for several reasons requires that data reports are up-to-date and timely. First, the degree to which a student is a risk for school failure, suspension, or alternative placement typically involves multiple school indicators including behavior, attendance, and grades as well as other data that provide information about the student's attachment to school, his relationships with peers and adults, any physical and mental health concerns, and conditions of home and family life that influence stability and vulnerability. All of these data points can be used for placement of students on the "worry list" and "extremely urgent list" and thus prompt assignment of a Student Support Coach and delivery of more intensive interventions as early as possible. Second, a combination of data helps adults create a holistic picture of a student's school and life experience and helps frame the development of comprehensive interventions that will address the multiple needs of students at risk. Blueprints of Tier 3 interventions, like a Comprehensive Student Success Plan, can be tracked to assess the combination of interventions that produce the most effective outcomes for students severely at risk.

Team Composition

The size of SIT teams will vary from school to school. Typically the team is comprised minimally of the lead social worker, lead counselor, psychologist, and lead discipline assistant principal. The SIT team may invite teachers, other Student Support Team members, and academic support team members to participate in individual consultations about students. Although the SIT is comprised of a smaller subgroup within the Student Support Team, all other Student Support Team members are likely to participate in parts of the weekly meeting when students on their case load are being discussed or when their specific expertise is required to determine or deliver a specific intervention. Alternatively, some schools have multiple SIT teams made up of teachers and support services personnel who work exclusively with a specific grade level. Often, a grade-level assistant principal, counselor, social worker, and special education coordinator form a team structure to service those students in need at that grade level.

Frequency of Meetings

We recommend that this group convene weekly for two hours. The work is layered and intensive, and we have found schools to need this time to accomplish a range of purposes. We have provided a sample agenda in Figure 7.2 that supports on task and productive conversations in the SIT.

Figure 7.2

Six Part School Intervention Team Weekly Agenda

At Least One Day Before the Meeting:

Part 1: Scan weekly discipline summary data to identify any new students who need immediate interventions, consultations, or Student Support Coaches and update case load roster.

Scan weekly progress monitoring reports of students on "worry list" and "urgent list" to assess trend lines and identify three to five students who are first priority for case conferences during the next meeting. Schedule case conferences and invite students' support coach, academic intervention specialist, behavior specialist, or other appropriate staff members to the scheduled conference time for each student who will be discussed.

Consult with others and identify one student who will be the focus of a Comprehensive Student Success Plan consultation during the next meeting.

Meeting Day Agenda *(2 hours total time)*:

Part 2: Facilitate at least three case conferences with prioritized students. *(15 minutes each)*

Part 3: Determine next steps for new students identified in Part 1: B. *(15 minutes)*

Part 4: Facilitate Comprehensive Student Success Plan consultation for identified student in Part 1: C *(30 minutes)*

Part 5: Consult with Dean or Discipline AP to identify any specific interventions that need to be scheduled for students who committed single or multiple violations involving bullying, harassment, and physical violence. *(15 minutes)*

Part 6: Consult with Dean or Discipline AP to review status of students assigned to out-of-school suspension or students who have had an extended absence for health or other reasons, and schedule transition protocols for returning students. *(10 minutes)*

Team Roles

- Lead Facilitator: Develops agenda and facilitates weekly meetings.
- Academic Intervention Specialist or Coordinator: Consults with the School Intervention Team (SIT) to help determine the most appropriate academic interventions and programs for students who are experiencing severe learning gaps that have become significant barriers to the student's capacity to function successfully in the classroom.
- Comprehensive Student Success Plan Coordinator: Schedules and facilitates Tier 3 consultations that focus on students with highest needs.

- Keeper of Real-Time Student List: Updates the roster of students identified on the "worry list" and "extremely urgent list" and ensures that students' coaches receive all data relevant to their students.
- Data Presenter: Gathers and culls weekly data to identify high needs students and review specific data about students to be discussed that week.

Collaborating With External Support Partners

Schools fortunate enough to secure additional student support services and programs through community-based organizations rarely anticipate the careful planning and coordinated management needed to avoid potential conflicts and confusion among and between internal student support staff and external partners. In working with school student support staff and external partners, we have witnessed several conditions that lead to inefficiency, ineffectiveness, and day-to-day tensions.

Frustrations surface when student support staff and external partners have neither discussed nor share a common mission for the services that they provide. Because support staff members are working in a school, rather than a clinical setting, the aim of all interventions and services should be directly connected to developing and strengthening behaviors and mindsets that will improve students' academic, personal, and social efficacy and enable them to function more successfully in school and the classroom. Another problematic condition emerges when team members use different criteria for assignment to caseloads. As a result, we have found an alarming disconnect in many schools where students identified on the weekly "worry list" have no access to case management services. In addition, support staff members who are contracted from various community organizations tend to operate unilaterally, using different intake procedures, communicating different expectations for students and families, and providing different protocols for interventions and progress monitoring. Finally, a lack of clarity around expected school responsibilities for all student support staff, beyond the delivery of direct services to student and family clients, creates unnecessary dissension.

The foundation for building greater consistency, effectiveness, access, and accountability among student support staff is the development of a memorandum of understanding (MOU) between the school district or school, the internal student support staff, and all external partners who provide student support services. An MOU creates broad and specific agreements that govern how student support staff members organize themselves and work collaboratively to create a viable multi-tiered system of supports and interventions for children and families that maximizes resources to improve students' academic and behavioral outcomes. Appendix D: Memorandum of Understanding Checklist for Student Support Team and Partners provides greater detail about the goals, roles, and responsibilities of SST members.

In closing, we want to reiterate the importance of these teams and colleagues working together interdependently and seamlessly. When they have arrived at a place where they hold and value that their collective work and energies will not only serve their students, but will help them provide the sophisticated and targeted interventions for each and every student that is in need of their thought, attention, and care, they will feel a greater satisfaction with their efforts. The work of these teams is sensitive and serious, and the quality of the relationships amongst and between these teams, will create the energy source that is needed to do this complex organizational work. "What we see is most influenced by what we have decided to be."[1]

---

[1] Wheatley, M., (1992) – Leadership and the new science: Learning about organizations from an orderly universe. San Francisco, CA: Barrett-Koehler.

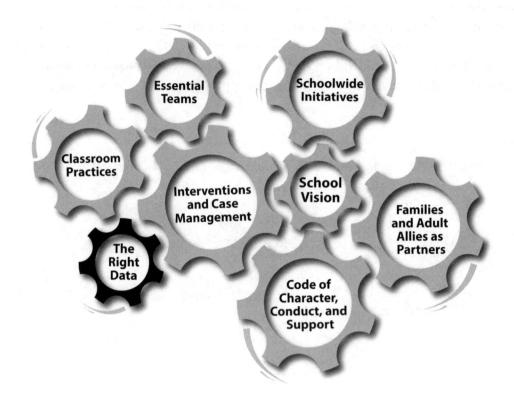

The Right Data

How do you collect, track, analyze, and use the right data to ensure that you can deliver the right responses?

CHAPTER OUTLINE

Introduction
Goals for Data
Barriers to and Solutions for Choosing and Using the Right Data
Sample Data Points

Introduction

Today school leaders are charged with the task of amassing detailed data on students, analyzing that data, and making data-informed decisions to improve their educational program, school climate and culture, and more specifically to increase student achievement and reduce disciplinary problems. There is no doubt that data is an important gear in a schoolwide discipline and student support model. What is not always so clear is how to make sure your school has the right data that truly supports an accountable and restorative discipline and student support model—data that is timely, accurate, complete, and easily accessible. While some of the data challenges that schools face are related to technology, staffing, or funding, the lack of a clear vision around the use of discipline and student support data within a strategic and inclusive data plan is often a more significant obstacle.

In many of the schools we are called in to support, we find databases that have been historically compartmentalized: academic data is housed in one system, attendance data in another, and behavior data in yet another. As a result, school staff members are often looking at fragments of a student's profile. We need to see a student's holistic data story in order to serve them well. Academic issues and behavioral concerns are often interrelated and addressing a problem usually requires an understanding of all of the contributing factors. A key premise of this book is that discipline and student supports should be integrated and that means the data must be integrated as well.

Ultimately, what schools need is a deep and broad picture of their collective data, allowing them to institute strategic schoolwide strategies that reduce discipline problems and implement interventions that help students who have lost their way get back on track. This chapter begins by clarifying the essential goals for a school discipline and student support data plan. Next, we detail seven common barriers that make it challenging to collect the right data and recommend possible solutions to jumpstart your thinking about how to improve the collection, processing, analysis, and use of discipline and student support data in your district or school.

Goals for Data

Discipline and student support data tools and systems must be designed in a way that enables staff to (1) submit and process behavior incidents to determine appropriate and timely consequences; (2) determine and deliver consistent, effective, and timely interventions; and (3) accurately monitor and assess students' progress during and after interventions. If your district or school struggles with any of these three components, it will be important to identify the exact data issues and develop a strategic plan to resolve them.

Discipline referrals are at the frontline of a discipline data system and key to achieving the above listed goals. In order to immediately process discipline incidents, assign appropriate school sanctions/ consequences, and determine and deliver aligned restorative interventions, student discipline referral data must be communicated in a way that is both standardized and detailed. Given the realities of a typical busy school day and teachers' demanding schedules, referrals need to be easy for staff to complete in a nominal amount of time. When referral data results in the consistent identification and classification of student behaviors, it is much easier to avoid disparate practices and respond in ways that are consistent and fair. This requires that the referral form mirrors the precise language found in a thoughtfully designed Code of Character, Conduct, and Support as we described in Chapter Six. In addition, a good referral form will provide a snapshot of the classroom strategies the teacher has already tried in their attempts to resolve the issue in the confines of their classroom. And finally, the information on a discipline referral form must be immediately available and digitally accessible to administrators and student support staff members so there are no lags in response time.

Many administrators with whom we work share their growing concern about the high number of office disciplinary referrals. In some cases, many teachers are referring students for low-impact behaviors that have a minimal or temporary effect on the individual, the adult, the group, or the learning environment. And, in our experience in working with Administrative Teams, they report that a small number of teachers tend to be responsible for the bulk of referrals. If teachers are referring students excessively, there will be an enormous amount of data to sift through, which inhibits administrators and student support staff to respond in a timely matter.

For example, if a school has a number of teachers submitting multiple referrals daily for Tier 1 behavior concerns, the sheer number of referrals that need processing bog down the system and limit the administrators' and student support staff's ability to respond effectively to more chronic or egregious behaviors. Professional development modules that focus on classroom management and discipline responses to Tier 1 behavior concerns as well as guidelines for writing and submitting clear and appropriate referrals will produce more streamlined and useful data.

An integrated data system that allows administrators and student support personnel to instantaneously see the complete profile of a particular student is the ideal. When current district software or compartmentalized data practices prevent this, schools have to find a way to bring the data together. District data software and interfaces may not be ideal, and we encourage those responsible to advocate for more integrated, efficient and flexible systems. Schools and districts have the capacity to work with software vendors to customize their data tools to better enable them to do their job. Please know that we are aware that transitioning to an integrated data system takes time and resources. Schools all over the country grapple with this challenge, and we appreciate that every school's context is different.

Many schools create their own internal databases for the purpose of tracking the status and progress of students. For example, we have worked with schools in a district in Oregon where grade level student intervention teams keep Excel spreadsheets that provide comprehensive student data for students on their "worry list" and "extremely urgent list." Students on the "worry list" are those who present persistent academic, attendance, and behavior concerns. Students on the "extremely urgent list" need immediate support because they are experiencing some kind of personal, behavioral, or family crisis. By using spreadsheets that are updated regularly by Student Intervention Team members or Grade Level Student Intervention Teams, they can immediately access a detailed data profile for each student that includes academic data, attendance data, state test data, behavior data, intervention plans, progress monitoring notes, classroom practices that resulted in student gains, family contact information, and more. Having all of this data at their fingertips is critical for diagnosing the root cause of the problem. It also facilitates designing, implementing, and tweaking interventions to ensure that they are achieving the desired outcomes for the students.

Additionally, the data system needs to function at the macro level as well as the micro level. It must be highly effective at uncovering schoolwide trends such as: the most frequent types of behavior problems, where and when the majority of incidents are happening, what groups of students are being referred, teacher referring trends, and success rates for interventions. With this kind of data, schools are poised to act. As described in Chapter Nine, the School Climate-Discipline Team plans and organizes schoolwide promotion and prevention initiatives, and the Student Support Team can develop needed interventions and make sure those interventions are working. When done right, the data become an essential tool for being able to actualize a system that is fair, accountable, and restorative. Such a system also provides evidence to the school community that the school's policies and discipline actions are sound and effective.

Barriers to and Solutions for Choosing and Using the Right Data

BARRIER #1

Referrals are Associated with Punishment

> **Possible Solution: Reframe the Concept of a Referral**
> It is important to make it clear to your staff that referrals are viewed as diagnostic opportunities that support further investigation, data gathering, and problem solving through collaborative consultation.

Barrier Defined

Too often, behavior referrals are only associated with punitive consequences that are expected to follow the submission of a referral. Submitting a disciplinary referral most typically serves as a student's ticket to the dean's office, the detention room, or an in-school or out of school suspension for inappropriate behavior that the student has exhibited.

Possible Solution

If we unpack the definition of referral, we actively choose a different destination. To "refer" is to direct to a source for help or information. A "referral" is the process of directing the person to an appropriate specialist or agency for a definitive intervention. Unfortunately, it is all too common for staff to see referrals in a one-dimensional way, as an end event instead of the start of a process. The goal of any referral should be to alert the student, parent, administrators, teachers, and student support staff that an academic, attendance, or behavioral problem has become a barrier to a student's learning and functioning successfully in classrooms or public spaces. When referrals are perceived more as a diagnostic tool, teachers begin to recognize that the referral process can support them as much as it supports students. If we capture the spirit of this idea of a referral, effective referrals would be less about meting out punishments and more about determining the right diagnosis in order to provide the right intervention so a student can turn around his or her behavior or academic performance. This shift in beliefs would also support earlier conversations about the student in question through a variety of consultations with administrators and relevant staff members, grade level teams, the School Intervention Team, or individual teachers and a Student Support Team member.

Considerations

Language about the multi-dimensional purpose of referrals needs to live in the Code of Character, Conduct, and Support. Staff members also need the opportunity to explore a more nuanced concept of referrals and think about this new paradigm with their colleagues so the entire school can develop a shared belief around the use of referrals.

BARRIER #2

A Paper Referral System

> **Possible Solution: Behavior Management Software**
> In the long run, the benefits outrun the costs of an integrated behavior system, and there are likely several options that complement your district's student information system.

Barrier Defined

The trail of paper office referrals and notifications, often filed away in a place that is inaccessible, makes efficient and effective management of behavior data impossible. The "paper trail" problem is often the biggest barrier to effective and efficient disciplinary and student support data management. Furthermore, the elimination of paper documentation is directly tied to removing many of the other barriers we identify in this chapter. If your school or district is still paper-dependent, review this list of problems with paper and note the challenges you have experienced.

- Someone has to input key data from submitted written forms into the school or district database. The backlog of unprocessed data can easily slide into weeks, and even months, of delays.

- When written data are transferred to an electronic database, it is often coded and transcribed inaccurately and incompletely. There is a "reductionist" tendency when written data are electronically transferred; precise detail morphs into vague descriptors that provide too little concrete information. In addition, only the most general incident categories like "suspension," "student removal from class," and "ODR" (office disciplinary referrals) may actually be disaggregated by grade, gender, race, students with disabilities, English language learners, etc. Thus, it becomes impossible to develop summary reports that capture "Who, exactly, is engaging in what specific behaviors, and where and when is it happening?" This critical information is needed in order to align assigned consequences to the right interventions.

- Turnaround time between submission of a referral and an administrator's response might be delayed for hours or even days. This is very problematic for dangerous or destructive incidents that require an immediate response.

- When submitted documentation is neither transparent nor easily accessible, the processing of individual referrals by different deans and administrators can vary wildly in the same building and across the district. For example, there can be variance of consequences assigned for the same behavior violation and the differing degrees of timeliness and thoroughness of follow-up investigation and notification to students and parents. Everything is hidden away, so issues around inconsistent and inequitable practices are very difficult to uncover.

- The only way for administrators, Student Support Team members, or teachers to get a quick status update about an individual student is to retrieve the student's file, which is likely to be stored in some cabinet in a locked room.

- When a staff member does review a student's file, every piece of paper must be touched and read. There are no summary reports that provide a quick snapshot of the frequency and range of concerns and incidents.

- Identifying and tracking students on the "worry" and "extremely urgent" lists becomes an incredibly tedious task when all one can bring to the table are individual file folders, which overwhelms well-intentioned student support staff and administrators.

- A paper system either excludes or slows down the process of closing the communication loop with a teacher regarding follow-up responses after an incident. Teachers rightly complain when there is no manageable or timely protocol that communicates to them what happened with the student after the referral and what steps they should take to support the student in their care.

Possible Solutions

Investigate behavior management software options and switch to a digital system. When making purchasing decisions for behavior management software, we recommend comparing products to see how well they deliver the following valuable features: (1) data can be integrated into the district's student information database, so there is no need for double-entry; (2) referral forms are comprehensive and easy to complete; (3) referrals can be customized to match the Code of Character, Conduct, and Support language; and record very specific behavior concerns and violations, and disciplinary consequences and interventions; (4) individual student reports as well as schoolwide and district summary reports of disaggregated disciplinary data can be easily generated; (5) all documents and reports can be printed out; (6) case management rosters can be generated; (7) assigned administrators receive a quick digital alert when a referral is submitted; (8) follow-up responses to teacher-submitted referrals can be viewed by referring teacher; and (9) the interface is easy to navigate, intuitive to use, and it takes minimal numbers of clicks to get what you need.

Many districts are involved in the process of transitioning to digital systems and might still be reliant on paper referral forms. We have worked with many urban schools that go ahead and purchase their own behavior management software package during the transition. Schools can purchase these packages "per head" at a very reasonable cost.

Considerations

In moving to a digital system, there is one situation where a paper system should be used in addition to a digital referral: when students are removed from the classroom or another location, a brief paper referral form should accompany the student and the more detailed digital office disciplinary referral can be completed within the next hour or two. In the interest of safety and prompt transitions, the paper referral form helps to ensure that students get to the right place in a timely manner.

We have learned that trying to customize your district electronic student information system to fix what it currently cannot do is not an efficient use of time or district funds. The results are rarely satisfactory, wasting significant amounts of time and money. We suggest organizing a task force to take on this project. The group should include the district or school technology coordinator, an administrator, a Student Support Team member, and some teacher leaders. This group needs to come to the table with a strong desire and commitment to resolve the data problem. They must also be prepared to be ambassadors of the new system for the staff at large.

Because of the nationwide spotlight on inequitable and ineffective disciplinary practices and inadequate disciplinary data management, many companies that offer student information system software now have sophisticated behavior management packages that complement and can be integrated into district student information systems.

Only One Referral Option

> **Possible Solution: Two Kinds of Incident Submissions**
> Provide a system for accurately recording and processing two kinds of data sets (1) observation notes about Tier 1 behavior concerns (low impact behaviors) for internal school use, and (2) official discipline referrals for Tier 2 and 3 behavior violations.

Barrier Defined

Having only one type of referral proves to be problematic because information about a student is likely to be shared and reviewed only after unwanted behaviors have become persistent and more difficult to address. When there is only one referral option and only one way of processing that referral, the system is not nimble enough to respond proactively.

Possible Solutions

When a school takes the steps to reframe the concept of a referral (Barrier #1) we strongly recommend that schools develop ways to record and process two disciplinary data sets: (1) observation notes about Tier 1 behavior concerns that are handled by the teacher for internal school use that are more diagnostic in nature, and (2) official office discipline referrals for Tier 2 and 3 behavior violations, which potentially involve a student's removal from the classroom. This solution works for a number of reasons. First, the act of submitting informal observation notes triggers a more proactive stance for intervening earlier and more strategically with students. A Grade Level Student Intervention Team can then use the notes for diagnostic consultation to develop interventions used among teachers who work with the same student.

Researchers at the Consortium for Chicago School Research and Johns Hopkins Talent Development Secondary have found that one of the most powerful strategies for student improvement was the early discussion and problem solving among and between student support staff and teachers who taught the same student.[1] When Tier 1 guidelines identify low-impact behavior concerns, describe suggested teacher responses, and encourage submission of follow-up observation notes, teachers are clearer about their responsibilities to handle the majority of problem behaviors in the classroom and more inclined to engage in early consultations with other colleagues.

A discipline story at Bronx Design and Construction Academy, NYC, provides an example of how this works. Teachers note their concerns about student behavior and classroom disengagement in an online behavior log that the dean of students and advisors review daily. Patterns quickly emerge, and when administrators, teachers, and advisors share this information, they can address situations before problems escalate. "We have many students struggling as they adjust to high school and our expectations here," says dean Adam Parades.[2] The process of submitting and discussing low impact behavior concerns early on has also prompted teachers to engage in more proactive classroom management strategies that help students reengage before minor incidents become major discipline problems.

A second rationale for distinguishing two types of submissions relates to compliance issues that surround official office disciplinary referrals (ODRs). By federal law, every disciplinary referral that involves removal of a student from the classroom or public space, must be investigated by an administrator using "due process" and must ensure that all accompanying documentation be submitted to the district and the state department of education for review.

Put simply, "due process" is the right to a fair hearing when students are accused of a violation of a rule or law. In *Goss v Lopez*, the US Supreme Court considered what due process means for students facing temporary suspension from school, as well as temporary removal from the classroom, because of their alleged violations of school discipline rules. The Court concluded that accused students must be afforded an informal hearing with school administrators before such suspensions are determined or after a student is removed from a classroom. Today, more and more districts are under close scrutiny by state attorney generals and civil rights organizations to ensure that schools comply with the provisions cited in the 1975 Supreme Court ruling. Figure 8.1 is a summary of key points from the 1975 ruling.

Figure 8.1

GOSS ET AL. v. LOPEZ ET AL.

SUPREME COURT OF THE UNITED STATES 419 U.S. 565

January 22, 1975, Decided.

Students facing temporary suspension have interests qualifying for protection of the Due Process Clause, and due process requires, in connection with a suspension of 10 days or less, that the student be given oral or written notice of the charges against him and, if he denies them, an explanation of the evidence the authorities have and an opportunity to present his side of the story. The Clause requires at least these rudimentary precautions against unfair or mistaken findings of misconduct and arbitrary exclusion from school.

There need be no delay between the time "notice" is given and the time of the hearing. In the great majority of cases the disciplinarian may informally discuss the alleged misconduct with the student minutes after it has occurred. We hold only that, in being given an opportunity to explain his version of the facts at this discussion, the student first be told what he is accused of doing and what the basis of the accusation is.

When schools restrict the use of official disciplinary referrals to Tier 2 and 3 behavior violations and use an alternate referring tool for Tier 1 behavior concerns, "due process" investigation becomes a more manageable workload. Having access to data from less formal documentation allows for more collaborative consultation between all staff, more open-ended problem solving, a greater emphasis on understanding root causes of the situation, and increased support to help students take actions to make things right.

Considerations

Teachers will need support and professional learning experiences so they can easily understand what behaviors necessitate Tier 1 documentation and responses versus an ODR. This will ensure that all students are treated fairly when these distinctions are being made. There are two important things to look for: (1) teachers with high numbers of referrals need to be observed and supported to help them become more skillful, and (2) teachers need to be assured that their submissions of official Tier 2 and 3 referrals will be supported by the administration and taken seriously. Otherwise, teachers will not document and refer students with the highest needs, and schools will not have the right data. We have found that an hour-long session, where administrators, teachers, and student support staff work side by side to analyze student behavior scenarios and talk through what types of referrals are appropriate for a given situation, is a minimum requirement for this to work.

Schools will also need to establish structures and systems for processing the new types of referrals. How will the Student Support Team or grade level teams review, manage, and respond to students who engage in persistent Tier 1 behaviors that do not warrant student removal, but do require additional attention and support? We recommend that schools develop a threshold that triggers a timely response. For example, a threshold of three to five incidents might trigger an alert to a designated member of the Student Intervention Team who would immediately schedule a problem solving and planning conference with the student and referring teacher.

BARRIER #4

Inaccurate and Incomplete Referral Data

Possible Solution: Overhaul Referral Forms

Redesign referral tools to ensure accurate, consistent, and sufficiently detailed data.

Barrier Defined

Imprecise descriptors of behavioral concerns and violations make consistent and equitable responses challenging. When the referral form provides no common language to help teachers accurately identify the type of behavior concerns or violation, staff will inconsistently label the types of misbehaviors. Alternatively, when a referral form is too simplistic, making it easy for teachers to check the "disrespectful," "disruptive," "disobedient," "disorderly," and "defiant" boxes it is impossible to get a clear understanding of the behavior violation. Without knowing the exact type of misbehavior and the circumstances surrounding that behavior, the Student Support Team has to do significant legwork to uncover the information that will enable them to align an appropriate consequence and intervention. The result is a discipline response that is either too slow or disparate.

Possible Solutions

Referral data must be detailed enough to ensure alignment between discrete unwanted behaviors and the most appropriate consequences and interventions. Therefore, it is important to design office referral forms that capture a descriptive picture of the violation and the behavior in a diagnostic and non-judgmental way. In addition to identifying the specific behavior using the Code of Character, Conduct, and Support descriptors, referral data should include:

- The referring adult
- The time of the incident
- The location of the incident
- The subject or course if the incident occurred in the classroom
- The room arrangement or learning context in which the incident occurred
- A place for the specific narrative (What exactly did the student say and do?)
- Other pertinent information that might include steps/interventions taken to change the behavior prior to writing the referral or a record of any parental contact

These are the kinds of details that would inform a solution. The referral should also provide space for the Student Intervention Team or administrator to identify actions taken after the referral was processed including assignment of consequences and interventions; and document arrangements for follow-up conferences involving student, parent, teacher, support team member, and/or administer.

Considerations

A revamped Code of Character, Conduct, and Support might be a necessary precursor to ensure that you have consistent and clear behavior language and categories to use in the forms. Also, consider how the language on the referral forms can reinforce the message that referrals are not a punishment but rather a tool for communicating concern to the Student Support Team. We recommend getting input and feedback from a wide variety of staff when designing a better referral form and some targeted professional learning sessions to support effective use of the form. Requiring the person filling out the form to document strategies they have used to try and support the student in the moment is also a way to prompt teacher accountability and inform the best next step. While you might be tempted to tweak the form multiple times to get it exactly right, faculty will get frustrated if the form keeps changing so consider making only one refinement mid-year or wait until the start of the new school year before making any changes.

BARRIER #5

Fragmented Data Lead to Fragmented Responses

Possible Solution: Integrated Weekly Student Data Reports
Combine behavior, attendance, and grades into weekly student reports that capture a holistic picture of each student and serve to coordinate response efforts.

Barrier Defined:

Here is what we know about students who underachieve, demonstrate academic performance issues, have the potential to drop out, and students who frequently have conduct issues. Researchers have identified absenteeism, low or failing course grades, and suspension, often in combination, as the three most critical factors that place students at-risk for school and life success. It is notable that these factors, including suspension, are also signs of student disengagement. Although suspension may be a direct result of student misconduct on the surface, the majority of suspensions begin in the classroom when teachers encounter students' reluctance, resistance, or refusal to engage in classroom learning and are unable to reengage students in the moment or provide sustained support to turn around behaviors and mindsets that impede learning.[3]

As we mentioned earlier, behavior, attendance, grades, and counseling data and referrals often live in different silos. They are often managed and processed by different people using different time frames to review data, resulting in the delivery of completely separate interventions. For example, attendance data often resides with an attendance clerk who disseminates it to the attendance committee in charge of addressing attendance problems. On another floor, an academic accountability coordinator may be providing standardized test data to specific teachers with no other context than that of the student's performance on a particular assessment. Down the hall, an RTII specialist is screening students in order to red flag multi-year literacy and math gaps and will use that data to determine academic interventions. In another office, the dean or discipline assistant principal is processing disciplinary referrals without access to vital academic data that may be a contributing factor to discipline problems in the classroom. In the meantime, no one may have the charge of reviewing every student's grades on a continual basis to spot single and multiple course failures or upward or downward trends in academic performance. The result is the "broken mirror effect" in which shards of data result in a fractured set of services that do not necessarily target the priority needs of the student.

In our experience with schools around the country, the process of assigning discipline consequences is often isolated because the discipline staff has limited access to data that would provide a fuller picture of the student. This all matters because students' problem behaviors can often be the first visible signs of learning gaps and disconnects with the task or the teacher. When responses focus only on "fixing" the discipline problem, rather than helping the student experience greater success in school, interventions may never help the student to develop the desired behaviors that are likely to lead to more positive engagement and academic success in the classroom.

Possible Solutions

On the outset, we want to acknowledge that very few schools and districts have the capacity to input and retrieve critical behavior, attendance, and grade data for individual students from a single database. That said, working with multiple databases does not preclude schools from developing inclusive student reports that provide a combination of data, thus, making it possible for administrators, teachers, and Student Support Team members to discuss students' challenges and progress holistically.

Research has shown that integrated data is a must. Over the past 10 years, researchers at the University of Chicago Consortium and Johns Hopkins Talent Development Secondary took on the task of identifying the most effective strategies for improving middle and high school students' academic outcomes through strategic use of the right data. Years of exhaustive collection, analysis, and discussion of data with school partners produced only marginal achievement gains until schools did three things. First, schools needed to build the capacity to produce weekly individual student reports that contained cumulative and weekly data about attendance, course grades, and major discipline problems. Second, schools had to figure out a weekly protocol and forum for discussing and addressing concerns that emerged from the weekly individual student reports. Finally, schools had to figure out how to share this information with students, teachers, student support staff, and parents in ways that promoted problem solving and effective interventions. When these three conditions were met, achievement levels for struggling students increased dramatically at the same time that their attendance improved and disciplinary problems decreased. The research showed that using just three data points, behavior, attendance, and grades, (think "BAG" check) to determine the right interventions and assess and monitor student progress produced far better outcomes.[4] Figure 8.2 illustrates this significant insight. Even in schools where weekly grades are not formally recorded, quick check-ins with teachers or grade level teams about a student's academic status can often place discipline problems within a more nuanced context and link desired changes in behavior to goals for improving academic performance.[5]

Figure 8.2

Essential Diagnostic and Intervention Data

Creating ways to funnel essential **Behavior,** **Attendance,** *and* **Grades** *(BAG) data into weekly student-level reports is a diagnostic and intervention game-changer. It enables school staff to connect the dots among multiple concerns and data points so that they can develop more coherent interventions when students' challenges become barriers to learning and school success. This is particularly important for students at highest risk and students who are experiencing multiple problems across academic, behavioral, and emotional domains. All adults who are teaching and supporting an individual student can use a holistic data set to determine the right set of interventions.*

When all staff members are using the same holistic student reports on a weekly basis, other benefits become evident. First, it enables School Intervention Team members to place students on the "worry list" and "extremely urgent" list earlier and more efficiently. Second, when all staff use the same data set to inform their support of individual students, the aim of all interventions, regardless of the specific focus, becomes abundantly clear: support students to develop, strengthen, and engage in behaviors that will improve their academic, personal, and social efficacy. When a goal like this is held by all school staff, adults' interactions with students are much more likely to focus on the future instead of the past, and communicate hope and confidence in the student's capacity to learn, and grow, and do better.[6]

Considerations

It is important to frame the integrated data report as a tool that will support teachers and student support staff to do the jobs they have already been tasked with, not as one more thing they have to do. To that end, every effort must be made to ensure it is a useful tool, easily updated, and that the weekly protocol is streamlined and efficient, resulting in the faculty feeling efficacious.

BARRIER #6

No System to Monitor and Track Student Progress During Interventions

> **Possible Solution: A Singular Intervention Tracking and Monitoring System**
> All Student Support Team members logging their intervention work in one system.

Barrier Defined

If we want to understand how to impact student behaviors, we need to systematically assess the outcomes of our actions. Unfortunately, many schools do not have systems in place to monitor and track student progress during and after interventions and even fewer schools track the overall effectiveness of the interventions that are being delivered. While special education personnel might be actively monitoring student progress, very few discipline deans, assistant principals, and other student support staff have a way of actively tracking the impact of their efforts and the intervention.

Possible Solutions

Only recently have districts and schools begun to think about how they systematically gather intervention data that helps them (1) track what Student Support Team members actually do with students and their families, (2) monitor student progress during and after interventions, and (3) assess the effectiveness of interventions delivered to different cohorts of students for different problems within different frames of time. Some districts choose to create a cloud-based spreadsheet in which Student Support Team members can log in specific data. Research indicates progress monitoring needs to be systematic and frequent. Academically, students are more likely to stay on track when weekly monitoring of grades becomes a universal practice. Behaviorally, weekly monitoring gives students a timeframe during which to focus on desired end behaviors and ensures that teachers are providing feedback within that timeframe.

Schools need to decide on one tracking and monitoring system that all Student Support Team members will use to log their interventions with students. One approach to documenting the delivery of single incident and longer-term interventions is to develop a fairly simple student intervention-coaching log using Google Docs, Google Sheets, or a Microsoft Excel spreadsheet housed on a secure network drive.

Considerations

Documenting what student support staff members are doing with students, providing weekly progress monitoring for students, and assessing the success of specific interventions may involve a set of brand new tasks and radically different expectations. Consequently, involving the entire Student Support Team in a discussion of the goals and rationales for implementing these new practices is essential. Some teams might decide to implement these tasks in stages, first ensuring that a weekly progress monitoring loop is in place for students receiving longer-term interventions and then later taking on the tasks of documenting all student support sessions and assessing intervention effectiveness.

BARRIER #7

Schoolwide Data Trends are neither Comprehensive nor Disaggregated

> #### Possible Solution: Detailed and Disaggregated School Climate Data and Schoolwide Summary Reports
> Identify school climate survey results and a set of schoolwide summary reports that capture and reveal essential data.

Barrier Defined

As a reminder, earlier barriers focused on the collection and processing of individual student data and reports. This last barrier focuses on schoolwide climate, disciplinary, and attendance data.

School attendance and disciplinary data reports are often not sufficiently disaggregated or summarized in ways that help reveal important trends, patterns, and concerns. If we do not understand the problem, we cannot address it. The goal of schoolwide data collection, disaggregation, and analysis should be to see the school clearly; to identify positive and worrisome trends and patterns; to trouble-shoot problem areas that require immediate attention; and to assess progress in meeting school improvement benchmarks and outcomes. Data sources should be broad and varied enough to provide enough data points to create complete pictures of the school and different groups of students.

Possible Solutions

We strongly encourage schools to develop a plan for collecting, disaggregating, and analyzing the right schoolwide disciplinary and school climate data at frequent intervals over the course of a year. Lifting up the right data depends on the prioritized concerns a school is trying to address and the time of year.

The National Center on Safe Supportive Learning Environments (NCSSLE) maintains a compendium of valid and reliable surveys, assessments, and scales of school climate. These surveys can assist educators in their efforts to identify and assess student, staff, and parent perceptions related to physical and psychological safety, discipline and student support, student-student and student-teacher relationships, and other conditions that create a positive learning environment and learning-focused culture. Identifying survey trends and highlighting particular areas of concerns can provide a platform for School Climate-Discipline Teams to develop schoolwide initiatives that closely match prioritized concerns and desired outcomes.

A Washington, DC middle school that was experiencing an alarming number of student fights and aggressive incidents involving staff members invited us to assess their data and help them design an effective intervention that would reduce the number of fights and aggressive incidents. With the School Climate-Discipline Team we took a granular look at their data, disaggregating it by gender, grade level, students with disabilities, students with multiple aggressive incidents, and the location where the incidents took place. Of the 47 incidents over a two-month period, each grade level had similar numbers of incidents, but over 70 percent of the incidents involved special education students and just eight of those students were involved in the majority of incidents. Furthermore, we discovered that a majority of incidents were committed in five classrooms. Without access to the disaggregated data we could easily have designed an intervention that would have had little impact. Instead, we pulled in the special education teachers and the teachers who taught the students with excessive numbers of incidents and developed a multi-part intervention that included (1) beginning and end of week check-ins with all special education students to set goals, develop strategies for dealing with anger and frustration, and to learn how to ask for help; (2) special education case managers working with the teachers to provide more effective learning accommodations; (3) weekly progress monitoring that included a parent-check and feedback from the faculty; and (4) a weekly check-in breakfast with the principal with the nine students with multiple incidents. The result was a 50 percent drop in fights and aggressive incidents in the first month after the intervention was implemented. The lesson was clear – the right data can guide us to the right intervention.

Sample Data Points

We have included a comprehensive list of data points that will help to uncover attendance, academic, and disciplinary trends in your school. Your most significant concerns should inform the data you want to collect, disaggregate, and analyze. Disaggregating your data by category will help you identify the most impacted groups, and enable you to determine the most effective interventions to meet the desired changes in student outcomes. Consider disaggregating your data using these categories:

- Grade level
- Gender
- Race/Ethnicity
- GPA quartile (4= top 25%, 3=26-50%, 2= 51-75%, and 1=bottom 25 %)
- Students with disabilities
- Students with 504s
- Students living with someone other than a parent/guardian
- English language learners
- Student who receive free and reduced lunch
- Neighborhood (this may be critical if students experience safety concerns to and from school)

The School Climate-Discipline Team needs to prioritize the type of weekly, monthly, grading period, semester, or annual summary reports that will be most useful in their efforts to reduce problematic behaviors, ensure equity, and build and sustain a safe, civil, and caring school climate. We would like to offer a question set that can be used for discussion and analysis of any of the data points.

1. What do you see? *I notice…; I see…; It says that….*

2. What are your interpretations and questions? *I imagine…; I think…; I'm curious about…; I wonder…; I'm puzzled by…; I'm surprised about….*

3. What do you think you know after examining the data?

4. What else do you want to know? What other questions do you have? What requires further investigation?

5. What are the two or three most urgent concerns that emerge from the data?

6. What are the desired student outcomes related to your most urgent concerns? What do you want to increase or reduce?

7. How would you use this data with the whole faculty? With individual teachers?

8. How might you use this data to improve how teachers handle discipline in their classrooms?

Attendance Data Points

Choose to review, analyze, and compare summary and disaggregated data collected within a specific time period (weekly, monthly, grading period, semester, or year)

Daily Attendance
Average daily attendance

Number/% of students with 98% / 95% / 90% / 85% / 80% / 60% or better attendance

Number/% of students with less than 60% attendance

Number/% of students with 3/5/10/20 absences per grading period

Late Arrival to School
Number/% of students who arrive more than ten minutes late to school 3/5/10/20 times per grading period

Student late arrivals by teacher (1st and 2nd period)

Tardies during the School Day
Total number/% of students who are tardy during the school day

Number/% of students who are tardy during the school day 3/5/10/20 times per grading period

Number of tardies by teacher

Number of tardies by class period

Individual Student Data
Three or more / five or more / ten or more absences per grading period

Five consecutive absences

Three or more / five or more / ten or more late arrivals including class period and teacher per grading period

Three or more / five or more / ten or more cumulative tardies per grading period

Three or more / five or more / ten or more tardies in the same class including class period and teacher per grading period

Three or more / five or more / ten or more class cuts after student has arrived at school including class period and teacher

Academic Data Points

Choose to review, analyze, and compare summary and disaggregated data collected within a specific time period (weekly, monthly, grading period, semester, or year)

Number/% of students at risk of failing 1 or more classes	Number/% of students 3 or more years behind grade level in reading
Number/% of students at risk of failing 2 or more classes	Number/% of students 3 or more years behind grade level in math
Number/% of students failing 1 course	Number/% of freshman on track and off track to complete 9th grade within one year
Number/% of students failing 2 or more classes	Number of students who are significantly credit deficient in 10th grade, 11th grade, and 12th grade

Discipline Data Points

Choose to review, analyze, and compare summary and disaggregated data collected within a specific time period (weekly, monthly, grading period, semester, or year)

Office Disciplinary Referrals and Student Removal	Assignment to Intervention Center (IC), In-School Suspension (ISS) and Out-of-School Suspension (OSS)
Total number of behavior / office disciplinary referrals and student removal	Total number of IC assignments
Top five behavior violations that warranted behavior / office disciplinary referral and student removal with corresponding numbers for each violation	Numbers of students with two, three, and five or more IC
	Number of 1-day, 2-day, 3-day, and 5-day ISS and OSS
Number/% of students with 3/5/10/20 or more referrals and student removal	Top five behavior violations that warranted IC, ISS, and OSS and corresponding numbers for each violation
Number/% of referrals and student removal by class period	Number/% of total IC, ISS and OSS involving student-teacher conflicts
Number/% of referrals and student removal by teacher	Number/% of total IC, ISS and OSS involving student-student conflicts
Number% of referrals and student removal by grade level team or department	Number/% of total IC, ISS and OSS involving incidents of extreme violence/aggression and incidents that seriously jeopardize student and staff safety
Mean average number of classroom disciplinary referrals and student removal submitted within a given time period	**Data by Student** Three or more / five or more / ten or more referrals
Mode number of classroom disciplinary referrals and student removal submitted (This refers to the number of referrals submitted by individual teachers that occurs most often from within a given time period)	Three or more / five or more / ten or more student removals
	One-, two-, and three or more IC, ISS, and OSS
	Top 10% of students with the most referrals, student removals, ISS, and OSS

Office Disciplinary Referrals and Student Removal *continued*	Assignment to Intervention Center (IC), In-School Suspension (ISS) and Out-of-School Suspension (OSS) *continued*
Range of referrals and student removal submitted by individual teachers from fewest to highest	Other Disciplinary Data
Number/% of total referrals and student removal that involve student-teacher conflict	Number of students who are walking the halls and public spaces without a pass by class period
Number/% of total referrals and student removal from the classroom	Number of students who are walking the halls and public spaces without a pass during announced and unannounced hall sweeps
Number/% of total referrals and student removal from public space incidents	Number of district hearings by violation
	Number of long-term suspensions and alternative placements by violation

Additional Options for Data Collection

- Classroom walkthroughs to focus on observable student and teacher behaviors
- Public space walkthroughs that focus on observable student and teacher behaviors

Considerations

A professional data report is not the end goal, and we certainly do not want to burden schools with more work. Our hope is that schoolwide data reports will serve as a valuable tool for understanding and impacting discipline problems at your school. For example, the data might indicate a peak time period or day for when the majority of referrals incidents are occurring. This allows your team to explore possible explanations and identify solutions. If one day of the week or a particular period of the day generates a markedly higher number of referrals, what might teachers and administrators do differently to lower the number of referrals at that time? For example, if it is revealed that 60 percent of discipline incidents happen in the hallways after lunch and during the period immediately following lunch, a school might explore ways to have more adult supervision in public spaces right after lunch and ask all teachers to meet and greet students at the door during the period after lunch.

After you have collected, disaggregated, and analyzed attendance and disciplinary data for at least one grading period, identify which summary reports to run systematically that are most likely to capture what you need to review regularly and vigilantly. These will generate the key data that will inform interventions and schoolwide practices.

[1] Farrington, C.A., Roderick, M., Allensworth, E., Nagaoka, J., Keyes, T.S., Johnson, D.W., & Beechum, N.O. (2012). Teaching adolescents to become learners. The role of noncognitive factors in shaping school performance: A critical literature review. Chicago: University of Chicago Consortium on Chicago School Research.

[2] Davidson, J. (2014). Restoring Justice. Teaching Tolerance, (47). doi:http://www.tolerance.org/magazine/number-47-summer-2014/feature/restoring-justice

[3] Iver, M. (2013). Early Warning Indicators of High School Outcomes. Journal of Education for Students Placed at Risk (JESPAR), (18), 1-6. doi:10.1080/10824669.2013.745375 Martha Abele Mac Ivera

[4] Farrington, C.A., Roderick, M., Allensworth, E., Nagaoka, J., Keyes, T.S., Johnson, D.W., & Beechum, N.O. (2012). Teaching adolescents to become learners. The role of noncognitive factors in shaping school performance: A critical literature review. Chicago: University of Chicago Consortium on Chicago School Research.

[5] Allensworth, E. (2013). The Use of Ninth-Grade Early Warning Indicators to Improve Chicago Schools. Journal of Education for Students Placed at Risk (JESPAR), 18(1), 68-83.

[6] ibid

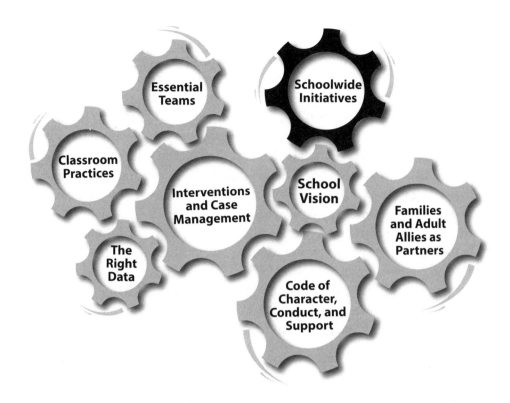

Schoolwide Initiatives

How do we prioritize and implement schoolwide promotion and prevention initiatives that will create an improved school climate?

CHAPTER OUTLINE

Introduction
Physical Environment
Pro-Social Interactions
School Bonding
Student Voice
Orientation and the First Month of School

Introduction

Perceptions of school climate reveal the heart and soul of a school — the extent to which every student and adult feels safe, respected, welcomed, and attached to the larger school community. School leaders have shared with us two challenges they associate with implementing schoolwide climate initiatives. One challenge is simply trying to balance efforts to establish an academically rigorous school culture with equivalent efforts to promote safety, order, good character and conduct, school bonding, and student voice. Bonding to school is one of the strongest indicators of healthy adolescent development and academic achievement.[1] School bonding involves two important ideas: *school attachment*, a student's emotional connections to peers and adults, and *school commitment*, a student's investment in the group, a student's self-identification with the values of schooling and achievement, and a student's pride in attending school.[2] The risk of focusing on common core curriculum and instruction as the exclusive remedy for improving student achievement comes at the cost of appreciating how the quality of the school climate influences student motivation and engagement.

The other challenge arises from questions about who organizes schoolwide initiatives and to what extent the staff are expected to participate in them. Even though the School Climate-Discipline Team, as described in Chapter 7, has the major role in prioritizing and organizing these initiatives, a positive school climate is the responsibility of all school stakeholders, including all staff, students, families, and invested community members. Schools that achieve 100% staff participation in schoolwide initiatives often do two things that generate their good will and enthusiasm. First, schools reach consensus about professional responsibilities beyond the delivery of quality instruction and services that feel fair and reasonable for every adult to carry out. Second, schools offer a menu that invites every staff member to choose a minimum number of schoolwide events and activities in which they want to participate during the school year.

This gear, Schoolwide Initiatives, focuses on Tier 1 activities, events, and strategies that support a safe, orderly, and attractive physical environment, promote pro-social behavior and communication within these spaces, strengthen school bonding, and increase student voice in the day to day life of school.

These initiatives have a universal reach in a school because these opportunities are accessible to every student and are intended to have an impact on every student. The chapter is organized into five sections, (1) physical environment, (2) pro-social interactions, (3) school bonding, (4) student voice, and a special section (5) student orientation and the first month of school. We are confident that the suggestions offered can help initiate a conversation about options that are most relevant to your school context. Many schools and districts strategically collect and use school climate data to leverage what is working; name the concerns; and identify, prioritize, and strategically plan initiatives that align with desired school climate outcomes.

Physical Environment

How we feel about the physical environment shapes how we behave in it and how we take care of it. The physical environment can potentially make adults and students feel safe and welcome, or afraid and alienated. Students respond more positively to places that are attractive and cared for, and thus, are more likely to do the right thing to help maintain them. A Carnegie Foundation report on urban schools concluded, "The tacit message of the physical indignities in many urban schools is not lost on students. It bespeaks neglect, and students' conduct seems simply an extension of the physical environment that surrounds them."[3] Focus, attention, and care for the physical environment can be part of a catalytic process of school development and improvement. Our hallways, lunchrooms, classrooms, foyers, and offices can inspire, engage, and shape the ways in which we move around the school community throughout the day. The intentional design of signage and arrangement of physical space communicates how we will live and work and learn together in our school community. It is critical to let students know at an assembly or town meeting how the entirety of the physical environment serves as a resource to support good conduct and purposeful learning.

Use of Space

Gathering Areas in Public Space: If positive social interaction among students is a desired goal, schools need to create inviting spaces where students can hang out, talk, and study together. Creating spaces that invite conversation and positive interactions among smaller groups of students supports critical communication and relationship skills. Think about how you can spruce up public spaces inside and outside the building. Some schools create carpeted conversation zones, install benches, and establish comfortable seating and table groups throughout public space areas. The change in atmosphere is stunning and communicates the message, "We know you like to hang out and be social so we are providing you inviting spaces to do this." It also communicates that adults trust students to use these spaces to engage with each other in productive ways. A principal in Denver, Colorado, with limited space, created "cozy corners" for students to sit and talk with each other. He paid particular attention to the wall space to make sure it had a piece of student art, or a photograph, and there was signage supporting students to understand the purpose of the space. Enlist students, parents, and staff members who have an eye for design to be part of this type of effort.

Study Spaces: Many schools establish "homework hall" two or three times a week for students who choose to stay late and complete work, or for students who are required to stay after school and complete work when they get behind in a specific course. This takes commitment from a group of faculty members who are willing to oversee this activity and create the spaces that are needed for students to feel focused, organized, and productive. The success of "homework hall" is as good as its implementation and monitoring. This structure needs to have rituals and routines, the environment needs to be pleasant and comfortable, and the adult(s) need to see this as a service to help students use their time wisely.

In order to move this forward, here are some questions to consider: In what ways does the room arrangement support independent work, small group work, and one-to-one conversations with adults? Is the room resource-ready? By this, we mean are there computers available, and is the room stocked with paper, pencils, and project supplies such as tape, glue, scissors, etc.? Are there postings for how the room will be used and/or an "expectations postcard" that explains the behavioral and academic expectations and the opportunity this room and time provide for the student to get back on track? Are there student ambassadors available to help students who are new to the homework hall make the transition?

Some schools pay faculty members a stipend to supervise homework hall. Teams, academies, and small learning communities can also establish their own homework halls. If students have no way home, they cannot stay after school. It is worthwhile to launch a campaign to get approval and funding for late busses twice a week for homework hall, tutorials, and other academic interventions.

Large Meeting Spaces: Physical arrangement of auditoriums and gymnasiums need to be reviewed prior to the school year. Visual postings, which are addressed later in this chapter, will help students learn appropriate conduct in large spaces more quickly. Equally important, assigned seating of student cohorts supervised by different adults results in organized and orderly gatherings, especially when the interests for doing so are explained to students. We worked with a school in Massachusetts, where once a week the cafeteria was changed into an assembly for 365 students. Chairs were arranged by grade levels, each group of 20 students sat with their advisor in an assigned set of rows, and clear pathways were designated to support traffic flow. At the end of the assembly, students were dismissed by grade and advisor cohort, and each student took their folding chair and placed it on a flatbed so the janitorial staff could easily move them. Students did this willingly after they were publically introduced to the janitorial staff who thanked them in advance for helping them with their job. The staff, of course, had to model, teach, practice, and assess this critical procedure over several weeks. But by the third week, it took only eight to ten minutes to move 365 students.

Cafeteria: The cafeteria is a place where schools have a real opportunity to consider how to arrange the room to support healthy social interactions, help students navigate the space with ease, and to meet behavioral expectations. We hear the concerns of so many leaders and teachers about the conditions of the cafeteria: the cleanliness, the noise level, the student behaviors, and students feeling alone and isolated amidst the crowds. Setting the stage for improved conditions in the cafeteria takes a committed group of staff and students who conduct a deep analysis on persistent concerns. In these discussions, staff and students talk about what is and is not working and share ideas for improving the cafeteria experience.

Creating a cafeteria plan that is approved by the principal and the School Climate-Discipline Team is essential. Putting procedures in place for issues such as transitioning in and out of the cafeteria, cleanup procedures, and noise levels need to be clear. Running smooth cafeteria sessions is all about having clear procedures. Students need them modeled and they need time to practice, self-assess, and receive feedback. In a middle school we worked with in Massachusetts the cafeteria hour runs like a well-oiled machine. The principal, leadership team, teachers, custodial staff and security personnel came together to design the cafeteria plan. Students had a practice week to get it right, and the adult supervisors in the cafeteria went through a training session to support healthy interactions with students. Finally, a committee of students, staff, and parents paid attention to the visuals on the walls and hung items such as photographs, the mission statement, and rules.

We would like to offer the following questions as you consider ideas for your own cafeteria make-over: How might you cordon off the cafeteria into clusters of tables that are marked by names, letters, or numbers? How do you creatively assign these tables to cohorts of students? How do students enter the cafeteria, get their food, and move to their assigned cluster? How does each cluster exit? What are their responsibilities for throwing their trash away, cleaning their space, and leaving no trace? We want to note that many of the cafeteria settings we have observed are woefully devoid of adequate trashcans.

Solutions to these questions prompt the need for explicit procedures that will promote the desired behaviors that you expect. If students are seated by cohort cluster, for example, they will need to practice choosing a seat within the designated area, cleaning up their area, and exiting by cluster. The supervision for table clusters needs to be systematically organized and include a staff discussion about ways to encourage civil conversation and appropriate behaviors. Often we see adults chatting with each other around the perimeter of the lunch room. It is critical that lunch supervision is constant, supportive, and friendly. Lunchtime supervisors need to be prepared to support students who enter the cafeteria presenting a range of emotions — some students cannot wait to be with their friends, while some may feel isolated, and others might be stressed from a bad morning.

Hall Passes: An organized hall pass system that has clear protocols is efficient, and easily implemented will ensure commitment from the staff and follow-through with regard to implementation. Hall walkers will take advantage of uneven enforcement, so be sure to get consensus from your staff. Inviting staff and student input when developing and/or fine-tuning the protocols for hall passes will support implementation efforts. Consider color coding hall passes by floor or building section so it is easy to identify the floor or area to which a student should be returning. Laminate these passes and be sure there is a procedure in the classroom where they are picked up and returned. Gather a group of students who want to participate in the design of the hall pass, laminate them, and deliver them to teachers to be used throughout the year.

Visual Postings

Mission, Core Beliefs, and Core Values: Many of the schools with whom we work have mission statements and core beliefs and values that are aspirational and inspiring. And, so often, they are not visually alive or at the center of critical conversations with regard to school improvement. Posting the mission statement and core beliefs and values in strategic places throughout the school enables staff and students to interact with them at critical moments and it keeps the spirit of the mission statement alive. While meeting with a principal and his leadership team in a school in upstate New York, we asked how the school's mission statement and core beliefs and values aligned with their goals for discipline. The mission statement was not in the room, neither posted on the walls nor at the table. When the principal retrieved the statement, it became apparent to the entire Administrative Team how valuable the statement was, and how important it is to have it front and center when making decisions. Where are the strategic places in your school setting to post a mission statement?

Schedule: Posting the daily schedule(s) in strategic places throughout the school can help many students feel anchored and enables them to move from one place to the next with more ease. It also helps teachers, security, and administrators engage in more productive conversations with students who might be loitering or appear confused. The large-scale schedule becomes a piece of data that can inform the conversation between the adult and the student to help them move along. *"I see that your seventh grade class is currently in science and that you have lunch right after. Have a good class and I will check-in with you at lunch. Thanks for moving along."* Students can be involved in posting the schedules, and in sprucing them up with artwork, photographs, or icons.

Six Big Rules: Thoughtful school leaders and leadership teams have spent countless hours creating school rules to support students to be self-directed, self-managed, and self-disciplined. Yet, we often do not see them posted in strategic areas of the school. Posting effective school rules in classrooms, in several places throughout a floor or wing of the school, in the cafeteria, in the foyer provides gentle reminders to students that this is the way we will conduct ourselves in this setting. Adults can proactively engage a student with the poster on rules when they see a rule about to be broken. *"Hey, Jamal! Good to see you. Let's take a look over here at this rule. Remember when we discussed this in your advisory meeting?"* Posting rules and keeping them alive will only be successful if the students and the staff have been involved in a dialogue about the reasons and interests for having the rules in the first place. In a school we worked with in Austin, Texas, an art class created icons for the rules. The principal met with the students in the class along with some upper classmen to brainstorm with the students what icons might work for the rules. The icons were then put in front of all students in their homeroom structure and voted upon. This inclusive process lends itself to students following the rules and increases staff commitment to enforcing the rules that shape important behaviors.

Photographs: Hanging photographs of day-to-day interactions of staff, students, and families and special traditions and events anchor us to times and places where engagement is visible, joy is alive, learning is evident, and relationships are valued over time. These photographs have the potential to be visual models for the ways in which we are expected to participate in school, in learning, and in relationships. A school we supported in Massachusetts has its halls lined with large photographs of their daily life. We have observed students at the school individually and in clusters pausing and talking about them, smiling and laughing, and some in cases students quietly reflecting as they study what they see. Powerful visuals evoke emotions, drive deeper engagement, and can potentially transform behavior. Choosing the right photographs is critical and takes an invested team of students and staff to guide the process. Cultural relevancy, authenticity, and visuals that capture the human experience are factors to consider. Why this photograph? What is it communicating to our school members?

Student Work: Posting students' work is a collaborative process with students and takes time, commitment, and ongoing attention and care. Work needs to be carefully chosen, and the visual display needs to be created, rotated, updated, and maintained. This cyclical process indicates that learning is ongoing and evolving. A middle school we work with in Denver, Colorado, is visually alive with student work. One can walk the hallways and classrooms and see the learning, thinking, voice, and choice afforded to students as they navigate their day-to-day learning environments. When student work is posted there is an inherent message that we value learning, we value students collectively and individually and what they bring to the process; both their successful and less successful efforts, not just their masterpieces. This strategy is not one we recommend without prior discussion as it takes the collected thinking of a committed group to explain the value of using this strategy, set criteria for posting student work, and ensure that students are involved in the process.

Attendance and School Discipline Updates: Posting monthly changes in attendance, referral, and suspension data invites staff, parents, and students to assess and celebrate a school's progress in achieving targeted improvements in student outcomes as a whole school as well as disaggregated by grade, gender, race, etc. Making and keeping this data public encourages school communities to continue implementing their attendance and discipline plans long after the September honeymoon period.

Pro-Social Interactions

Thousands of social interactions among and between students, staff, and parents happen every day in a school. At a very basic level, healthy relationships foster warmth; set the stage for physical, emotional, and intellectual safety; and result in students learning a complex set of verbal and nonverbal skills to communicate their feelings and negotiate a range social interactions more confidently. When adults nurture relationships and model healthy communication in a variety of formal and informal settings, they are providing students with a foundation for developing critical social and emotional competencies.

Faculty Meet and Greets

We are often asked to evaluate a school's climate and culture, which includes their public spaces. One winter morning, a team of us watched a principal and key staff stand at the entrance of the school in upstate New York, meeting and greeting students as they entered. With smiles all around, good mornings, high fives, and fist bumps, the students had the opportunity to make a transition from their home culture or bus culture to their school culture. Some students approached the principal to shake his hand. We learned that this was a ritual in the school. The morning hallways were calm, orderly, and marked with adolescent chatter. This school had a consistent team greeting students. In other schools, staff members are invited (that means every adult in the building) to volunteer several times a year to be part of the morning welcome team that meets and greets students as they arrive in the morning. We have also seen high schools where upperclassmen serve as greeters. In all cases, the adult or student greeters need to be trained on the meet and greet protocol and learn how to engage students who might enter school already looking a bit low, anxious, or agitated. Students notice the difference when friendly adults are visible in public spaces and when someone is there to greet them in the morning. This morning ritual has the power to change the attitude of a student as she/he begins her day.

If you have a student leadership team that shares responsibility for improving school climate and culture, invite them to join with the School Climate-Discipline Team to generate ideas for official student "meet and greets" several times every semester. Here are some ideas that other schools have implemented:

- Pass out buttons that contain a phrase or symbol that is associated with a schoolwide campaign around issues of respect, diversity, violence, harassment, etc.

- Hand out a "quote of the day" to every person who arrives in the morning. This can be done at ritualized times of the year. Many students hang on to these, tape them to their lockers, or use them as bookmarks. One school created a bulletin board and over the course of the year the quotes grew and students started to add their own.

- Welcome students and pass out a reminder for a specific schoolwide event: a service project; spirit week activities; activities that that are part of a special week-long focus or theme.

- During exam week, pass out energy bars (no nuts) and wish everyone well.

- Pass out special ribbons designating schoolwide promotion and support of a particular cause or conviction. For example, some schools pass out purple ribbons on the day before prom as a reminder not to drink and drive.

Administrative Team and Teacher Hallway Presence during Transitions

Schools where adults are strategically placed and where every teacher stands at the door during transitions see dramatic improvement in the way students move from one class to the next. Clear protocols help expedite hallway traffic and promote safety, respect, courtesy, and friendliness. Here are five options that adults might consider to make hallways and other public spaces safe, respectful, and civil:

1. Require everyone to wear ID badges. For some students and families/adult allies, ID badges may trigger concerns about the school becoming a "police state." However, given the times in which we live, for safety reasons alone, ID badges make sense. Some schools color code ID badges by grade level, which can give adults an instant picture of who is traveling in public spaces. Moreover, in large schools, where it is impossible to know every student, it can feel totally unreasonable to expect adults to remind students to lower the decibel level, take off their hats, clean up their language, slow down, or move on to class, if adults have no way of knowing who students are. Calling students by name is the beginning of civil, decent, and respectful interactions.

2. Create a public space map that helps you identify the hallways, stairwells, and "hang-out spots" where students are most likely to congregate, goof off, or engage in over-the-top behaviors. It will also help you to identify peak periods when congestion is at its worst. This is where the adults need to be strategically placed and trained in how to interact with students who start to engage in behaviors that disrupt the safety of others.

3. Create a weekly schedule in which all adults in the building sign up for a public space posting during the same periods on the same day(s) every week. Stationing the same personnel in the same spot is crucial so adults become familiar with the students and traffic flow in their area. Every adult in the school stops what they are doing between classes and supports an orderly change of classes. Here is one way to divide supervision of different public space locations:

   - Faculty members are stationed outside of their classrooms during periods when they teach to meet and greet their students.
   - Faculty members are stationed near stairwells during periods when they are not teaching.
   - Guidance, support staff, administrators, and classified staff are stationed at exits, entrances, and trouble spots where congestion and dawdling are major problems.
   - Security personnel and school aides use a map of the school to configure "walkabouts" for each person that will ensure coverage of the whole building between class periods.

   This takes initial planning up front and the commitment of all staff to fully participate and follow through with implementing a public space improvement program. In our experience, when staff members are presented with public space incident data and also have an opportunity to analyze staff, student, and parent culture/climate survey data that reveals significant issues with public space, more often than not, most staff will get on board to make the school more safe for students and for themselves. Teachers need to see that administration is at the helm of this work. Once the plan is designed and the bugs of the plan are worked out, staff and students experience order and calm and a positive and spirited energy during transitions.

4. Conduct hall scans. A hall scan is a ritualized procedure carried out by a group of administrators, safety personnel, and other staff members who "walk-through" the entire building at random times during the day in order to keep traffic flow of students clear of congestion, encourage students to move to class in an orderly manner and arrive on time, and identify and process students who are in public spaces during class and without permission so that chronic "hall walkers" can be assigned appropriate consequences and interventions. An administrator is identified to become the hall-scan coordinator. A schedule is created for announced and unannounced daily hall scans for the first four to five weeks of school, and thereafter at strategic times during the year (e.g. after long weekends, holidays and vacations).

5. Ask teacher leaders to facilitate table discussions with small groups of faculty on the topic of "Getting Students' Cooperation to Follow Public Space Expectations." The discussion might include the following topics:

    *   What do you want your more visible and vigilant presence in public spaces to communicate? Consider the goals of your interactions with students in public spaces—what is most important? *"We're glad you're here and we want to support you to get to class on time and promote a safe, orderly, friendly atmosphere."*

    *   Review school rules and public space expectations so you can clearly communicate those expectations to students. Name specific behaviors, both for adults and students, which promote safety, civility, and respect. Name specific behaviors that "cross the line" of safety, civility, and respect. Agree on the expectations that all adults are willing to support and enforce.

    *   Review specific procedures you want adults to use when they witness behaviors that "cross the line" of safety, civility, and respect.

    *   Invite the group to discuss the differences in tone, language, and demeanor between these two approaches: (1) demanding immediate obedience in ways that are hostile or aggressive and can turn a minor infraction into a major incident or confrontation, and (2) reminding and asking students to cooperate in a friendly way.

    *   Provide examples of ineffective and effective responses as shown in Figure 9.1 and have groups of teachers, administrators, security staff, and others to come up with additional scenarios that will help adults help students do the right thing in the moment.

Figure 9.1

Responses

"Asking for Trouble" Responses	Effective Responses that invite cooperation and self-correction
"Take that hat off right now, this minute!" "It's you again! How many times do I have to tell you to move your behind to class?"	"Love that hat and you need to find another place to put it right now." "The clock's running. I know you don't want to be late."

- Facilitate conversations with all students about issues of respect, civility, and responsible behaviors in public spaces and share the plan to support their transitions throughout the day. Ideal discussion times might include during a designated class period, homeroom or advisory session, or assembly or town meeting.

Schoolwide Communication

Students, families/adult allies, and staff members want to be part of the communication loop that keeps everyone informed of what is going on in the life of a school. All community members want to feel connected and engaged. Some of the schools have this down to a science, where they have a set of complementary communication structures and venues to ensure they are reaching all the constituent groups through their preferred or only mediums. In a school we worked with in Austin, Texas, the principal and staff member responsible for communications made sure that the following structures were seamlessly connected: the school website; a monthly newsletter for parents, staff, and students; a wall-size calendar in the foyer decorated with art, events, holidays; a weekly email to the staff from the principal and leadership team; and a Sunday evening phone call that was recorded and released to all families about the upcoming week in Spanish and English. These overlapping structures had similar information, and in some cases new and updated information.

More often than not when we talk with staff members, the communication structures in the schools are fractured. We offer the following questions to consider: Who is the gatekeeper of all communications? How might you engage a group of students who like to write, draw and gather information? What are the monthly deadlines for updating communication in all venues? We recommend that they start small, routinize the structures, follow through, and stay the course. A school community will feel nurtured, cared for, and more invested if they are kept abreast of what is happening around them.

School Bonding

As discussed earlier in the chapter, school bonding, both *attachment* to students and adults at school and *commitment* to the values of school, offers a powerful antidote to student disengagement, apathy, and absenteeism. The structures, strategies, and activities in this section foster a sense of belonging, inspire school pride, and reinforce a student's identity as an invested member of the school community.

Homerooms, Homeroom Cluster Groups, or Advisory Groups

Most schools have a homeroom structure and some schools have a very powerful advisory program in place. This is a time where the same group of students comes together daily or two to three times a week to check-in with the adult who is their caretaker. School leadership has an opportunity to step back and consider how a homeroom structure and/or advisory program supports a positive respectful and engaging school climate and to what end? What are the goals? How have we involved staff and students in the conversation about the reasons behind these structures? What are the roles and responsibilities of students and staff, so that we can maximize the time whether it is 10 minutes, or 30 minutes in the case of advisory? Students in these structures have a place to be known and feel connected. They get questions answered, they might make a friend over time, or find a resource to help them with one of their classes. They may get fed, have a chance to share a concern, and have an adult help them get to the right resource. This connection is about listening, leaning in, and learning about the students entering their room. A school we worked with in Colorado had an extended homeroom each morning for 10 minutes. It was a highly ritualized time for the students where they signed in, shared breakfast, sent in attendance to the front office, and reviewed the upcoming day. It was a tone setter.

Everyone Participates!!

From the perspective of promoting positive student behavior and fostering feelings of attachment and commitment to school, a number one priority should be ensuring that every student is engaged in something at school to which they attach personal meaning and expression. All youth development opportunities, whether classified as co-curricular, extra-curricular, sports, service learning, student leadership, peer education initiatives, or special projects, performances or submissions in electives or core classes, share some common features: a sense of belonging and membership; a strong peer group; student initiated, designed, and directed activities; frequent and regular contact with the same group of students or adult over an extended period of time; opportunities to develop new skills and mastery; a strong sense of purpose; and opportunities for teamwork.[4]

Students who participate in some meaningful activity at school have higher grades, higher graduation rates, fewer disciplinary problems, and more focused future aspirations.[5] "Participation in extracurricular activities in high school appears to be one of the few interventions that benefit low-status, disadvantaged students – those less well-served by traditional educational programs – as much as or more than their more advantaged peers."[6]

Here are two very different strategies for making this happen for every student. The first comes from an Anchorage, Alaska, high school that discovered that 20 percent of their students were involved in multiple school activities while the other 80 percent participated in nothing. They also found out that many students had afterschool obligations that prevented their participation. The student council and interested teachers designed a survey to find out what students were most interested in, matched up adults to sponsor activities that made the cut, and created a one-hour activity period once a week within the school schedule. Some offerings stayed the same while others changed on a quarterly basis. The result? Everyone had something they had chosen to do, from more traditional student activities to a club focused on creating intricately beautiful flies for fishing season. Who knew that 200 kids in Alaska would sign up for salsa dancing?

Lyons Township High School in LaGrange, Illinois, wanted to boost participation of "outlier" students and students from lower-income communities within the school district. They did three things that increased extra-curricular and co-curricular participation to 93 percent. First, students carried out a "join up" campaign every fall. Second, at the end of every quarter, when students reflected on their academic progress they also reflected on what experiences during the quarter, both academic and non-academic, had special meaning for them and identified specific school activities in which they had participated. Third, advisors followed up with students who had no activity entries by engaging them in conversations about what might be blocking their involvement and discussing what might be the best thing to try on and try out.

Sustaining the effort to ensure that each and every student is attached to an extra-curricular activity takes time and planning. It also takes adults checking in on all students to encourage them to find an interest, take a risk, and try something. Earlier we addressed the homeroom structure and the advisory structure. In both cases, there can be ritualized times of the year when adults share options with students and schedule "sign-up sessions" along with check-in sessions to see how things are going mid-semester. Adults need to convey to students that these experiences are valuable and that there is a place for every student to participate. There also needs to be a monitoring structure to assess student engagement and follow through.

Whole School Assembly and Town Meetings

Ritualized school assemblies and/or grade level town meetings that are regularly scheduled, have purpose, are highly structured, and come with anticipation of a shared tradition or surprise support order, engagement, curiosity, and celebration. Every school setting is unique and the physical environment needs as much attention as the content of the assembly or town meeting to ensure focus, attention, and care for those in attendance and those facilitating the assembly or town meeting.

Town meetings can be organized within a team, a grade level, or a combination of several classes. They serve many purposes, including discussion of issues when it is critical for everyone to hear and discuss the same information at the same time, such as a serious incident; when there is a significant change in school personnel or policies; or when an external event in the community impacts the life of the school. Town meetings are also a time for students to share their concerns about problems and provide a time to generate resolutions.

Schools that have successfully integrated assemblies and town meetings into their communities understand the importance of identifying the goals for such a gathering. They also recognize the critical and ongoing planning, persistence, and patience it takes to ritualize them, and embed them into the school schedule as a key structure in support of a healthy school climate. They ask these questions: Where is it held and what is the intentional seating arrangement? What are the rituals and routines? What is the structure for the anchor experience within the assembly? What is the protocol for student involvement? What are the roles and responsibilities of the adults and what does supervision look like?

We do not want students and staff to just show up, we want them to look forward to the opportunity to come together as a community—to have a shared experience. We witnessed a principal and student assembly team open the year by previewing the structure for the fourteen assemblies that would take place: the purpose of the assemblies, some of the highlights on the schedule, and the rituals of entering, opening, closing, and exiting to return to class. In this particular case, they had music playing while students and their advisor moved to their assigned seats. The name of the song and artist was projected on screen. A student welcomed the community and asked for a moment of silence *"to help us make the transition into the assembly, to gather our focus and attention."* The agenda for the assembly was projected. They ended the assembly by thanking the presenters and asking the school to give a round of applause to those who organized and facilitated the assembly. They projected when they would see them next time around and thanked them for their attention and focus. They introduced the exit protocol and dismissed by sections and rows. The rows were numbered so the facilitator could say *"Rows one and seven please make your way to your next class."* This takes a lot of time up front, but once the rituals and organizational structures are put in place, assemblies and town meetings can be a powerful place to honor, celebrate, and inspire.

Celebrations and Acknowledgements

Acknowledging students' growth and effort over time sends a message to students that *"We notice your efforts and successes."* This honoring of specific achievements results in students feeling cared for and encourages students to continue to put forth time and effort. For example, many schools recognize those students who make the Honor Roll. We have also seen schools recognize students who have made measurable progress in improving their GPAs from one grade report to another. Principals have invited these students to attend a special lunch or dessert where they receive a certificate. In another school, teachers submitted the name of one student from each class whom they wished to honor for their efforts to turn around their attitude and/or their performance in class over the course of a grading period. These students were invited to a special celebration breakfast and school staff rotated throughout the school year and contributed breakfast treats, so every staff person participated at least once a year.

Consider end-of-week or end-of-quarter appreciations or acknowledgements where students share out loud in a circle, on paper, on post-its, or in graphic form an appreciative statement. Schools rotate periods for this 10 to 15 minute activity; so if a school has a seven period day, every teacher is committed to one Friday every seven weeks. This translates in 20,000 minutes when students and teachers pause to share a highlight of the week, something they are proud of accomplishing, someone who has helped them, someone who has stood up for a person or a principle, or someone who made class more interesting or intellectually challenging, etc.

We recognize these efforts take time and a School Climate-Discipline Team that is interested in coordinating them. What is most critical is to find structures that honor a range of students for the incremental changes they are making on their journey as adolescents. The structure needs to feel viable and ritualized, because students will come to love these gatherings and count on them.

School Spirit Day and Weeks

School spirit events can promote school pride and community identity; support a common goal; or affirm a schoolwide value, belief, or principle. Or they can just be about fun, providing a good excuse to break the routine, lighten up, laugh and enjoy each other's company. The problem is that school spirit activities are usually designed, marketed, and carried out by a few students who often represent only one group of students in the school. A School Climate-Discipline Team needs to ensure that it represents a diverse range of students and staff in the school community. As you think about broadening the appeal of and participation in school spirit activities, you might use these questions as a starting point for assessing and reimagining school spirit days.

- What purposes do you want school spirit activities and events to serve?
- What types of events would involve and engage the entire school community?
- Make a list of current "school spirit" activities and events? How often do they happen? Who coordinates them? Who actually participates in them? Are there any patterns or trends that stand out when you look at your data? How are they inclusive of the student population?
- How might different groups sponsor different events for different grade levels?
- As you brainstorm ideas, think about the purpose it might serve, and the groups to whom it would appeal the most.
- If your school's improvement plan contains goals related to school climate, check to see if your ideas align with your school improvement goals.
- As you prioritize and select events, keep asking, *"What will it really take to pull this off and achieve the goals of the event?"* Specifically ask:
  - Who needs to be a part of this effort?
  - Who is going to coordinate and organize it?
  - Who is going to publicize it?
  - How will you get your friends interested?
  - How much time do you need for planning?
  - What resources do you need?
  - When is the best time of the year for this event?

Figure 9.2 offers examples of school spirit events and activities:

Figure 9.2

Activity Chart

Purpose of Event or Activity	Description of Sample Events and Activities
School Pride	Academic Pep Rallies that celebrate schoolwide academic improvement, individual and group accomplishments, academic competitions, the big push before finals or state exams, etc.
	Pep Rallies for the "other teams" at school that do not get the same visibility and support as football and basketball.
	Awards and Recognition Day: Multiple venues throughout the day where students receive awards, notes, recognition, cheers, etc. for their academic achievements and improvement, personal accomplishments and talents, and contributions to the school and larger community. Every student gets recognized whether it is a personal note from one adult in the building to the announcement of the Valedictorian.
Community Identity	Alumni Week: All kinds of activities that welcome and celebrate former students and connect alumni and current students in conversations around life after high school.
	School Redesign Week: For high schools which are developing a redesign plan/smaller learning communities, all members of the community participate in surveys, discussions, and design labs to ensure that every voice has been heard.
	The First Day of School: Make the first day of school special for everyone, inviting parents, community members, and civic and business leaders to participate in activities that welcome back students and staff, promote learning and education, and communicate a commitment to support all young people.[7]
Support for a Common Goal or Cause	Community Wide Literacy: Literature Circles in all English classes composed of students, faculty members, parents, and community members who have read the same book or text.
	Project Share: Your ticket for entering school is a donation of food, books, or toys to be distributed to families in need.
	Support our Troops: A day that honors community members and alumni serving in the military with opportunities to write letters and cards, or buy pins and ribbons that support families.
Affirmation of schoolwide value, belief, or principle	Service to the Larger Community: Schoolwide participation in National Service Day.
	Tolerance and Diversity Week: Afternoon student-led workshops and a Personal History Museum. Everyone brings an artifact or a photo of an artifact that represents their cultural history/identity.
	Democratic Practice and Civic Responsibility: Voter Registration Day
Gotta have some fun!	Advisory/homeroom team competitions: Pictionary, Building the Tallest Tower, Indoor Table Olympics.
	Grade Level or Division Talent Shows.
	Dance Week: Dance students are on hand every day at lunch performing, teaching, and encouraging students to get up and dance to all kinds of music.

Student Voice

Student voice initiatives refer to "those pedagogies in which youth have the opportunity to influence decisions that will shape their lives and those of their peers either in or outside of school settings. Understood as the capacity to act in a way that produces meaningful change in oneself or the environment, agency is the key to student voice." Time and again, research has shown that the more educators give students choice, control, challenge, and collaborative opportunities, the more motivation and engagement are likely to rise.[8]

For many students, the number one issue they care about at school is how they are treated by students and adults. Involving students in school governance, school improvement initiatives, and disciplinary processes can have a positive impact far beyond the students who are directly involved in any specific initiative. A restorative orientation toward discipline places students at the center of situations that involve collaborative decision making and problem solving. Student agency is enhanced every time students partner with caring adults to resolve a conflict, improve a current reality, do something better, or make it right. Developing opportunities to promote student voice does not just improve school climate; student voice enhances student's personal growth and maturation, supports individual identity development, and increases attachment to school.[9]

Figure 9.3 illustrates a spectrum of student voice opportunities.[10] Think about these questions as you look at the chart and assess the current reality in your school.

1. For each cluster of student voice opportunities (from "expression" to "leadership," annotate student access to these opportunities in your school.

O	= most or all students have access on a regular basis
△	= high achieving students have access on a regular basis
□	= many students have hit and miss access
◇	= a few students have limited access (*and who are the few?*)
X	= this opportunity is not yet present in our school

2. Consider the reasons why students have more access to some opportunities and not others.

3. Consider the reasons why some student sub-groups may have access to some opportunities while others do not.

4. Specifically identify the student leadership opportunities that are available to your students. Approximate how many students are directly involved in these opportunities.

5. How do adult leadership and teacher expectations influence and/or limit student voice opportunities and influence and/or limit who participates in these opportunities?

Figure 9.3

Spectrum of Student Voice Oriented Activity

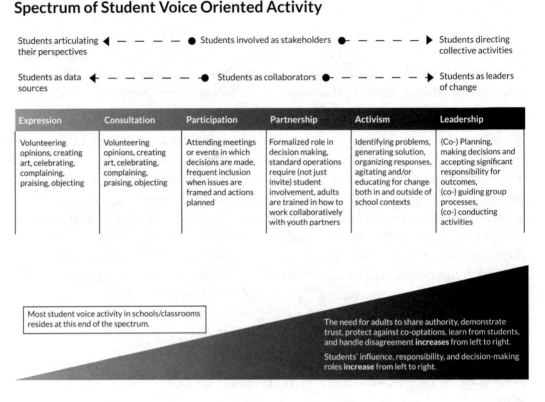

Eric Toshalis & Michael Nakkula. 2012. Motivation, Engagement, and Student Voice: Students at the Center Series. Boston, MA: Jobs for the Future. Adapted and used with permission.

Many of the student voice strategies we share with you align with the continuum. Engaging Schools consultants have helped support student voice opportunities in middle and high schools across the country. We offer multiple options because we know school contexts vary. We have also selected options that both students and adults have found to be most powerful and compelling in leading school change.

Junior and Senior Leadership Courses

We have worked in many high schools that offer an intensive Youth Leadership opportunity as an elective course during the school day, during a "zero" hour, in an after school course for credit, or as a certificated service learning project. These students are in the driver's seat learning all of the necessary skill sets to plan and facilitate freshman orientation activities; serve as "buddies" to at-risk freshmen; co-lead freshman advisories with ninth grade teachers; facilitate peer education workshops focused on bullying, harassment, violence, intergroup relations, and dating relationships; become trained to serve as restorative group conferencing co-facilitators, peer mediators, or peer listeners; organize and coordinate schoolwide events and campaigns that promote a respectful, caring, and inclusive community; and lead class lessons and discussions about the school Code Of Character, Conduct and Support. All of these initiatives require a significant long-term commitment from students and intensive training. Thus, packaging these opportunities into a leadership course where students earn credit or a certificate creates a reliable flow of new student leaders from year to year.

Positive Action Community

This is a less formal, less intensive structure that supports the same kinds of student leadership initiatives that are part of leadership course. Positive Action Communities (PACs) can include as many as 50 students and five to 10 adults who form a partnership to focus on one issue or initiative for an entire year or identify three or four on-going projects from which team members can choose. In addition, this team may serve as the "go to group" to help trouble-shoot and generate solutions to specific issues that are prompting concern and complaint (cafeteria decorum and dirty bathrooms, for example). Groups meet weekly or biweekly and much of the training and planning to carry out specific initiatives happens during the summer or at weekend retreats. Groups like PAC can also serve as a conduit to discuss issues with the larger faculty and with the student body through grade level and town meetings. Betsy Revis, a PAC student member from Huntington High School, on Long Island, New York summarizes her experience this way. *"The best thing that has happened to me since I joined PAC is now I am a member in a group where I can make a difference in my school and in the community. PAC has put more students and teachers on the same page."* A PAC advisor noted that *"One of the first things we did was have PAC students and teachers make separate lists of the ways that students are disrespectful to adults and a list of ways that adults are disrespectful to students. Both groups independently had the same list of actions, from a teacher rolling his eyes when a student asks a question to a student cursing at a teacher when they are frustrated. So, when we realized that both groups knew what the problems were and wanted to fix them, we were already on our way to making real changes."*

School Climate Student Advisory Board

Identify a group of 12 to 15 students representing all grades and all student groups who meet with the principal and some members of the School Climate-Discipline Team on a monthly basis to confer about new practices, policies, and initiatives, engage in problem analysis and problem solving related to issues that directly impact students, and make recommendations to the School Climate-Discipline Team and the Administrative Team. Sometimes, this group may be "on call" to serve as a clearinghouse for sharing and passing on information to their peers related to rumors, safety issues, and serious incidents that impact the entire school community.

Cross-Age Mentors for At-Risk Students, English Language Learners and Students with Disabilities

For young people who struggle academically, who feel vulnerable in a sea of faces where everyone else looks more confident and comfortable, or who simply feel a little lost in high school, having an older friend at school who already "knows the ropes" can be a game-changer. Cross-age mentoring involves a match between a younger student and an older student who provides support, friendly advice, and encouragement through effective role modeling and consistent direct contact over an extended period of time. Research shows that peer mentoring has the power to increase school connectedness, strengthen feelings of self-efficacy, foster improvements in grades and pro-social behaviors for mentees and improve mentors' interpersonal communication, empathy, problem solving, and moral reasoning skills.[11] In comparison to adult-youth mentoring, cross-age mentoring may show more robust outcomes for mentees because peer mentors meet more often with their mentees than adult mentors. In addition, the power of positive peer bonding is such a strong developmental benchmark for many young people, especially when there is at least a two year difference in age.[12] Keep your eyes and ears open to match up two groups of students in particular: younger students with persistent academic problems, attendance, and discipline problems and juniors and seniors who have turned themselves around after a shaky start at the beginning of high school. Two other pairings are worth noting. Matching a novice English Language Learner (ELL) student with a fluent ELL student can help decrease emergent English language learners' feelings of anxiety and bewilderment. Another inspired match emerged from a physical education department's concern that in large classes, teachers felt that they were not providing adequate support for some of their students with disabilities. They created a "buddy" system that was so successful that it turned into a full-fledged peer-mentoring program. In all of these examples, intensive training is needed for the mentors. Schools have provided a retreat for students and a bimonthly support group to troubleshoot and offer support. In some schools, the adults responsible for the mentoring program shadow the mentors a least two to three times a year to offer coaching.

School Climate Surveys, "Get the Pulse" Focus Groups or Student-Led Presentations to Faculty

Too often, the data from annual school climate surveys for students and teachers is never shared or pursued. We have supported schools to use a four-step process involving students that moves from data analysis to action recommendations. First, a group of students and staff review the data to identify positive findings and specific issues of concern. Second, the same group crafts a set of follow-up questions to ask students and teachers to gather multiple perspectives and a better understanding about issues that the groups finds most compelling. Third, the same group is trained to conduct separate focus groups of students and teachers using a consistent format for recording the data. Fourth, the same group analyzes the data and students present their findings and recommendations to the faculty. This process surfaces priorities that need to be owned by a group of staff members and students, so they can create a viable work plan. A progress-monitoring tool needs to be designed and implemented and updates on progress need to be communicated via the school's communication structures.

Outliers Lunch and Learn

In many secondary schools, the students who have the toughest time at school do not have a voice that is heard and considered. We have witnessed life-changing conversations when administrators, department chairs, and or deans take the time to have lunch with small groups of students who are experiencing the most challenges at school. These are often students in crisis who have compelling stories that go untold. The simple act of paying attention and listening not only builds adult empathy and understanding, but these conversations have the potential to change policies and practices, particularly related to how to better serve this group of young people. These students are often identified by homeroom supervisors, advisors, student intervention teams, and administrators. This takes a coordinated effort, and a review of student data. A sensitive adult must check-in with these students to invite them to a lunch and learn session, and then facilitate these sessions.

Student-Faculty Forum

A student-faculty forum addresses issues of mutual concern to students and teachers; discusses possible changes in school policies, schedules, courses and curriculum; and makes recommendations for action. Student-faculty forums are composed of rotating faculty members and student representatives from homerooms or advisories who are responsible for sharing information and soliciting feedback from their classmates to bring back to the forum. A forum generally meets on a monthly or bi-monthly basis, depending on the urgency and number of tasks presented to the forum to tackle.

Orientation and the First Month of School

Orientation, the first day, the first week, and the first month of school all offer opportunities for culture building that shapes the rest of the year. These initiatives require all hands on deck to plan how to introduce and review important schoolwide procedures, policies, and practices. This is the time when leaders, student support staff, teachers, and non-certified staff set the tone for a positive school year by strategically rolling out the behavioral and academic expectations for each and every student. Questions to consider:

- What are the ways we support developmental transitions from one grade to the next?
- What interactive processes might we put in place to have staff and students review the school code of character, conduct, and support, particularly student expectations, rights, and responsibilities?
- What communication structure and venues will we use to highlight, discuss, and clarify important changes in schoolwide rules, policies, procedures, scheduling, and use of facilities?

- How might we generate anticipation and excitement about learning expectations, experiences, and opportunities across the school linked to each grade level?
- What common messages do you want to communicate to the entire school, and what specific grade level messages feel most important?

Engagement in proactive thinking about the specific events and activities before school opens and during the first month will help make all students and families in your school feel welcomed. This is especially true for new students and their families. Ideally, orienting all students to their new school year includes less time spent in large group assemblies and much more time in town meetings, advisories, highly structured homerooms, and classrooms facilitated by key administrators, teachers, Student Support Team members, and student leaders. Using interactive formats like circle games, turn-and-talk, and trios is likely to reduce feelings of isolation and awkwardness by ensuring that students get to know some of the other students and the adults during these community building activities. Keep in mind the prosocial goals that you want to promote and set aside time for activities that help establish the values of cooperation and positive peer relationships. Finally, be sure to provide a time when students can ask questions or write down their questions anonymously and have them answered.

All students need to be oriented to their grade as they make a transition into another school year. This often goes unnoticed for students who are not sixth and ninth graders. Middle and high school orientations before school opens typically range from a half day to two whole days. We have found that setting aside monetary stipends and blocks of time in the summer for a few school staff members and student leaders to plan, prepare all materials (including directions and scripts for specific activities), and rehearse a "walk-through" make the difference between a highly engaging, high spirited grade level orientations, and the "sit and get" version that can leave new and returning students uninspired and disconnected.

Orientation sessions for incoming sixth and ninth graders are especially critical as these students are usually entering a new school and a new culture. We offer the following Student Orientation Check List as illustrated in 9.4 that can guide a school climate -discipline team to identify and prioritize essential activities that can take place before school officially opens, during the first month on designated class periods, or at class meetings with whole grade level teams. Many of the activities can be student-designed and student-facilitated, offering powerful leadership opportunities for older students.

Figure 9.4

Student Orientation Activity Checklist

Assembly Activities (Keep these activities to 20 minutes or less in any one setting, remembering that one of the reasons to even include a few assembly activities is to teach students how to enter, where to sit, and how to exit.)	**Q and A and Text-Driven Activities** (Foster a learning-focused culture from Day 1 by ensuring that students read, write about, and discuss some brief texts)
Welcome / Agenda for the day / Message from principal and key adults who work with incoming sixth or ninth graders. Three things you should know about our school that communicate our mission and values and three things that make our school different, special, unique. Introduction of vice-principal, dean, counselors, and student support staff who will work with sixth or ninth graders. Dos and Don'ts skits performed by teachers and student leaders to explain the school rules and expectations. Inspirational speaker / rally. Preview of extra-curricular, after school activities, and sports presented by student leaders.	Navigating the daily / weekly school schedule, especially if the school is on an A/B block schedule. Review of schoolwide rules, norms, consequences, and interventions so that new students and families know "what will happen if…" Clarifying schoolwide student expectations, rights, and responsibilities. Who can help me? Where do I go for ____? What does freshmen on track mean? Why grades matter (credits, courses, testing, etc.)
Logistics and Building Walk-Through (This requires well-planned timing so groups of about 30 students can rotate from one venue to another.)	**Activities that Promote Grade Level Identity and Group Building**
Navigating the school building / school tour. Lockers and locks. Cafeteria procedures and protocols. Media center procedures and protocols. Walk-through of student's personal schedule near the end of orientation program. This is a brief opportunity for students to meet their teachers using a modified schedule of 10 minutes per class with three- to five-minute intervals to navigate from one place to another.	Introduction to advisory and advisor / graduation coach or introduction to home-room teacher within the grade level. How grade level teams work. Introduction to agenda books / daily planners. Group building games with other students in same advisory or same core class involve fun, non-threatening participation. Special lunch with "home-base" teacher or advisor / graduation coach.

Family/Adult Ally Orientation Activities (Provide families/adult allies with three different times when they can attend a 90 minute to two hour orientation: in the morning, in the afternoon, and in the evening.)	Activities that Promote Conversation, Reflection, and Goal-Setting for Students
School rules and expectations; what your child should know. Family/adult ally and student rights and responsibilities. What does "freshmen on track" mean (credits, courses, testing, etc.)? Why grades and attendance matter / Interim and quarterly progress reports. Curriculum and schedule overview. Communicating with your child's teachers. Roles of "home-base" teacher or advisor, grade level vice principal, dean, and Student Support Team. What is normal during this transition? What should I know? What should I expect? Supporting your child's success / Homework, study habits, goal setting. Post-secondary planning. What to discuss with your child after this session.	College-and-career readiness (How do I imagine and plan my future? What should I be thinking about?) Service learning (if this is a school requirement.) What I need to know to be "school smart" (study skills, qualities of a good student, what do I need to be and do my best?) Making healthy life choices (sleep, nutrition, stress, managing your emotions.) Completing personal learning profile and student information. Personal reflections / Q and A / What am I looking forward to? What am I a little anxious about? Feedback board / End of day or week reflections.

Passport to School

This is an excellent orientation activity for incoming sixth or ninth grade students that comes from Westerville North High School in Ohio. If you work on grade level teams, create a passport that all students receive. During the first quarter, students are expected to collect items that they attach to pages in their passport, get their passport stamped by various staff, and provide evidence through signatures and notes that they participated in various activities or found out specific information about the school, its graduates, its programs, the building and grounds, etc. Provide enough options so students can make choices about the items they complete. You might want to set a goal of a specific percentage or number of items that every student completes by the end of the first quarter.

At the end of the first quarter, take some time to share what students did and what they found out. Also invite students to give feedback about the ways this project helped them get connected to more people and become more familiar with their new school environment.

Launching the First Day and the First Week

Here are a few suggestions for the School Climate-Discipline Team that can form the beginning of a first-day and first-week to-do list:

- Decide who is in charge of welcoming returning and new students and parents who have not officially registered yet.
- Decide what visual artifacts and tools you want posted in public spaces and in every classroom.
- The first day back from summer is a big transition for most students. Create lists of dos and don'ts with the faculty that focuses on pacing the roll-out of curriculum, schoolwide expectations, group building during the first month, and Tier 1 practices that promote positive behaviors and engaged learning.
- Be clear about the adult supervision that is expected in public spaces during the first couple of weeks for two reasons. First, you want to set the tone for fostering safe and civil spaces by ensuring the visibility of friendly adults who are encouraging a smooth flow of traffic from place to place that includes morning entry, passing time between classes, the cafeteria, and end of day exit. Second, new students in the building are likely to need some help getting around during the first few days.
- Invite school staff and student leaders to serve as Welcome Ambassadors during the first two or three weeks of school by wearing a badge in school colors that says, "Ask me. I can help." It's a great way to communicate that "our school is a friendly place" and help new students navigate the building.
- Provide clinics and a designated "trouble-shooter" to ensure that all staff members are prepared to submit disciplinary data electronically.
- Have an end-of-day check-in with faculty after the first day to share highlights of the day, provide updates on rooms, repairs, and schedules, and offer faculty an opportunity to submit urgent questions and technical or classroom issues that need to be addressed immediately.
- Create a schedule of administrative visits to classrooms to provide a personal welcome to every student. Ideally, choose one period during the day and during the first few weeks have different administrators visit all classes during the period.
- Plans for family engagement during the first month of school are communicated to families, adult allies, staff, and students.

By the End of the First Month

- Assess disciplinary procedures and protocols to decide what needs to be adjusted or tightened up.
- Review and trouble shoot any glitches in the use and submission of electronic disciplinary data.

- Be sure that you have accurate student and parent contact information for every student, including the identification of an adult ally if the parent is absent or unable to serve in a parenting role in the moment. Schools accomplish this through home visits and conferences with students.
- Using your early warning indicators, identify students on your "worry list" who will require more intensive Level 2 and 3 academic and behavioral interventions.

Any reader might duly claim overload after reading this chapter. The scope of schoolwide climate initiatives is vast and varied, covering the gamut from safety issues to youth development. This chapter, in particular, is a testament to the inspired work of schools across the country. Their stories demonstrate how collaborative efforts can make a difference for so many young people. We hope you have been inspired too.

---

[1] McQueen, M. B., Boardman, J. D., Domingue, B. W., Smolen, A., Tabor, J., Killeya-Jones, L., ... & Harris, K. M. (2015). The National Longitudinal Study of Adolescent to Adult Health (Add Health) Sibling Pairs Genome-Wide Data. Behavior genetics, 45(1), 12-23.

[2] Libbey, H. P. (2004). Measuring student relationships to school: Attachment, bonding, connectedness, and engagement. Journal of School Health, 74(7), 274-283.

[3] Carnegie Foundation for the Advancement of Teaching. *An Imperiled Generation: Saving Urban Schools. Princeton*, New Jersey

[4] Tierney, W. G. and Colyar, J. E. (Eds.) (2006). Urban high school students and the challenge of college access: Many routes, difficult paths. New York, NY: Peter Lang Publishing.

[5] Broh, B. A. (2002). Linking extracurricular programming to academic achievement: Who benefits and why?. Sociology of Education, 69-95.

[6] Millsap, R. E., & Everson, H. T. (2005). Everyone Gains: Extracurricular Activities in High School and Higher SAT Scores.

[7] (see www.firstdays.org)

[8] Toshalis, E., & Nakkula, M. J. (2012). Motivation, engagement, and student voice. The students at the center series, 1-42., Jobs for the Future

[9] Boekaerts, M. (2011). What have we learned about the social context-student engagement link. Teachers College Record, 113(2), 375-393.

[10] Toshalis, E., & Nakkula, M. J. (2012). Motivation, engagement, and student voice. The students at the center series, 1-42., Jobs for the Future

[11] Garringer, M., & McRae, P. (2008, January 1). Building Effective Peer Mentoring Programs in Schools: An Introductory Guide.

[12] Karcher, M. (2007). Research in Action: Cross-Age Peer Mentoring. www.mentoring.org/downloads/mentoring_388.pdf

[13] Carnegie Foundation for the Advancement of Teaching. An Imperiled Generation: Saving Urban Schools. Princeton, New Jersey.

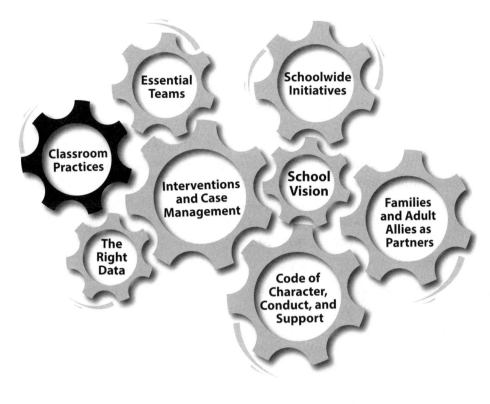

10

Classroom Practices

What are the teacher mindsets and practices that build engaging and well-managed classrooms, align with an accountable and restorative approach to schoolwide discipline and student support, and ensure every student to academically succeed in school?

CHAPTER OUTLINE

Introduction

Principles of Promotion, Prevention, and Intervention to Support Learning

A Framework for Strengthening Conditions for Learning

Using the Framework to Prioritize Universal Practices That Provide a Platform for Professional Learning

Introduction

Where change is concerned, the teacher is clearly the key."[1] Teachers are first in line to navigate and support the adolescents in their care and are responsible for creating the conditions for high performing classroom communities where students can learn and grow. They face the daily challenge of teaching students who come to school with different profiles, passions, problems and a range of adolescent behaviors and energy. It is hard to imagine any other job as demanding as one that calls on us to teach and support every adolescent effectively, particularly in urban settings where the complexity and intensity of students' needs can sometimes feel overwhelming. We hold deep regard for middle and high school teachers who come to school every day committing their best efforts to meet these challenges.

At the same time, we have to face 20 years of disciplinary data that reveal inequitable treatment of alarming numbers of young people while achievement data during the same period indicate virtually no improvement for secondary students who are chronically underperforming. The data tell us that good hearts and good work are not enough to change the downward trajectory that millions of adolescents experience as they move from elementary to middle and high school. This chapter invites the reader to consider the mindsets and practices that can enable every secondary teacher to:

- Build engaging and caring classrooms;
- Establish safe, orderly, and well-managed classrooms;
- Align their practices to a restorative and accountable approach to discipline and student support; and
- Support every student's social and emotional development and academic success.

Student engagement and classroom management play equal and powerful roles in supporting safe, supportive, and productive learning environments. Highly successful teachers use relevant and challenging curricula to foster deep learning through engaging and rigorous instructional strategies, meaningful products and assessments, and student voice and choice. However, high quality instruction is not a substitute for effective classroom management. Effective classroom managers "(1) develop caring, supportive relationships with and among students; (2) organize and implement instruction in ways that optimize students' access to learning; (3) use group management methods that encourage students' engagement in academic tasks; (4) promote the development of students' social skills and self-regulation; and (5) use appropriate interventions to assist students with behavior problems."[2]

Principles of Promotion, Prevention, and Intervention to Support Learning

Teachers who are adept at establishing routines and procedures to support self-directedness and are equally skilled at redirecting and responding to misbehaviors, rarely have the need to send students out of class. More specifically, we think reductions in suspension and student removal from the classroom depend on a teachers' capacity to implement key principles of promotion, prevention and intervention as shown in Figure 10.1.

Figure 10.1

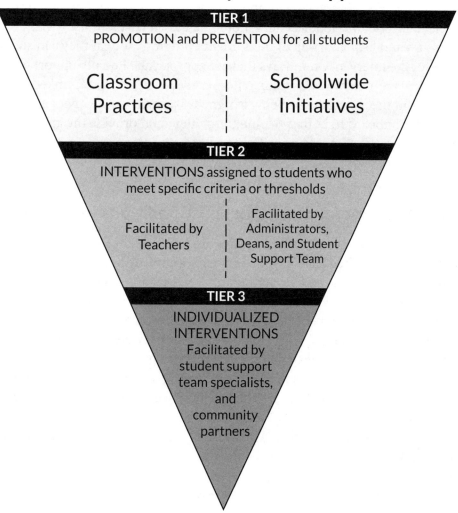

Tier 1 practices **Promote** engaging and well-managed classrooms by fostering students' self-management, social efficacy, and academic mindsets and habits of learning. Tier 1 practices **Prevent** and defuse most disciplinary incidents and potential student-teacher conflicts through high student engagement, strong student-teacher relationships, consistent instructional supports, and strategies that prompt redirection, self-correction, and re-engagement. These practices can be implemented in any classroom, in any subject, at any grade level.

Tier 2 practices begin with teacher-facilitated academic and behavioral **Intervention and subsequently may involve other specialists or administrators to** help students get back on track when they experience academic and behavioral challenges that become barriers to learning. Principles of promotion, prevention, and intervention in the classroom align with a restorative and accountable approach to schoolwide discipline and student support, building a common language for supporting all students at the school and classroom level.

Although Tier 3 interventions occur outside of the classroom and are likely to involve an academic or behavior support specialist, a social worker or counselor, or special education liaison, teachers should be informed about the specific intervention and kept apprised of the student's progress, so that they can support the goals of the intervention in ways that are appropriate. Equally important, when students re-enter the classroom after receiving interventions linked to being removed from the classroom or being assigned a suspension, teachers need to be sensitive and onboard to both welcome the student and provide the appropriate support to assist the student's transition back into the classroom.

A Framework for Strengthening Conditions for Learning

While the last two decades have not resulted in improved outcomes for most secondary students, they have produced a very optimistic body of research for shifting teacher mindsets and strengthening teacher's practices and efficacy, especially with students who experience significant internal and external barriers that make positive attachment to school and academic achievement more challenging undertakings. To this end, this chapter provides a framework in Figure 10.2 of a carefully selected array of teacher mindsets and practices that align with five major strategies for working effectively with adolescents. They are (1) engaging in developmentally appropriate practice; 2) engaging in culturally responsive practice; (3) providing targeted instruction and support for students who are at-risk of school failure; (4) providing targeted instruction and support for students with disabilities; and (5) engaging in effective classroom management strategies.

Figure 10.2

A Framework for Strengthening Conditions for Learning

Classroom Conditions for Learning

	Promotion and Prevention	Intervention
Strong and Caring Teacher Presence	Authoritative and collaborative teaching style Voice and non-verbal communication Cultural competence Depersonalizing and normalizing typical adolescent behaviors	
Personalized Relationships	Meet and greet at the door Learning and using every student's name Value-added feedback and confidence Boosters Personal Check-ins Knowing your students	
Instructional Organization	Attention, silence, clear instructions Procedures and routines Group facilitation and group building Instructional pacing Student voice and choice	
Engaging and Rigorous Learning Protocols	Incorporating independent think time and purposeful social interaction in ways that foster students' academic, emotional, and behavioral engagement	
Physical Environment	Purposeful furniture arrangement Essential classroom postings Learning tools and supplies	
Academic and Behavioral Supports and Interventions	Academic and behavioral expectations and academic press Anticipating learning gaps Student mindsets and habits of learning A listening culture Academic and behavioral coaching and conferencing	Teacher facilitated academic and behavior Tier 2 interventions
Restorative and Accountable Discipline	⟶	A step by step guide when behavior problems arise Defusion and de-escalation strategies and protocols

It is worth noting that the same practices that support critical conditions for learning are also linked to increases interest, participation, effort, investment, attention and good will for adolescent learners. They are often referred to as "high impact" practices, so named because their "effect size" is significantly larger than the vast majority of research-based practices and result in more significant gains in achievement.[3] You will also notice that the vast majority of practices fall within Tier 1 Promotion and Prevention principles, affirming the importance of emphasizing proactive strategies to support disciplined, high performing learners.

As you review the framework, we invite you to think about the essential mindsets and practices you want teachers to make visible, particularly during the first month of school, which is critical to establishing a strong classroom culture. We recommend that administrative leadership teams work with grade level teams or teacher cohorts to intentionally allocate time during the first weeks of school to establish a strong classroom culture, which will support and sustain their students' growth and development over the next nine months. We collaborate with many principals who use a version of the framework as a guide for "first month look for's" in every classroom. This supervision practice has two large benefits. On one hand, it establishes a baseline for instructional expectations and gives faculty permission to front load the teaching and practice of essential routines, procedures, and learning protocols that build a strong community of learners. On the other hand, a "first month look for" checklist enables administrators to intervene quickly and provide coaching and support to teachers who are struggling, so that they can re-establish order before ineffective teaching practices become entrenched.

Strong and Caring Teacher Presence

Teaching presence is the combination of attitudes, outlook, and demeanor that teachers wear most often and most visibly. This includes how teachers exercise their power and authority, how teachers approach potential conflict, how teachers sound, and how teachers communicate what they believe and value, and what they want to defend and protect. Some aspects of teaching presence are like a second skin. Others are harder to come by, requiring time and practice in order to express aspects of one's teaching persona with authenticity and confidence. We placed "strong and caring teacher presence" first in the framework intentionally. One's teaching presence often overrides a teacher's instructional competence as the lever for garnering students' trust and reaching and teaching many adolescent learners. The ways in which teachers of adolescents communicate their authority, care, and beliefs in students' capacity to succeed will directly impact how young people respond and whether they will take on the mantle of a cooperative and engaged learner.

Authoritative and Collaborative Teaching Style

A teacher's power and authority create the opportunity to influence, inspire, guide, coach, and shape the behavior of others. For adolescents, some sources of power and authority are far more effective than others. Authoritative teachers make extensive use of referent power (power through relationships and identification with an authority figure) and expert power (power through special knowledge and skills that someone desires or respects). They use their power to assert their right and responsibility to create a learning environment that is first and foremost a safe place for everyone. Being in charge means asserting that all students will be supported to learn and achieve and that everyone (including the teacher) deserves to be treated with dignity and respect.

Researchers agree that authoritative teachers exhibit a strong presence through clarity of purpose, a strong resolve to meet their goals, and a high commitment to providing academic and behavioral guidance.[4] They also show a deep commitment to meeting the developmental needs of adolescents by modeling respect and trust rather than demanding it.[5] They establish a community of "we" rather than "us vs. them," putting in place practices that invite teachers and students to become partners in the classroom. Sharing responsibility for learning shifts the emphasis from my classroom to our classroom, and from "what I am teaching" to "what you are learning." Authoritative teachers know the risks of insisting that adolescents do everything "my way". They are more likely to provide options for how students can meet important learning goals and academic expectations.

Finally, one's communication style is likely to impact a student's willingness to attend, engage, and cooperate. Adolescents respond more cooperatively and positively when teachers use a collaborative communication style that engages students and teachers in responsive listening and dialogue, invites problem solving and negotiation, and communicates high support, helpfulness, flexibility, and understanding.[6]

In contrast, and far less effective, teachers who systematically take an authoritarian stance often rely on officious power (power through "office", title, status, position, and legal/contractual obligations is recognized and respected) as a primary source of their authority—in other words, "I am the teacher; you are the student, and this is the way it's going to be." Teachers who take an authoritarian stance also tend to use coercive power (to control and punish by means of verbal threat, berating, insults, sarcasm, classroom removal, detention, and suspension) to establish order and control student behavior by commanding obedience, demanding respect, and exhibiting low to no tolerance for questions about rules, procedures, or processes. Student misbehavior, mistakes, and missteps are often viewed as violations of the teacher's authority. Classroom instruction tends to be teacher directed, and interactions with students tend to be more formal, distant, or adversarial. The need for control overpowers the spirit of cooperation and the importance of developing positive relationships. What's more, pushing one's own goals and agenda exclusively tends to devalue the goals, needs, interests, and feelings of others.[7]

Voice and Non-Verbal Communication

The way we use our voice and physical presence tends to build rapport and engagement or break connections with students. Over 65 percent of communication involves our non-verbal presence, the messages we send through our eyes, facial expression, gestures, and the physical movement and placement of our bodies.[8] Effective teachers develop a predictable physical presence that serves most classroom situations—eyes receptive, steady and focused, an interested and pleasant facial expression that avoids emotional extremes of no affect or highly charged affect, a centered and relaxed posture, and limited physical movement. All of these things help communicate self-confidence and self-control. When a more dramatic physical presence is served up sparingly, it holds the power to capture students' immediate attention and interest.

Because so much of teaching is presenting, questioning, discussing, explaining, and encouraging, we cannot overestimate the critical role that voice plays in a teacher's performance. Maximizing the use of our voice in the classroom is like playing a musical instrument. Voice pitch (low to high), volume (a whisper to a scream), pace (slow to rapid), inflection (placement of emphasis), and enunciation all shape our verbal expression. We modulate or adjust these aspects of voice to match different teaching contexts.

Teachers do well to cultivate at least two types of teacher voice. Credible voice is the voice of authority that we use when we are giving instructions, establishing routines, redirecting students, or explaining a critical concept or skill. The voice tends to stay in a lower pitch with little modulation and curls down at the end of a sentence. (Example: *Clear your desks so you are ready for _____.")*[9] Approachable voice is more invitational, encouraging, or enthusiastic. It accesses a more varied modulation and usually curls up at the end of a sentence. (Examples: *"Are you okay?" "Let's see if we can work this out." "Wow! This is different interpretation. Say more about that."*) Effective teachers of adolescents make a conscious effort to match their voice and non-verbal communication to an authoritative and collaborative teaching style.

Cultural Competence

Cultural competence in schools is a life-long process of developing mindsets and practices that enable educators to fully participate in diverse communities of adults and students and successfully teach all students across a range of diverse cultures and differences. Countering inequitable treatment of young people and disproportional practices of harsh punishments and exclusion requires a holistic effort to address five interdependent aspects of cultural competency. They are (1) self-understanding of one's own culture; (2) knowledge, recognition, and appreciation of human diversity; (3) understanding the biases and dynamics that shape interactions with others; (4) the courage to change and adapt new mindsets and practices; and (5) implementing inclusive and culturally responsive practices.

Understanding one's own culture: This involves unpacking one's own cultural identity, ethnicity, family background, beliefs, and values to explore the sources of our assumptions about human diversity, learning, and discipline. These experiences shape our sense of what we value, who we are, where we situate ourselves into family, school, community, and society, and how we interact with students.

Knowledge, recognition, and appreciation of human diversity: This includes a recognition that all types of cultural differences have a profound influence on our lives; specific knowledge of students' cultural backgrounds and communities that affect their dispositions, attitudes, motivations, and approaches to learning; and an appreciation that people of different cultures learn different ways of communicating, behaving, and problem solving. Our deep understanding of human diversity leads to an "unequivocal faith in the human dignity and intellectual capabilities of every student"[10] and the capacity to see and hear what is happening in the classroom from the perspectives of different students.[11]

Understanding the biases and dynamics that shape interactions with others: This includes an awareness and identification of *explicit* and *implicit* personal, systemic, and institutional cultural biases that may influence the "discipline gap", our impressions of and responses to students of color, and a recognition that these biases are part of our history.[12] These biases affect how we do our work and impact our interactions with adults and students across cultures. Biases are grounded in historical cultural experiences that continue to impact the dynamics between cultural groups nationally and within local communities. From the perspective of the classroom, regular reflection is the means to examine the cultural lenses that affect everyday decisions, from the texts and materials we choose to the behaviors that prompt our immediate approval or frustration.

Changing and adapting new mindsets and practices: This involves the courage to confront and then move beyond our personal discomfort, resistance, anger, or fears in order to improve our practice. Embracing this mindset indicates that we are willing to adapt or adjust the way we work with students and colleagues to take into consideration cultural differences.

Implementing inclusive and culturally responsive practices: The capacity to shift practices in the classroom is the result of embracing a culturally competent mindset. The practices in the framework align with the theory and research behind culturally responsive teaching. Four other culturally responsive classroom practices are worth noting: (1) explicit support and guidance for how to "do school" by learning the "cultural capital" of school success. Specific examples include direct teaching and practice of test-taking and study skills; how-to guidelines for presenting oneself, one's thinking, and work to the group; and matching appropriate communication and behaviors to the setting;[13] (2) the deliberate introduction of stories, texts, people, places, and visible symbols that reflect the cultural heritages of different ethnic groups; (3) making connections between content topics and student's experiences, families, peers, neighborhoods, and cultures; and (4) countering disproportional disciplinary practices by reframing discipline problems into teaching-learning problems, treating student removal from the classroom as the last resort rather than the first or most convenient response; and reconnecting with the students after disciplinary action in order to put the incident in the past and move forward with good will.[14]

Depersonalizing and Normalizing Typical Adolescent Behaviors

Adolescents (particularly between ages 12 and 16) are far more likely than younger children to challenge adult authority, break rules, question school policies, and behave aggressively toward peers and adults. Rudeness, provocative speech, and noncompliance are, indeed, normal adolescent behaviors. Responding effectively to these typical behaviors first requires a mindset that enables us to depersonalize and normalize what adolescents (between the ages of 10 – 19) do and say.

Teaching is, in many ways, the most personal of professions and something of a paradox. On one hand, our personal relationships and emotional connections to students are the very things that can increase students' attachment to school and learning. On the other hand, when students are emotionally charged, behaviorally challenged, or just goofing off, they need to count on us to be emotionally objective. When we resist the temptation to view students' actions and speech as personally offensive, we are less likely to become highly charged ourselves and more likely to sustain a steady focus on what we can do immediately to help a student re-engage or self-correct. Handling conflictual situations in a manner that displays self-control and calm earns students' respect and provides a role model for their emotional growth.

From the disciplinary research base, we have put together some key strategies that help teachers to depersonalize.

- Decouple the student's behavior from anything to do with you. *"Misbehavior on the part of students usually has little to do with a specific teacher."*15 Try imagining a reason for the unwanted behavior that is unrelated to disrespect or a personal attack. (You can think to yourself and say the following: *"This is not about me; it is not personal. I wonder what might have triggered this behavior?"*)
- Take in a full breath, find your relaxed posture, and ground yourself with the knowledge that you have the skills and strategies to re-engage the student.
- Remind yourself not to be surprised when adolescents make mistakes. Reassure yourself and your students that mistakes and missteps are normal, we all say things sometimes that we really do not mean, and we are all capable of making a quick recovery and getting back on track.

If you need to speak, use an economy of words and a voice that is steady, low key, and matter-of-fact.

Personalized Relationships

Many students invest in school because of the presence of trusting and caring relationships with teachers—because they have a sense that "you've noticed me; you've understood me; you know me." Particularly for adolescents who are underserved and underperforming, students of color, and students who live in poverty, the quality of the student-teacher relationship and a teacher's commitment to know each student individually will often determine a student's willingness to learn and cooperate in the classroom.[16] "Many behavioral problems ultimately boil down to a breakdown in teacher-student relationships: the causes of many classroom behaviors labeled and punished as rule infractions are, in fact, problems of students and teachers relating to each other interpersonally."[17]

Empirical evidence has established a link between student-teacher relationships and students' sense of identification with school. Students who reported feeling cared about by teachers felt a greater sense of belonging in school, valued academic work, and had higher levels of behavioral engagement. Students characterized teacher-caring most commonly to mean that teachers were concerned about them as a person outside of school and communicated openly in a warm and friendly manner.[18]

This practice encompasses the specific moves a teacher makes in order to get to know each and every student as an individual. Barriers to successful learning become more pronounced when we teach students as if they were all the same. Practices of personalization enable teachers to affirm their students' cultural identities and "meet learners where they are in terms of their capabilities, interests, attitudes, and other intrinsic motivational considerations."[19]

Meet and Greet at the Door

Students tell us how much it means when teachers hang out by the door saying "Hello" and greeting them by name before class begins. "Meet and greet" does not need to happen every day—two or three times a week is fine—and varying what you do and say at the door heightens students' anticipation and curiosity.

In the beginning of the year, for example, when you are trying to match names to faces, ask them to say their names as they walk into class so you and the other students can hear and repeat them. If you have students who speak other languages, ask them to write and pronounce "hello" in that language so you can make different "hellos" part of your greeting repertoire.

Learning and Using Every Student's Name

Respect begins with saying and pronouncing a person's name correctly. A person's name is at the heart of one's identity. Saying a student's name reaffirms a sense of self and the feeling of being known. Invite teachers to share strategies that enable you to learn every student's name within the first two weeks of school and enable students to learn each other's names. In addition, consider ways to incorporate students' names into day-to-day instruction. For example, when summarizing a discussion, teachers can mention students' names and refer to comments they made earlier that contributed to a better understanding of the topic.

Value-Added Feedback and Confidence Boosters

Value-Added Feedback is about the deed, not the doer. Effective feedback puts the focus on what a person did or said and how he or she did it. It incorporates specific language that indicates what was seen, heard, felt, or experienced. Feedback comes in many forms. The emphasis here, however, is on positive feedback that strengthens student-teacher relationships, fosters students' perception of their own competence, and increases the value that students place on learning. The most powerful type of positive feedback is "value-added" feedback when we link students' personal qualities to specific behaviors and academic efforts that you notice and appreciate.

> *"I noticed how you completed your last three labs. You tackled every part of each lab. That showed real perseverance."*

> *"I saw how you encouraged other students in your group to come up with more ideas. I appreciate your leadership."*

> *"Before you started on your project today, I noticed that you took the time to check the machinery and get all of your tools out before jumping in. That shows me you've got great self-discipline. You know what to do without being told."*

Giving value-added feedback through written post-it notes, personal phone calls or texts to students, or "sunshine calls/texts/emails" to parents can be the one thing that can jumpstart a change in a student's outlook and performance in the classroom.

Students' perceptions of competence and their prediction of success strongly influence motivation and effort. Particularly for learners who struggle and students of color, confidence boosters such as a teacher's words of confidence and encouragement can help ward off "stereotype threat" and a fixed mindset of "I'm not good at this." When students do not believe in their capacity to succeed, their motivation plummets to zero. What you do and say depends on what you observe. When discouragement is temporary and connected to a specific academic task, your responses need to communicate your confidence in students' capacity to work through it.

> *"I know this is challenging and I know you can do it."*

> *"I'm confident you can do this. Thanks for giving it a try."*

> *"Remember when you _____. You really showed yourself that you could do it."*

In cases of persistent discouragement and disconnection, the relationship has to come first, and specific academic interventions come later. It may take weeks or even months to make a connection that can enable you and the student to get to the sources of discouragement and figure out a plan that can help her turn it around. Think about one thing you can do every single day that creates a personal connection with the student (a physical gesture or light touch for students who are receptive, written or verbal words of support and encouragement, a small act of kindness and generosity whether it is sharing a lunch or giving student something that shows you know what interests them). Whatever you choose to do should communicate these messages:

"I won't give up on you. I'm here to help and support you when you're ready."

"I'm glad to see you today."

"I know you can right yourself and get through this difficult time."

Personal Check-ins

"The key to being a teacher who can build engaging and well-managed classrooms is to know her students. You have to know every single one and have a relationship with every single one. I think that one thing that really allows me to work hard is knowing that my teacher knows where I am in life at that moment. If they don't know me, I will tend not to work as hard for them."[20]

Students are more likely to trust teachers and fully engage in learning when they feel known, heard, and valued by their teachers. Teachers who use personal check-ins regularly, informally, and systematically get to know students as individuals and learners, build rapport, and create a positive class culture. Check-ins take anywhere from ten seconds to a minute, and the compounding impact of regular check-ins results in high returns with regards to relationship building. Personal check-ins often uncover clues that help us understand how to best support students with their emotional, academic, and behavioral needs. Personal check-ins enable teachers to connect with students and establish positive relationships and trust. Check-ins also provide an opportunity to better understand the lives and learner profiles of each student. Teachers make time for check-ins during Meet and Greet at the start of class; during independent student work time; at the close of class while students are packing up; when class energy is noticeably high or low; and when encountering students outside of class in hallways, the lunchroom, etc. For more specific scripts and examples, please see Appendix F: Personal Check-in Protocol.

Knowing Your Students

Knowing students well is the key to unlocking their motivation, effort, and academic potential. How might this be possible when secondary faculty are teaching as many as 150 students at any given time? We would like to offer four discrete practices that enable teachers to gather information that supports teaching to individual students' needs and interests. These practices can be embedded in any classroom at strategic times during a week, month, semester, and year. They are most impactful when they become ritualized and students expect that their opinions and perspectives will be heard and considered. Teachers can learn about their students by soliciting written responses, inviting students to share their own experiences and opinions within academic content discussions, and ritualizing opportunities to acknowledge individual students and the group.

- At the beginning of the school year use surveys, journal entries, and post-its to solicit information from students about their learning profiles, their interests, their vision of a good teacher and a great class, and what will help them when they struggle academically.

- Throughout the year use question prompts for quick-writes and journal entries that provide opportunities for students to connect their personal stories, opinions, and perspectives to curricular texts and topics. At the end of a lesson, learning unit, or grading period, solicit feedback that invites students to assess their own learning, make suggestions, and share their likes and dislikes about the class and the course.

- Pose questions, dilemmas, and problems that place students at the center of a situation in which their experiences and identities inform their responses.

- Incorporate rituals that include a Monday gathering that invites students to share a brief response to a question prompt about themselves or celebrate monthly birthdays, student of the week, kudos and appreciations, and personal and academic benchmarks that recognize individuals and the group.

Instructional Organization

Instructional organization involves a teacher's planning and preparation before a lesson is ever taught. The degree to which teachers organize classrooms for effective learning has a huge impact on student discipline. "Responses to disciplinary problems can only restore order. Effective classroom management (instructional organization) creates order."[21] The practices that follow give individual students and the group a roadmap for how to function for high performance.

Attention, Silence, Clear Instructions

A teacher sets the stage for engagement and participation by implementing consistent visual signals and verbal and physical cues for getting students' attention, ensuring silence when it matters, and providing clear verbal and written instructions for each task. Consistently incorporating these practices garners cooperation and commitment by providing clarity of expectations and captures student's focus for learning, allowing teachers to simultaneously manage individuals and the group.

During observational rounds where we sometimes observe up to 25 classrooms in a day, we notice that teachers who do not have effective strategies for getting attention, silence, and giving clear directions, struggle with classroom management. The good news is that teachers who make these three areas a priority will see marked gains in student on-task behavior within a matter of days.

Getting the Group's Attention: Whole group instruction begins with getting the group's undivided attention quickly and quietly so that student focus becomes automatic and immediate.

- When you are ready to begin class…
  - Stand in the same place every day, or
  - Use the same signal every day, or
  - Say the same thing every day, or
- If you are playing music, turn it off.
- Use a timer, chime, hand signal, rain stick, thunder tube, or unusual word (for example, sikiliza, which is the Swahili word for "interested silence") as a cue for students to listen up as a whole group, switch partners, transition to the next activity, return to original groups, or put away materials.
- Let students know at the very beginning of your instructions, what your cue will be that signals for them when to begin. For example, "*When I say "Please Begin."….you will stand and find a partner who…*" and then say "*Are you ready? Ok… Please Begin!*" or "*Let's do it.*" Or "*Okay, folks. Time to use your smarts. Go for it.*"

Getting Silence When Silence Is Required: If we do not insist on silence when we are speaking to the whole group, we can slide into the awful habit of talking over students. This often begins unconsciously, and then suddenly we are aware that our voice is getting louder and harsher, more students are talking, and fewer and fewer students are actually listening. None of us want to be trapped in the habitual loop of requesting silence, speaking louder and becoming more frustrated, demanding silence again, repeating oneself, and finally yelling at the group to "Be quiet." Another pitfall is saying "I'm waiting…I'm still waiting" for five minutes until eventually getting silence. We offer a few targeted strategies:

- Work on securing uninterrupted silence for very short periods of time for three to five minutes and work up to a 20 or 30 minute block of silence. Be sure to identify specific activities during which absolutely no noise is permitted, and invite students to discuss why silence is a reasonable and a necessary expectation for these activities.
- When practicing the discipline of sustained silence, any noise, however muffled, cannot be part of the mix. When any noise or side-bar talk begins, stop talking, still your body, take a relaxing breath, use your signal for silence and wait until silence re-emerges. At this point, peer pressure among students usually kicks in and students will rally to your attention.

Giving Clear Instructions: Clear instructions help sharpen students' focus on the learning task and provide clarity for what to do in the moment.

- Always provide at least two different ways for students to process and understand instructions.
- When you begin teaching a new group of students, keep tasks simple and instructions very brief for a few weeks. (*"Read _____ and write down _____ while you're reading."*)
- If you use both verbal and posted or a copy written instructions, make sure the wording mirrors oral instructions that may be a bit more detailed. Written instructions may include a sample product, demonstration, or model of what to do, or a visual or graphic depiction of steps.

To confirm student understanding, you may ask students to pair-share in order to paraphrase and clarify instructions; request an instruction summary from a random student; or allow a minute to take a few questions after initial instructions. Here is a sample sequence for giving instructions:

1. Name the task and describe how the task links to the learning outcome of the lesson or unit, and explain the purpose for the task in student-friendly language.

2. Explain step-by-step what you want students to do using simple but precise language.

3. Explain how students will do it, what materials they will use, and how much time is allotted.

4. Explain what the final product, presentation, or report should look like or sound like at the end of work time.

Procedures and Routines

All teachers use spoken and unspoken classroom procedures, such as how to enter and exit class, how to clean up and put away resources, or how to work with a partner. Procedures enable students and the teacher to establish a systematized method for completing the same task consistently time and time again. Sometimes middle and high school teachers feel their students should already know what the procedural expectations are in a typical class: *"This isn't elementary school. Shouldn't they know this stuff?"* The reality is that each day middle and high school students navigate the varied expectations of six to seven teachers, increasingly complex learning tasks, and more and more intricate social interactions. They need teachers to model, teach, practice, and assess targeted procedures in order to co-create and help maintain a safe, orderly, and engaging learning environment. Taking the time up front to identify and explicitly establish classroom procedures empowers students to navigate their social and learning experiences with increased independence and success and allows teachers to plan proactively for common issues before opportunities for unwanted behaviors arise.

Suggestions for Teaching Procedures:

*   Consider inviting students to help you develop classroom procedures. Students are pretty quick to suggest the easiest way to do something in the least amount of time with the least amount of hassle.

*   Ask students what some of the reasons might be for the procedure. Discussing the reason(s) for the procedure with your students results in their commitment to following through on the procedure because they understand the purpose.

*   Teach the procedure, model it in front of the group, and have students practice the procedure until all students are able to meet your expectations.

- Assess implementation and provide corrective feedback as you continue to hold students accountable to your expectations. It is only a procedure if at least 90 percent of students follow it seamlessly.
- Create charts and visual reminders of important procedures. When students slip, you can simply point to the chart, so they can figure out for themselves how to get back on track.

There are a variety of different types of procedures that support a high-performing classroom. Transition procedures include entering and exiting class, the use of passes, and a protocol when students are tardy to class. Procedures that maintain a clean and orderly classroom involve procedures where students clean up and put away materials, and how to use special tools and equipment. Learning procedures systematize the use and distribution of classroom resources, the collection of assignments, and specific guidelines for labs and studio work. Student work procedures routinize how students use interactive notebooks, what students can do when they have completed assignments, guidelines for revisions, and what students do when they miss assignment deadlines.

Group Facilitation and Group Building

Effective 21st century teachers recognize that teaching involves many roles beyond that of an instructor who is fully prepared every day to teach the content of their curricula. Intentional efforts to strengthen one's role of a group facilitator is the starting point for creating a learning environment that helps build cohesiveness, a common purpose, cooperation, and interdependence within the group. Key facilitator skill sets include constant scanning of the group to "read" what it needs in the moment; making observations about what one is seeing and hearing; holding the group accountable to norms of expected behavior, spending more time observing, coaching, and listening to the group than the group spends watching and listening to the teacher; checking in and problem solving with the group when many students seem to have lost focus, appear confused, or display low or negative energy.

Teachers use these facilitation skill sets in the service of building a cohesive learning community, a high-impact practice linked to increased student achievement. Yet, what does it take to actually establish a cohesive classroom in which students respect each other, listen to each other, cooperate with each other, and learn from each other? Although the development of group norms, expectations, and procedures is a good start—it is not enough. Deliberate attention to incorporating group building processes and activities sends students a message that a high functioning group is not merely a means to master content, but is, in fact, an end in itself.

Groups bond when they experience a sense of belonging and satisfaction from making a collective effort to achieve group goals or solve problems successfully. As students feel more connected to the group, they are more likely to invest in becoming responsible and productive group members. When the bottom line is "sink or swim together" students have a genuine stake in supporting each other's efforts and successes, resulting in fewer disruptions and discipline problems and greater cooperation and collaborative work habits.

We offer three group-building strategies that strengthen classroom cohesion:

- **Intentional Pairs and Trios Assignments** during the first month of school ensure that every student has had at least one opportunity to work with every other student in the class.
- **Group Challenge Problems** involve the whole group or teams in high-energy experiences in which they work collaboratively to solve a problem that often requires a combination of content knowledge, academic and social skill sets, strategic thinking, leadership, and effective communication. These kinds of team building activities ignite group identity immediately.
- **Group Circle (or Class Meeting)** enables the teacher and the group to engage in "real time" dialogue, problem solving, negotiation, and compromise to discuss day to day classroom issues and make decisions that impact student learning and the learning environment.

Instructional Pacing

Intentional and skillful pacing is essential for sustaining student engagement from the beginning of the class period to the end. Within any given class period, teachers need to consider and artfully sequence a variety of strategies, grouping formats, and instructional supports throughout each lesson. What learning strategies will support the target learning outcome for the class? How much time might be assigned to the different tasks within the period? What grouping formats will support social, cognitive and emotional engagement? What instructional supports will help the group and individual students stay focused and on task? For example, in a 50-minute lesson a teacher might start with a three-minute independent "reflect and connect," followed by a "turn and talk" to process it, then a whole group debrief. Next a brief 10-minute mini lesson might introduce a video stream related to the content, followed by a five-minute paired exercise in which students prioritize key concepts from the video. Midway through the class, the teacher might get students up and moving by distributing examples to pairs of students who post their examples beneath the key concepts. A 15-minute independent learning task involves students in a text protocol "read and respond" that deepens understanding of the concepts. The teacher takes five minutes to invite students to share their written responses to the text and closes the class with a two minute preview of homework applications and tomorrow's lesson.

Student Voice and Choice

In resilience research, students at risk of school failure who finally experience school success repeatedly mention teachers who deliberately and creatively provided them with choices about *what* they learned and *how, when, where, and with whom* they might learn it. By providing choice, teachers make student voice central and make learning differentiated and relevant – connecting content and skills to students' interests, identities, development, culture, and aspirations. Doing so builds students' sense of agency, academic motivation, and capacity for self-expression and supports each and every student to reach targeted learning goals. Developmentally, choice is a compelling factor that supports adolescents' growing need for autonomy.[22]

We are indeed aware of the ways that common core standards and state testing realities can constrain student choice. However, we encounter teachers who have learned how to engage in "both-and" teaching, offering choices in the curricular content, the learning process, and/or product that demonstrates what students have learned while also meeting the same target learning outcome or common core standard for all students.

One of the most powerful ways to introduce content choice is crafting curricular content into open-ended problems with multiple solutions in which students select specific content and materials to complete the task. By content we are referring to academic knowledge, academic skill sets, topics or themes, and materials. Examples of offering content choices might include multiple topic options for practicing a particular skill; or giving students a choice of readings, graphics, on-line videos, or case studies to complete in order to gain specific content knowledge. Process choices (how a student learns) might include keeping a digital or paper journal, choosing which text protocol or note taking strategy to use with a required reading, several options for processing and mastering key unit vocabulary, or the choice of roles within a cooperative learning project, mock trial, simulation, or case study. Product choices, the way a student demonstrates what they have learned, might include the option of using digital media, hand constructed visuals and text, or narrative writing to show understanding of key unit concepts; or, a unit test that allows students to choose three out of five questions to respond to in order to show mastery of a specific learning outcome.

Choice can also provide a way to calibrate the appropriate degree of challenge for a wide range of student learning profiles in any given class. In contrast to "free choice" which allows students to self-select any task or product from a menu, "guided choice" directs different students to options that meet the same standard but vary in complexity and sophistication to accommodate a range of students' current academic knowledge and skill sets. In an era when assessments focus more on proficiency than excellence, guided choice is a way to foster both rigor and engagement for students who already excel in a particular academic discipline. Developing "guided choice" is particularly viable when teachers have opportunities to collaborate with "course alike" faculty to generate a range of task and product options for meeting important standards within their course content.

Engaging and Rigorous Learning Protocols

Whole books (including some of Engaging Schools' own publications) focus on this single topic; our aim here is to identify key features of engaging and rigorous learning protocols that have the highest impact on student achievement. High impact protocols incorporate independent think time and purposeful social interaction in ways that foster students' academic, emotional, and behavioral engagement and ensure that students' thinking results in high quality responses, products, and presentations. These protocols support students to (1) access and master complex content and skills, increase knowledge and understanding, develop a product, or demonstrate a proficiency; (2) use metacognitive skills to determine effective learning strategies to accomplish a task; (3) utilize social skills to communicate and participate effectively in a group; and (4) demonstrate emotional competencies and academic mindsets that foster self-regulation, perseverance, and high performance.

These protocols can range from simple "turn and talks" as illustrated in Figure 10.3, to carefully sequenced tasks that involve texts, movement, or manipulative materials to more complex cooperative learning experiences that involve trios and quads.

Figure 10.3

Example: Turn and Talk Basics

1. Design an engaging prompt aligned to a learning goal / target outcome / objective.

2. Determine method for pairing up students.

3. Display the prompt.

4. Direct students to the displayed prompt that pairs will respond to. Tell pairs the time frame for completion. Ask pairs to jot down their response.

5. Circulate, monitor, and support students as needed.

6. Announce time check at half-way point and when there are a few seconds remaining.

7. Use a signal to get the group's attention and call on pairs to share their responses with the whole group.

High-impact protocols often "game up" the curriculum by turning learning tasks into direct problem solving experiences that boost student interest, emphasize higher-order thinking, and build students' capacity to collaborate. In all cases, protocols require a compelling question or problem, high structure, and a carefully scaffolded sequence of directions. When teachers provide saturated opportunities to model, teach, practice, and assess a new protocol, it becomes part of students' procedural memory as they use it more often and more effectively.

Physical Environment

This is familiar ground in most schools, particularly when a new school year begins. The act of physically interacting with one's environment engages students at the most basic level.

Purposeful Furniture Placement

Invite teachers to think about placement of their desk, student files and supplies, an area for conferencing and tutorials, and a general seating arrangement that will enable them to see everyone, see the door, and move easily from student to student. Furniture placement shapes how students learn, so an important first month task is teaching students how to rearrange furniture quickly and quietly to accommodate different modes of learning: whole group presentation, demonstration, and mini-lesson; pairs, trios, and quads; and a discussion circle or square in which everyone can see each other.

Maximizing space to support engagement, social interactions, and independent work is key to creating a learning focused culture that feels safe, supportive, and respectful. We worked with a group of middle school teachers in Albuquerque, New Mexico, to create a floor plan for how they intended to use the square footage of their classroom. We used one classroom as a lab of sorts and had small groups of teachers work together to create a plan for optimizing the use of the space. Each group presented their plans and interests behind them. As a result, every teacher had several models from which to work. Teachers had time to draft their plan, had formal meetings with an assistant principal and department head to review the plans and made final changes to the plan based on the conversation. Prior to the opening of school, and once the plan was approved, staff had a half-day to organize their rooms. All classroom plans were reviewed again mid-semester to discuss successes and mid-course corrections.

Essential Classroom Postings

Postings of school rules, classroom expectations, and important procedures serve as visual reminders of community norms and also support students to self-correct immediately. Postings of daily agendas, essential questions, target-learning outcomes, and unit products in student friendly language serve as advanced organizers that provide students with a "heads up" of where they are going and what they are doing.

Learning Tools and Supplies

Having the right tools and supplies handy and organizing and distributing them efficiently can make a good learning experience an even better one. A guiding question for stocking the classroom might be: "What materials will help every student learn and increase student engagement and active participation in the teacher's context?"

Academic and Behavioral Supports and Interventions

We have integrated academic and behavioral supports and interventions because so many situations in the classroom may appear to be "discipline problems" when in fact, the root causes of many misbehaviors we see stem from academic learning gaps or disengagement, the lack of clear procedures and protocols, tasks that are a mismatch for some students, or a student's confusion about what to do.

Academic and Behavioral Expectations and Academic Press

Classroom expectations like schoolwide expectations (see Chapter 6) communicate the beliefs we hold about what students are capable of doing and achieving; they convey confidence in the students' capacity to succeed and thrive in school and life; they provide enduring guidelines for how we present and express ourselves and how we should behave. Classroom academic and behavioral expectations may be worded more specifically than schoolwide expectations to address learning contexts in different courses. What matters most, however, is holding all students accountable to meet classroom expectations and providing an array of supports that show students how to reach them. Here are a few examples.

- I expect all of you to pass this course. If you put in the effort, I am confident you will pass.
- I expect you to make our classroom a good place to learn by being friendly, helpful, respectful, and good-humored with others.
- I expect you to develop a growth mindset by setting goals, monitoring your progress, working hard, and making your best effort.
- I expect all of you to work with each other cooperatively and do your fair share of the work.
- Sometimes you might make poor choices, and make mistakes. I am confident that you can recover and get back on track.

"Academic press,"[23] a phrase coined by researchers Lee and Smith, are the high-impact strategies that teachers use to push all students to meet universal classroom expectations and complete high quality work. When these strategies are embedded in every learning unit, they help close the gap between learners who are successful and those who, in the past, may have logged a history of turning in low-quality and incomplete work. Examples of academic press include:

- Class and student goal-setting; transparent progress monitoring and recording and student self-assessment/reflection;
- Supporting every student to complete and/or revise several work samples to a high quality level in every course during every grading period;
- "No recorded grade until_____" means that no official grade is recorded until work is completed and/or corrected; and
- Office hours, homework club, acceleration sessions (to get a jump-start on new material), remedial sessions (re-teach, review, more practice), question and answer clinics, and after-school specials (to work on projects or provide extended learning time for completion).

Anticipating Learning Gaps

Anticipating learning gaps before they happen is the anecdote to frustration and failure. Traditional remediation for struggling students imposes interventions after students have failed. It is more productive, however, if teachers anticipate areas of difficulty before students approach new material. Part of that anticipation is knowing which students have identified learning disabilities, which have limited English proficiency, or how students have previously performed in class. Teachers should also be aware of which concepts and ideas have been difficult for classes in the past, where student misperceptions or confusions have been particularly strong.[24]

By anticipating when the lesson content, skill instruction, or learning processes might feel daunting or frustrating for particular students or the whole group, teachers can proactively plan for what to do when students are not learning and ensure that every student has the right supports to master content at all levels. Strategies can be as simple as giving the class or individual students a "heads up" for what to focus on before the lesson, previewing challenging content-specific vocabulary, or developing special instructions, resources, or modifications that will encourage more reluctant students to engage fully in the lesson.

Another critical strategy is determining early warning signs (academic performance/behavior indicators) that forecast potential academic struggle and failure that then prompt specific interventions that teachers facilitate during regular class time, during guided study periods, during teacher conference hours, or before or after school. For example, a combination of quiz scores, completed practice problems, and exit tickets might serve as the "red flag" in an algebra class for students who are struggling with algebraic word problems. For teachers, the mindset of anticipating that some students will require more coaching and support has the added benefit of reducing stress and feelings of being overwhelmed.

Student Mindsets and Habits of Learning

The University of Chicago Consortium on Chicago School Research has identified specific academic mindsets and academic behaviors (habits of learning) that enable students to experience academic mastery and also prove to prepare students to be college and career ready. Teachers deliberately model, teach, practice, and assess a set of academic behaviors (*organizing materials, participating, studying*), mindsets (*"I belong in this academic community; my ability and competence grow with my effort; I can succeed at this; this work has value for me"*) and social-emotional competencies (*self-awareness, self-management, social awareness, relationship skills, responsible decision making*) that develop habits of discipline, participation, and personal, interpersonal, and group efficacy.[25]

Researchers in the field of social and emotional learning have amassed unequivocal evidence that explicit teaching and practice of social and emotional competencies such as relationship building, self-awareness, self-management, and responsible decision making—results in improved attitudes about self, others, and school; more positive social behavior; few problems with conduct; less emotional distress; and ultimately greater academic success.[26] Students who develop these skills are less likely to participate in high-risk behaviors and are more able to persevere through academic challenges.[27]

We offer an example from a Denver school that reveals how a faculty tackled the mindset and the learning habit of "Being Prepared to Learn." Teachers were frustrated with students repeatedly showing up to class late and without their necessary materials. They decided students needed to learn what it meant to be prepared for class. They generated common language to communicate and remind students of their expectations for being "Prepared to Learn." Then each teacher spent ten minutes exploring and clarifying for their students exactly what it meant to be "Prepared for Learning" in their subject area/course. All teachers reinforced their expectations with visual postings located near the door to their class that they referred to regularly to help students self-monitor as they walked into the classroom. An example of a visual support is shown in Figure 10.4:

Figure 10.4

**Being Prepared to Learn
is important for your**

Success at School!

Prepared for Learning in <u>Social Studies</u> Means:

You are sitting in your seat when the bell rings.

•

You have your Interactive Notebook and
a writing utensil out and on your desk.

•

You are ready to start the Reflect and
Connect the minute the bell rings

•

You are open to listening and
learning from your peers.

A Listening Culture

A listening culture communicates that "We are interested in and curious about your development. We are going to work hard to understand you, consider perspectives and be fair in our response."

When we listen in active, empathic, and nonjudgmental ways, we learn how our students are grappling with their own situations. "Young people learn from what adults do, not what we say should be done. If we want to be listened to, we need to set a good example ourselves."[28] When adults in a school community engage in restorative listening, students are given the opportunity to think and reflect, and they will come forward with a more open mind to try to understand the choices that they made or at least lean in to think with us about their situation and problem solve around it. This listening culture leads to relationships anchored in trust and good will.

Belinda Hopkins, author of "Just Schools," uses the term, "a listening school" to describe schools that commit to a restorative orientation to discipline and student support.[29] Listening and speaking responsively are the basic building blocks of all restorative supports and interventions.

The process of responsive listening and speaking involves a dual focus. On one hand, you are listening—taking in the thoughts and feelings of another person, and doing this, to the extent possible, without filtering what you hear and see through your own lenses. On the other hand, you are speaking—reflecting back the speaker's words and feelings as accurately as you can without putting your own opinions into the mix. Hopkins reminds us that this reciprocal process takes "a great deal of restraint and skill."[30]

In a listening centered culture a teacher navigating a classroom discussion might sound like, "So that statement in the text seems to have upset you. What are others thinking about that?" Or a teacher fielding questions during a mini lesson in a listening culture might say, "So I'm hearing from several of you that problem number 12 was challenging. Tell me more about what is making balancing this particular equation confusing." Both examples demonstrate the way a classroom with a listening culture is dominated by questions and paraphrasing as opposed to commands and directives.

Academic and Behavioral Coaching and Conferencing

Responsive listening and speaking are also the cornerstones of conferencing—a high impact practice that strengthens personal relationships with students and positively impacts the culture of the classroom. For teachers, particularly, making time available for conferencing can be challenging. It is an intentional practice that takes time to schedule and requires a belief that conferencing is a practice that is worth the teacher's time. Some teachers strategically schedule slots of independent work time each week in class during which they confer with individual students. They might also set up a corner in the classroom that provides a bit of privacy and is out of hearing range of other students when the teacher speaks quietly.

Other teachers set aside lunch and planning periods to conference privately with individual students. Systematically scheduling times to conference demonstrates to students the teacher's desire to truly listen to understand and support.

Conferencing is an opportunity for personalized coaching. When teachers serve in the role of personal coach for students it communicates their investment in each student's personal development and well-being as well as students' daily mastery of academic content. A skillful coach, first and foremost, believes in a student's capacity to accomplish the task, solve problems, and make good decisions. Effective coaches communicate, "I'm on your side and on your case."[31] In a coaching role, teachers provide encouragement and concrete feedback, push for quality and high performance, listen responsively, and help students recover and restore themselves when they are struggling.

One-to-one conferencing: Whether the format is a brief academic or behavioral check-in or a more extended Tier 2 problem solving and planning conference, conferencing gives students the personal attention that they crave at the same time that it supports students to engage in metacognitive reflection and problem solving that foster self-management and responsible decision making. All types of conferences provide opportunities to strengthen student-teacher relationships. We want to highlight behavior and academic check-ins, because these kinds of brief conferences can be used every day in the classroom. We have included a Problem Solving and Planning Conference Protocol in Appendix G.

Behavior Check-ins: When a student is off-task, a quick informal behavioral check-in can gently guide students to self-assess and re-direct their behavior. These one-to-one, question-based check-ins communicate care, respect, and high expectations for on-task, respectful behavior in your classroom. The question format keeps the conversation positive and is helpful for immediately diagnosing and addressing the actual cause for the misbehavior. Behavior check-ins help students re-engage in learning by addressing low-impact off-task or negative behavior immediately; understanding the reasons behind students off-task behavior; helping students become more self-aware and able to self-regulate; and normalizing mistakes and missteps using a respectful, matter-of-fact, no drama voice and tone. Please see Appendix H for a Behavior Check-In Protocol.

Academic Check-ins: The informal academic check-in used daily as a tool for formative assessment, allows teachers to assess what a student is learning, doing, or thinking at a particular point in the lesson or unit. The one-to-one simple three-question format is intended to help students practice metacognition and gain confidence in their capacities as independent learners. (1) What are you working on? (2) How is it going? and (3) What are you going to do next? These check-ins also help teachers target their academic supports and interventions resulting in a class culture where high levels of thinking and learning are both expected and supported.

Academic check-ins help teachers determine what students are learning, doing, or thinking related to academic skills and content; help students practice important metacognitive skills; provide opportunity to address confusion, misunderstandings, or support the correction of errors; and provide specific positive feedback when a student's thinking is on track. Check-ins can become an established routine during student independent work time. Please see Appendix I for a detailed Academic Check-in Protocol.

Teacher Facilitated Tier 2 Academic and Behavioral Interventions

> *"As the people who know the students best—and are most accountable for their success or failure—teachers are best suited to identify students at risk and assist them."*[32]

When learning gaps and unwanted behaviors persist, teachers intervene with the goal of helping them to take responsibility to learn and practice behaviors and strategies that will close learning gaps and support desired target behaviors. Teacher-facilitated interventions have several benefits. First, the closer an intervention is to the time, space, and persons affected by the situation, the more likely the intervention will achieve desired results. Sending a student out of the room does not solve the problem that prompted a student's removal and potentially can impact the trust the student has with the teacher. Second, when teachers communicate directly with parents about the situation and the intervention, most parents are eager to do what they can to support their children's academic progress and positive behavior in school. Finally, when teachers establish predictable interventions and students know ahead of time "what will happen when_____," interventions become part of a natural learning cycle in the classroom and students tend to enter the process with less drama and resistance.

Typical teacher-facilitated academic and behavioral interventions almost always involve some kind of problem solving and planning conference. See Appendix G for a Problem Solving and Planning Conference Protocol. These conferences with a student may also incorporate the following:

- A required meeting with the teacher outside of regular class time to re-learn important academic content, learn and practice specific procedures, habits of learning, or academic or social skills. A workout session involves side-by-side instruction and coaching.
- Feedback and daily or weekly progress monitoring that enables both the teacher and the student to assess the student's use and practice of a desired target behavior or skill.
- Developmentally appropriate modifications that match behavior and root causes.
- Parent notification, discussion, problem solving, and progress monitoring via phone, email, text message, or letter.
- Standardized intervention protocol when students are failing at five weeks, the quarter, or the semester.
- Creating a weekly plan for supporting students who struggle removes the guesswork involved in figuring out, "When will I ever find the time to do this?" We encourage teachers to think about setting aside ritualized times

during the weekly classroom schedule for individual conferencing and tutorials. Setting aside at least one office hour before or after school, at lunch times, or during a prep period every week for student conferencing, development of behavior and learning contracts, progress report check-ins, parent contacts all have the potential to impact positive relationships with students coupled with increased academic performance.

Restorative and Accountable Discipline

It is no surprise the most typical unwanted behaviors in the classroom that teachers want to address more effectively are Tier 1 low-impact behavior concerns, minor problems that do not jeopardize student safety or put learning at a standstill because they cause serious disruption of the entire classroom community. Figure 10.5 outlines specific low impact behaviors.

Figure 10.5

NON-COMPLIANCE

Does not follow directions
Does not comply with classroom rules, norms, and procedures
Refuses to respond to school staff directives, questions, or requests
Does not bring necessary materials to class

NON-COMPLETION AND NON-PARTICIPATION

Does not attempt or complete assigned work
Does not maintain focus on task at hand
Does not participate in learning activities

DIFFICULTIES WITH SOCIAL INTERACTIONS

Demonstrates difficulty with getting along with others
Does not work cooperatively in small and large groups
Initiates or joins in "side bar" conversations, interrupting, blurting out, talking out of turn
Engages in teasing, taunting, name-calling

DIFFICULTIES WITH SELF-REGULATION

Does not work silently or independently without bothering others
Seeks attention inappropriately
Throws small objects, not directed at others and without physical injury to others or the classroom
Makes excessive, distracting, or disruptive movements or noises

DIFFICULTIES COMMUNICATING AND MANAGING NEEDS, THOUGHTS, AND EMOTIONS

Expresses needs and emotions inappropriately
Does not accept correction and feedback without a fuss
Misinterprets instructional and social cues
Engages in confrontational arguing or back talk
Demonstrates difficulties empathizing with others and accepting other points of view

Unfortunately, these same low-impact behaviors are the very behaviors that prompt the vast majority of student removals from the classroom and discretionary suspensions. Most of this chapter focuses on practices and mindsets that will, in combination, prevent and reduce the number of these kinds of incidents in the classroom. Nonetheless, what teachers ask for and what administrators want to provide for their teachers is a simple and clear step-by-step process when these behaviors do occur. We have provided a version of that in this section.

The other big discipline concern that arises in our work with teachers and administrators is the need to strengthen teachers' capacity to defuse and de-escalate highly charged or confrontational situations. We have included a brief guide to defusion and de-escalation here as well.

A Step by Step Guide When Behavior Problems Arise

Most of the practices in the framework promote conditions for learning that help students stay focused and engaged. Figure 10.6 illustrates scaffolded steps to address behavioral concerns. Step 1 of this guide enables a teacher to first use the briefest of responses when students lose focus temporarily with the aim of re-engaging the student immediately. Sometimes one response in not enough, so Step 2 involves a second attempt to redirect the student. Steps 1 and 2 emphasize Prevention with the aim of keeping minor missteps from becoming major disciplinary incidents. Step 3 involves a teacher-facilitated Intervention to determine the source of the problem and make a more deliberate plan to address it. Steps 4 and 5 involve support staff when a student's behavior warrants removal from the classroom or triggers the need for a consultation with other teachers and student support staff to determine a more comprehensive Intervention.

Figure 10.6

A Step-by-Step Guide for Addressing Behavioral Concerns

Tier 1

Step 1:

When a Behavior Concern Arises:

1. Name the Concern to Yourself: _____

2. Identify One Immediate Goal for this Situation:
- Re-engage student in learning?
- Defuse emotional upset?
- Defuse confrontational behaviors?
- Stop hurtful or aggressive behaviors?

3. Try One or More In-the-Moment Responses:
- **Proximity, Physical Prompts and Cues:** Try proximity first. 90 percent of misbehaviors stop when a teacher moves into close proximity of the students who are misbehaving. Next, use body language to signal to the student that they need to think about their behavior and self-correct. When you want to redirect one student or a small group, pivot toward the students; square up and stand straight, or lean in close and slightly at an angle; make eye contact and put on your "flat face" (relaxed but showing no emotion); freeze and focus your attention for a few seconds.
- **Visual Prompts and Cues:** Point to directions, process steps, reminders, time messages, etc. posted around the room or on the board.
- **Verbal Reminders:** "Take a look at the steps posted on the board and figure out what you should be doing now." "Okay, group, what do we need to finish today before you leave class?" "Let's remind each other – what should we see and hear when we work in small groups?" "Two more minutes before we gather back as a whole group and share."
- **Positive Directives:** "Let's all lower our voices as we enter the classroom. Thank you." "Eyes front, please" "Please take your assigned seat, put your notebook and text on the top of your desk, and begin working on the Warm Up. Thank you."
- **Postpone and Revisit:** "I see you're too upset to focus right now. Take a minute to re-group and I'll check back in with you in a moment."
- **Insist on Problem Solving:** "You have a choice here. "You're welcome to _____ or _____. Take 60 seconds to think about it and decide."
- **Observational Feedback/Acknowledging Feelings:** "I see_____" "You look_____"
- **Open-ended Behavioral Check-in Questions:** "What can I do to help you?" "What do you need to get back on track?"

4. When Student Re-engages: Provide positive reinforcement and feedback. Examples: "I noticed that you made a responsible choice. Or "Thank you for _____, it helped our class to continue learning."

Step 2

If Student Does Not Re-engage Within a Minute:

1. **Assess What is Impeding Student Learning:** Task mismatch? Confusion about what to do? Skill gap? Frustration? Distraction? Personal distress or emotional crisis?

2. **Facilitate a Quick Behavioral or Academic Check-in:** Conduct a brief one-to-one conversation to determine the cause(s) of the behavior and support the student with problem solving to improve their behavior.

3. **For Low-Impact Concerns, Use Logical Consequences:** Change of seats, loss of classroom privilege, in-class "time-out", short "time-out" in partner teachers room, a written reflection or picture that may or may not go home, informal parent contact.

4. **Document the Misbehavior and Your Attempts to Support the Student:** Use your own method of tracking the behavioral concern.

5. **When Student Re-engages:** Provide positive reinforcement and feedback.

Tier 2

Step 3

If Student's Behavioral or Learning Difficulties Persist:

1. **Arrange to Meet with the Student Outside of Class and Engage in a Problem Solving and Planning Conference:** Following the protocol, work with the student to identify the desired end behaviors, and develop a behavior plan.

2. **Contact Parent:** Inform parent about the behavior concern and the plan.

3. **Monitor Student's Progress for Three or More Weeks:** (See Appendix J for sample Progress Monitoring Tools).

4. **Submit Documentation to the Dean or AP According to Specific School or District Policy.**

Step 4

If Student's Behavior Warrants Removal From the Classroom Because the Behavior has Seriously Impacted the Ability for Other Students to Learn or has Jeopardized the Physical or Emotional Safety of Others:

1. **Follow Your School/District's Procedure for Having a Student Removed From Class.**

2. **Document or Submit a Referral in Accordance with School or District Policy.**

3. **Engage in a Brief Restorative Conference When Student Returns to Class:** Welcome student back and communicate your belief in his/her capacity to be successful in your class moving forward.

4. **Monitor Progress of Desired Target Behaviors as Needed or as Requested by the School.**

Step 5

When Pervasive Behaviors Seriously Impede a Student From Functioning Effectively in the Classroom:

1. **Document Student Behaviors and all Teacher Actions:** Use this to manage the behavior and provide interventions.

2. **Consult with Dean, Social Worker, or Counselor and Your Grade Level Team:** (or colleagues who also teach the student) to discuss concerns about student, share your observations, and develop an intervention plan. If applicable, complete a formal request for support from the school's Student Intervention Team to request the school's support with developing a more comprehensive intervention plan.

Defusion and De-escalation Strategies and Protocols

When a student is overtly upset, frustrated, aggressive, or angry, our immediate goal is to defuse their emotions and help them calm down. Defusion and de-escalation strategies and protocols will help students work their way to an improved emotional state, so they can access the reasoning, problem solving, and cognitive part of their brain. When students are highly charged, upset, or angry, teachers need to be ready to depersonalize the situation by keeping emotionally objective. The goal is to acknowledge a student's feelings in a one-to-one interaction that is as private as possible using words of care and reassurance that will help students restore their emotional equilibrium so that they can pause and think about their next move that can help them re-set and re-engage.

When students are physically explosive, teachers need to acknowledge that the safety of the class is jeopardized, direct the explosive student to move away from others and toward the door, and use school protocols to ensure care for the explosive student and ensure safety for the rest of the class. When students are argumentative or confrontational, the most important move *is not* "picking up the rope" and arguing back, explaining one's response, or answering questions that draw the student into further conversation. The hallmark of de-escalating these kinds of potential power struggles is making a brief, matter of fact statement that communicates that the teacher will not engage with the student in the moment. Then the teacher closes the interaction, and moves on with instruction. Please see the Defusion and De-escalation Protocol Appendix K.

Using the Framework to Prioritize Universal Practices That Provide a Platform for Professional Learning

Developing a set of shared or "universal" classroom practices is a primary task of any initiative to improve schoolwide discipline and student support. When we say "universal" we mean all teachers in the building are on board, committed to implementing a specific practice with consistency and fidelity, and using common language to teach these practices to all students. By "practices" we mean very specific actions, protocols, or strategies that are visible to students and any educator walking into a classroom. Improved student outcomes connected to changes in discipline and student support policies are more likely to be achieved when teachers have extensive opportunities to participate in high quality professional learning that is "problem-specific and user-centered."[33]

We acknowledge that garnering the good will of faculty to commit to doing the same thing in specific contexts, and in some cases doing it with exacting precision, can be a "heavy lift." However, as school reform researchers, Larry Cuban and David Tyack remind us, this *is* the work that schools must do. "Changing where it counts the most—in the daily interactions of teachers and students—is the hardest to achieve and the most important."[34] When *problems of practice* are the focus of professional learning, a combination of data and dialogue is used to identify an instructional issue or problem that is directly observable, actionable by school staff in real time, and identified as "high leverage" because it makes a significant difference in student learning.[35] The practices in our framework meet these criteria. Schools that introduce the concept of universal practices thoughtfully begin this process by choosing to implement just one or two high leverage practices that secure the greatest interest among the faculty.

Faculty teams need opportunities to explore and discuss the rationale and benefits of a specific practice, gain a thorough understanding of how and when to use it, and explore ways to track and monitor their use of the practice over time. Instructional rounds, guided by principles developed by Richard Elmore, enable observers to collect descriptive/non-evaluative data on the practice which is then synthesized and reviewed by teams to learn "what works, for whom, and under what set of conditions."[36] Data is shared and analyzed, and inferences, explanations, and conclusions are drawn to inform the next stage of work in a continuous cycle of inquiry. School leadership teams might use the framework we have provided as a tool for prioritizing problems of practice that the whole school is willing to tackle. Here are two examples of what this might look like.

CASE STUDY #1

Problem of Practice Revealed by Data: Disengagement and Non-participation

Systematic classroom observations revealed that the highest frequency of unwanted behavior at a high school in Wisconsin was non-participation. While they were not being disruptive, a number of students were disengaged, shut down, and not participating or doing classwork. For the most part, teachers were allowing students to be disengaged and at the same time teachers were becoming alarmed at how the behavior seemed to be spreading. Other students had begun to notice that it was okay to occasionally "check-out" if they did not feel like doing school on a particular day or during a particular class. Teachers were beginning to send students out of class because they "refused to work". The observation data also revealed that classes were slow to start, with lessons beginning two to eight minutes after the class start time.

Universal Practices Adopted: Meet and Greet and Engaging Class Start

First, all teachers committed to meeting and greeting students at the classroom door so they could continue to build relationships with students and communicate with each student individually to set the stage for their active participation during class. For example, a student who was previously disengaged would be greeted with, "Maria, welcome! Thank you for coming on time. Today is the climate change debate and I'm looking forward to hearing your thinking." At the same time, the faculty decided to look for ways to ramp up engagement at the start of class.

The first five minutes of any class are an opportunity to capture the interests of students, support a smooth transition into your classroom, and set the stage for active student participation and effort. Many teachers at the school already started class with a "warm up" or a "reflect and connect" but they were not necessarily engaging and were frequently the same thing day after day. After examining research around the importance of student engagement, teachers at the school committed to starting every class on time and in a way that would support student's cognitive, social, and emotional engagement in learning. The leadership team supported this effort by providing professional learning opportunities where staff experienced how to effectively facilitate a variety of engaging "reflect and connect" activities, shared ideas with colleagues, and received resources to support their planning. Teachers also had collaborative planning time and explored ways to ritualize their daily "reflect and connect" activities to ensure variety but make planning manageable. For example, a math teacher picked one day a week to share and analyze a shocking statistic, while an English teacher picked one day a week to show a strange or bizarre photo accompanied by a See, Think, Wonder Thinking Routine to support students' analytical thinking. Students quickly began to notice that their teachers were investing time and energy to make their lessons engaging, which built good will and strengthened student-teacher relationships.

Finally, the teachers agreed to establish the expectation that all students would participate in every class and they also committed to addressing students who were off-task or not participating by using visual cues, invitations to self-correct, and if needed one-to-one behavior check-ins to suss out the root cause of the disengagement. Within just a few weeks, follow up classroom visits revealed that the number of students off-task or not participating had decreased by more than half.

CASE STUDY #2

Problem of Practice Revealed by Data: High Numbers of Classroom Removal for Low-impact behaviors

Analysis of the discipline data by the School Climate-Discipline Team revealed that the 80 percent of students who were sent out of class for low-impact behaviors that included: sidebar conversations, blurting out, distracting others, not bringing necessary materials, and/or refusing to do assigned classwork. The data also revealed that the majority of these incidences were happening in the ninth and tenth grade with teachers who had less than two years of experience in the classroom. Further disaggregation of data revealed that the 60 percent of students had IEPs or 504 plans and were receiving special education services.

Universal Practices Adopted: Clear Classroom Expectations, Invitations to Self-correct, and Behavioral Check-ins

The School Climate-Discipline Team, which included the Dean, an AP, the special education (SPED) coordinator, and several ninth and tenth grade teachers, met to discuss the problem and brainstorm solutions. It was noted that after a significant turnover in faculty in the last two years, many of the new teachers might need some support with foundational classroom management strategies and understanding the referral process and what behaviors warranted removal. The special education chair also noted that SPED teachers needed a better way to communicate with classroom teachers about the students on their caseloads so they could more closely monitor their progress.

The School Climate-Discipline Team developed a year-long professional learning plan that focused on preventing most discipline incidents and student-teacher conflicts by learning and practicing initial moves that would stop minor issues from becoming major incidents. In addition, the team established a Google based spreadsheet for ninth and tenth grade to track the behavioral concerns and teacher interventions for students who had received three or more referrals. The SPED coordinator and the Dean would closely monitor this Google spreadsheet so they could stay on top of students that might need immediate or additional supports and interventions.

Initially, during a teacher collaboration time, teachers worked on plans to communicate or co-construct classroom expectations with their students. Then all teachers created and posted visual supports to reinforce expectations. Next, teachers explored and discussed three initial strategies to use for inviting students to self-correct when they were exhibiting low impact misbehaviors: proximity, visual cues and signals, and neutrally voiced questions. Teachers were also explicitly informed of the specific behaviors that warrant classroom removal and the expectations for how a teacher should keep a log of any behavioral concerns and the classroom based interventions they are using so they can share those with the Dean or a SPED case manager before a problem escalates. Ninth and tenth grade teachers also received training on adolescent development, effective communication strategies, and a protocol for doing an in the moment behavioral check-in that would support them with building relationships with some of their more challenging students while simultaneously helping them determine the root cause(s) of the misbehavior. This was followed up by professional learning sessions that focused on de-escalation strategies to prevent and defuse potential student-teacher confrontations.

Throughout this process, the SPED case managers worked with their students to make sure they understood the classroom expectations in their various classes and coordinated additional supports and interventions with teachers as needed.

In this chapter, we have attempted to distill a set of teacher mindsets and practices that hold the most promise for improving classroom management, addressing disciplinary incidents effectively, and supporting students to develop increased personal, social, and academic efficacy. The goal of creating a schoolwide accountable and restorative approach to discipline and student support will depend on teachers' capacity and commitment to adopt these mindsets and practices.

---

[1] Jullan, M., and Hargreaves, A. (1996) What's Worth Fighting for in Your School? New York: Teachers College Press

[2] Evertson, C., & Weinstein, C. (2006). Handbook of classroom management: Research, practice, and contemporary issues. Mahwah, N.J.: Lawrence Erlbaum Associates.

[3] Hattie, J. (2014) Visible Learning, Tomorrow's Schools, the Mindsets that Make a Difference. http://www.slideshare.net/xarxatic/tgls-hattie

[4] Wubbels, T., & Levy, J. (1993). Do you know what you look like?: Interpersonal relationships in education. London: Falmer Press.

[5] Marzano, R. (2003). What works in schools: Translating research into action. Alexandria, VA: ASCD.

[6] Evertson, C., & Weinstein, C. (2006). Handbook of classroom management: Research, practice, and contemporary issues. Mahwah, N.J.: Lawrence Erlbaum Associates. Chapter 8: Student-Teacher Perspectives on Classroom Management, pp. 181-219.

[7] Wubbels, T., & Levy, J. (1993). Do you know what you look like?: Interpersonal relationships in education. London: Falmer Press.

[8] Burgoon, J.K., Buller, D.B., & Woodall, W.G. (1989). Nonverbal communication: The unspoken dialogue. New York, NY: Harper and Row.

[9] Powell, W., & Kusuma-Powell, O. (2010). *Becoming an emotionally intelligent teacher.* Thousand Oaks, CA: Corwin Press.

[10] Gay, G. (2010) Culturally Responsive Teaching: Theory, Research, and Practice. New York: Teachers College Press.

[11] Laura Rychly, L. and Graves, E. (2012) Teacher Characteristics for Culturally Responsive Pedagogy, Multicultural Perspectives, 14:1, 44-49, DOI: 10.1080/15210960.2012.646853

[12] Gregory, A., Skiba, J. and Noguera, P. (2010) The Achievement Gap and the Discipline Gap: Two Sides of the Same Coin? Educational Researcher 2010; 39; 59

[13] Gay, G. (2010) Culturally Responsive Teaching: Theory, Research, and Practice. New York: Teachers College Press.

[14] Noguera, P. A. (2007). How listening to students can help schools to improve. Theory Into Practice, 46, 205–211.

[15] Marzano, R. (2003). What works in schools translating research into action. Alexandria, Va.: ASCD.

[16] Evertson, C., & Weinstein, C. (2006). Handbook of classroom management: Research, practice, and contemporary issues. Mahwah, N.J.: Lawrence Erlbaum Associates. Chapter 8: Student-Teacher Perspectives on Classroom Management, pp. 181-219.

[17] Marzano, R. (2003). What works in schools translating research into action. Alexandria, Va.: ASCD.

[18] Tschannen-Moran, M., Bankole, R.A., Mitchell, R.M., & Moore, D.M., Jr. (2013). Student academic optimism: A confirmatory factor analysis. *Journal of Educational Administration, 51*(2), 150-175.

[19] Adelman H. and Taylor, L. (2001) Enhancing classroom approaches for addressing barriers to learning: Classroom focused enabling. Washington, DC: Center for Mental Health Services, U.S. Department of Health and Human Services.

[20] Doda, N., & Knowles, T. (2008). Listening to the voices of young adolescents. Middle School Journal, 39(3), 26-33.

[21] Evertson, C., & Weinstein, C. (2006). Handbook of classroom management: Research, practice, and contemporary issues. Mahwah, N.J.: Lawrence Erlbaum Associates.

[22] Developing Adolescents: A reference for professionals (2002) American Psychological Association. Washington, DC.

[23] Lee, V., & Smith, J. (1999). Social support, academic press, and student achievement: A view from the middle grades in Chicago. Chicago, IL: Consortium on Chicago School Research.

[24] Support Struggling Students with Academic Rigor, A Conversation with Author and Educator Robyn Jackson by Rick Allen. Educational Leadership. August 2012, volume 54, number 8, pages 3-5. ASCD.

[25] Farrington, C.A., Roderick, M., Allensworth, E., Nagaoka, J., Keyes, T.S., Johnson, D.W., & Beechum, N.O. (2012). Teaching adolescents to become learners. The role of noncognitive factors in shaping school performance: A critical literature review. Chicago: University of Chicago Consortium on Chicago School Research.

[26] Civic Enterprises., Bridgeland, J., Bruce, M., & Hariharan, (2013). The Missing Piece: A National Teacher Survey on How Social and Emotional Learning Can Empower Children and Transform Schools. Collaborative for Academic, Social, and Emotional Learning. Chicago: Author.

[27] Battistich, V., Schaps, E., Watson, M., Solomon, D., & Lewis, C. (2000). Effects of the child development project on students' drug use and other problem behaviors. Journal of Primary Prevention, 21(1), 75–99.

[28] Hopkins, B. (2004) Just Schools: A Whole Approach to restorative Justice. Jessica Kingsley Publishers, London and Philadelphia.

[29] Ibid.

[30] Ibid.

[31] Lieber, C. (2009). Getting classroom management right: Guided discipline and personalized support in secondary schools. Cambridge, MA.: Engaging Schools.

[32] 32 Ballentine, R. and Gaines Pell, A. Intervention as an Inside Job. Educational Leadership. October 2010, volume 68, number 2. ASCD.

[33] 33 Bryk, A., Gomez, L., Grunow, A. and Lemahieu, P. Breaking the Cycle of Failed School Reforms, Using Networked Improvement Communities to learn fast and implement well. Harvard Education Letter. Volume 31, Number 1, January/February 2015.

[34] Tyack, D. and Cuban, C. Tinkering Toward Utopia: A Century of School Reform (1997) Cambridge, MA: Harvard University Press.

[35] Teitel, L. and Elmore, R. (2009) Instructional Rounds in Education: A Network Approach to Improving Teaching and Learning. Cambridge, MA: Harvard Education Press.

[36] Bryk, A., Gomez, L., Grunow, A. and Lemahieu, P. Breaking the Cycle of Failed School Reforms, Using Networked Improvement Communities to learn fast and implement well. Harvard Education Letter. Volume 31, Number 1,January/February 2015.

11

Interventions and Case Management

How do we systematically provide restorative and accountable interventions to all students who need them?

Introduction

Promotion and prevention practices, the focus of the prior three chapters, are essential for reshaping a school's discipline and student support model. More than preventative efforts are necessary to meet the challenges of our students with significant needs. When high-impact behaviors go unchecked, other students, whole classes, and the school staff are all affected in ways that can erode the school's ability to establish a safe and productive learning environment for everyone. Finding good solutions is not easy. Yet, when schools marshal their resources to develop an organized system of timely interventions that address a wide range of academic, social, and emotional issues, the frustrations that arise from feelings of "just putting out fires" can be replaced by a quiet confidence that the staff is poised to provide the right supports to help students turn around. Students who come to school with considerable personal and family difficulties, who feel marginalized by acts of conscious and unconscious bias at school, or who simply experience school as a daily struggle, all need our best efforts to support their continued growth and development during adolescence.

This gear focuses on an integrated approach to providing interventions for Tier 2 and 3 behavior and academic challenges. We cannot overstate the importance of committing to a shared goal for all restorative and accountable interventions and student support services and would like to offer this statement of purpose: *"The aim of all restorative interventions and student support services is to nurture students' healthy development and resiliency; develop and strengthen behaviors and mindsets that will improve students' academic, personal, and social efficacy; and enable all students to be successful in school and the classroom."* As we have mentioned in other chapters, a single aim for student support held by all staff eliminates contradictory practices and mixed messages that arise when discipline and student support live in separate silos. A common goal galvanizes the collective belief that administrators, Student Support Team members, teachers, and other non-certified staff are all on the same side, on the same team, and want the same outcomes for our students.

This chapter reviews the importance of aligning Tier 2 and 3 interventions to Tier 2 and 3 behavioral violations. This is followed by a description of the Intervention Center, a schoolwide discipline structure that enables schools to manage and oversee students during the processing of disciplinary incidents and the provision of immediate supports and interventions. Then we turn to restorative interventions and offer nine examples of intervention strategies that, together, address most of the issues that students who are at-risk experience at school. We pull it all together by detailing a step-by-step process that describes how a school might respond to different discipline scenarios from the incident to the intervention, and describe a case management structure that helps to organize the work. We close with a look at personalized programs for students with the highest needs.

Alignment of Tier 2 and 3 Behavior Violations and Interventions

As noted in Chapters two and six, a key to providing the right support to students is aligning the appropriate interventions to specific behaviors that prompt Tier 2 and Tier 3 school sanctions/consequences. Student support staff members need to feel prepared to deliver two types of interventions to students. The first are short-term interventions aligned to a single incident of a serious behavior violation. These incidents include teasing, inappropriate language, fighting, bullying, inappropriate use and misuse of school equipment, hallway and public space misconduct, verbal aggression against school personnel or between students, and damage to personal or school property. Interventions aligned with these incidents enable students to repair relationships; make amends, offer restitution, or engage in an action of apology; reflect more deeply about the impact of a student's actions on the school community through writing and conversation; and/or provide targeted social skill building and practice related to a desired end behavior. After students have been assigned a school sanction/consequence, administrators have several choices for moving the process from the school sanction/consequence phase to the intervention phase of a disciplinary incident. Sometimes the administrator hands off the intervention to a specialist who delivers standardized mandated interventions in response to specific behavior violations. Anti-bullying skill building sessions following a bully incident would be an example. At other times, administrators will either consult with members of the Student Support Team to explore the best possible intervention or hand off the determination of the intervention to the School Intervention Team.

A Three-Tiered System of Support

TIER 1 PROMOTION and PREVENTON
for all students

TIER 2 INTERVENTIONS
assigned to students who meet
specific criteria or thresholds

TIER 3
INDIVIDUALIZED
INTERVENTIONS

The second type of interventions is longer term and targeted to students whose behaviors place them on the "worry list." These students often fall into three categories: students who present chronic Tier 1 behavior concerns after teachers have provided classroom supports and interventions; students who engage in multiple Tier 2 and Tier 3 violations, and students who are experiencing a combination of academic, attendance, behavior, and mental health challenges that seriously jeopardize their well-being and success at school. Longer-term interventions are usually delivered by a staff member who serves as the student's support coach and manages that student's case; confers with the student to create a plan for the interventions; and meets with the student on a regular basis to provide counseling, coaching, targeted skill building, behavior replacement training, and progress monitoring that support the goals of the plan. Schools need to consider the threshold of incidents and referrals that prompt placement on the "worry list" and assignment to longer-term interventions. Over time, as the Student Support Team discusses the effectiveness of various interventions used to address specific behaviors and social and emotional challenges, teams usually establish a standardized array of interventions that they are prepared to deliver.

Intervention Center

A critical structure for immediately responding to students with high needs and Tier 2 and Tier 3 behavior incidents is an Intervention Center (IC). The IC provides a central location for managing disciplinary incidents and students in need of more intensive support. The IC can serve multiple functions within a school, by serving as the intake location for students who (1) need to be removed from the classroom or who have engaged in serious incidents of public space misconduct and need to be temporarily removed from that space; (2) have been traveling in public spaces without permission during class periods and are temporarily removed to the IC for processing before returning to class; (3) are upset and angry and have received a "reset pass" to meet briefly with a Student Support Team member to cool down and regain their equilibrium so that they can return to class ready to learn; and (4) have been assigned to the IC for a designated period of time, such as a class period, half day, or whole day, during which students are picked up to participate in scheduled conferences or assigned interventions with administrators, Student Support Team members, and/or teachers.

The success of an Intervention Center is as good as the people supporting it. The IC coordinator needs to be highly skillful when communicating with emotionally charged students and have a calm, capable demeanor so he or she can manage a variety of tasks and disruptions at once. At any given time, one Student Support Team member needs to be "on call" and present in the IC on a rotating basis to assist where needed and address more explosive or crisis situations as they arise. Ideally, APs, deans, and other student support personnel "float" in and out of the IC to stay on top of situations that require immediate attention. The IC coordinator oversees the intake and processing of all students who are sent to the IC and also serves as a kind of broker who contacts others who need to meet with a student immediately. Specifically, they might contact an administrator who will need to investigate and process serious behavior violations. Or, they might need to communicate with a student's support coach who can facilitate a cooling down conference with a student who is highly charged and explosive. See Appendix L: Intervention Center Coordinator: Roles and Responsibilities.

There are many benefits of establishing an Intervention Center. All students are initially directed to one place. This means no more informal "stop and drop" when teachers ask an administrator or Student Support Team member to "take this student and talk to them," which is rarely an ideal opportunity to provide a quality intervention. A single intake location also fosters consistent treatment of young people and a consistent intake protocol that begins with an Intervention Center Referral form that a student brings with them to the IC, and includes an Intervention Center Reflection and Return form that students complete during their stay in the IC. In addition, the IC becomes a central location for Student Support Team members to find students whom they are seeing for an intervention. Because there is only one intake log book, it also becomes easy to identify "frequent fliers" who need to be discussed at the next School Intervention Team meeting. Most importantly, no students or their documentation get lost. Please see

Appendix M for the Intervention Center Referral Form, and Appendix N for the Intervention Center Reflection and Return Form.

Tier 2 and 3 Restorative Interventions

Restorative interventions require students to own the problem, reflect on the impact of their behavior on themselves and others, and understand the reasons the behavior was unskillful, unacceptable, or inappropriate. Interventions engage students in some action or learning process that will enable them to correct behaviors, repair relationships and the harm they have done to others, learn desired replacement behaviors, or restore their good standing. We offer examples of several intervention strategies that address the most typical student issues that arise. More individualized and intensive Tier 3 interventions like a comprehensive student success plan are created through extensive consultation with the School Intervention Team or the grade level office team and are likely to involve a combination of many intervention strategies. In all cases, progress monitoring will be required to measure the impact of the intervention and assess what additional measures might be needed to support the student. While the context of the intervention will drive the design of the monitoring tools and process, the universal expectation to provide progress monitoring will enable Student Support Teams to identify the interventions that work most effectively and efficiently.

Example Interventions

Academic Interventions: If behavior problems are rooted in school failure, a strategic plan to assess the student's learning gaps is needed to provide the right academic interventions. This process might start with a consultation with the student's teachers, a universal screening assessment, a special education evaluation, or diagnostic testing with psychologist. At this point, the Student Support Team can determine the most appropriate academic interventions in addition to those provided by the teacher. Typical academic interventions include required academic support and recovery protocol when students are failing or at-risk of failing a course; assigned placement in "flex time" academic clinics during the school day for 5 five weeks up to the remainder of a semester; required tutoring/homework hall facilitated by rotating teachers; and specialized recovery and remedial programs for students with multiple failures and students whose math and literacy skills lag years behind grade level proficiency.

Workout Session with Teacher: For many Tier 2 behaviors the best intervention might be one delivered by the classroom teacher. In a workout session with a teacher, a student would be required to spend time with one or more of their teachers outside of the regular class setting to learn and practice the skills or behaviors that they are lacking. For example, a student (or a group of students) might spend thirty minutes, one day a week, for three weeks working with his science teacher to preview the weekly science lab in advance and identify the appropriate behaviors and expectations for interacting with lab partners and the equipment. Workout sessions with teachers are highly effective for two big reasons. First, they can target key academic skills as well as behavior skillsets within the context in which the student is expected to perform. And second, the closer the intervention is to the problem, the more likely that the intervention will be successful.[1]

Restorative Conferencing: Restorative conferencing is the foundation of a restorative approach to discipline. Restorative questions can serve as the foundation for any restorative conference.

- What happened? (What was your role in what happened?)
- What were you thinking and feeling at the time?
- Who else was affected by this? How?
- What have been your thoughts/feelings since then? What are you thinking/ feeling now?
- What do you want to do to make things right?
- What can I (others) do to support you?
- When a situation like this comes up again, what actions might you take next time?

A restorative conference can be facilitated by a teacher, a Student Support Team member, or small team. The conference structure supports the student with unpacking the problem or issue and helps them think for themselves about possible strategies and solutions through collaborative brainstorming. The open-ended question format in these conferences helps the student develop self-awareness, social-awareness, and problem solving skills.

A Problem Solving and Planning Conference is an essential restorative conference. While it might seem more expedient to tell the student what to do and "fix" the problem for them, the long-term goal is to strengthen the students' self-discipline/ self-management skill set. Actively collaborating with the student in the solution process also strengthens the student-teacher relationship and garners a student's goodwill to commit to the desired behavioral change. In Appendix G, we have included a protocol for a Problem Solving and Planning Conference that can be used by teachers, administrators, or Student Support Team members. We have also included a Restorative Group Conference Protocol in Appendix O.

A change of courses, schedule, or teacher: There are unique situations where it might make sense to change a student's schedule or class. For example, you might do a course change if diagnostic data reveal the student should be placed in a different leveled math class to gain the underlying skills and knowledge that are preventing success in her current math class. In some cases, a schedule change is a step you take combined with other interventions. For example, if you separate two students who have been fighting by switching one to another class, you have not solved the problem, but merely limited the frequency in which the problem might occur. To be truly restorative in nature, you would want to couple it with a mediation conference or have the two students participate in life skills group. We also caution schools to limit the option of transferring students out of classes because of poor student-teacher "chemistry" to those situations that truly appear to be irreconcilable.

Assigning a coach/mentor/advocate: Student assignment to a counselor, youth advocate, special education case manager, external partner case manager, or Student Support Coach is the organizational means to oversee a student's intervention plan and monitor a student's progress during the plan's implementation. However, we also recognize that assignment to someone designated as the student's support coach or peer mentor is a powerful stand-alone intervention strategy. For many students who are at-risk, daily face-to-face contact and a trusting relationship with either an adult or a student peer who is "on their side and on their case" serves as the catalyst for showing up to school more often, taking the role of a student more seriously, and engaging in fewer behaviors that raise alarm bells. This is especially true in middle and high schools that do not have any type of advisory system where every student is assigned to an adult who takes responsibility for personally supporting the students to whom they are assigned. We encourage every Student Support Team member, dean, and administrator to serve as a Student Support Coach for at least one student. This ensures that everyone involved in delivering key components of discipline and student support are able to share first hand experiences of working long-term with one student. See Appendix C for Guidelines for Student Support Coaches.

It is also noteworthy to mention that Student Support Coaches do not necessarily need to be drawn only from the cadre of Student Support Team members. Every school has teachers who can and will take on this role if the school can figure out reassignment and scheduling adjustments that allow the time and space for teachers to make this commitment. One strategy schools can utilize is inviting teachers to apply to serve as a coach for three students in place of the typical compulsory "supervision duty" requirements. Another strategy is to set aside .2 FTE time of a teacher's contract to serve as a coach as well as provide saturated academic supports for a designated number of students at academic risk.

Mediation or Restorative Group Conferencing: These are protocols that provide a highly structured opportunity for all parties involved in an incident to come together and resolve outstanding issues. Both protocols promote community values by building a sense of the community's capacity for resolving conflict and restoring relationships.

The goal of mediation is for the disputants to constructively work out differences in a way that solves the problem and preserves the relationship. Mediation is voluntary. Disputants agree to have mediators facilitate a process in which the disputants reach a win-win solution and agreement. Mediators do not offer solutions or advice. The mediator's role is to encourage problem solving between the disputants so that disputants generate their own solution. Mediations are often used when there is a conflict between individual students, between groups of students, or between student and staff member. In Appendix P we have included a detailed Mediation Protocol.

The goal of a restorative group conference is to empower the targeted person, the offender, the family, and community members to seek a constructive resolution to the incident by giving them a voice and a shared responsibility for the outcome. The intent is to address the underlying causes of the offending behavior, foster awareness and understanding of the human impact of the behavior, and have the offender take full responsibility for her behavior, and in engage in some action to make things right. Administrators use restorative group conferences for high-impact incidents that have seriously harmed or threatened the safety and well-being of individuals and groups or have jeopardized the safety, functioning, and reputation of the entire school community.

Most mediation and restorative practice programs require 12 to 20 hours of training to ensure adequate skill acquisition, practice and feedback, and development of an implementation plan. Schools need to have at least two or three people who "hold" these programs and build capacity and commitment within the school to use these processes regularly. *Circle Forward: Building a Restorative School Community* by Carolyn Boyes-Watson and Kay Pranis is an excellent resource that offers comprehensive step-by-step instructions for how to plan, facilitate and implement the use of a wide array of restorative practices within the school environment.[2]

Life Skills Groups: These small groups are facilitated by a member of the Student Support Team. Students systematically participate in groups for a semester or more. Topics might include anger management, gender empowerment, leadership development, or countering bullying and harassment to name a few. Students acquire critical skills that will help them be more successful and these groups also serve to provide students with a positive peer network.

Behavior Replacement Training: Students who get in the most trouble at school are likely to experience some combination of social, developmental, and cognitive delays as illustrated in Figure 11.1. Interventions that help close these gaps aim at teaching knowledge and skills needed for competent daily living and school success. Although some of these gaps can be addressed through mediation and Restorative Group Conferences that are prompted by single incidents, these processes do not provide the saturated practice needed for students to learn and use desired social skills and mindsets habitually.

Figure 11.1

Social, Developmental, and Cognitive Gaps
Adapted from *Teaching Adolescents to Think and Act Responsibly: The EQUIP Approach*[3]

1.) Social skill deficiencies

Social acquisition deficit. (I do not know how.)

Social performance deficit. (I can do it, but choose not to do it in specific situations.)

Social fluency deficit. (I can do it, but do not always know when or where to do it and to what extent to do it.)

2.) Developmental delays and differences

Diminished empathy/perspective taking.

Diminished/immature moral judgment.

Erratic frontal lobe functioning. (CEO of the brain) that does not fully develop in most boys until late adolescence/early adulthood.

3.) Cognitive distortions (thinking errors)

Egocentric biases that result in:

- A disregard for the views and rights of others.
- Fixed belief that self and others cannot change.
- Minimizing or mislabeling harmful behaviors.
- Assuming the worst in others and blaming others.

The basics of behavior replacement training forms a sub-set of the larger domain of social and emotional learning and emerges from Albert Bandura's social learning theory.[4] This intervention has been refined and tested by prominent researchers like Arnold Goldstein and John Gibbs *(Skillstreaming the Adolescent: New Strategies and Perspectives for Teaching Prosocial Skills, Aggression Replacement Training: A Comprehensive Intervention for Aggressive Youth, and Teaching Adolescents to Think and Act Responsibly: The EQUIP Approach)*, Catalano and Hawkins *(Theory of Anti-Social Behavior), and* Roger Weissberg *(The Impact of Enhancing Students' Social and Emotional Learning)* who have all spent decades investigating strategies that will help adolescents increase protective and resiliency factors, reduce anger and aggression, and strengthen social and emotional competencies. The principles underlying behavior replacement training emphasize the importance of (1) setting clear expectations with specific instructions; (2) using modeling to discuss and understand the importance of the skill; (3) coaching the individual to try out the skill through the use of frequent prompts; (4) engaging individuals in role playing, behavioral rehearsal, and discussion of scenarios; and (5) offering abundant positive feedback or reinforcement for small improvements in social behavior.

Behavior replacement training within the school setting helps close the social, developmental, and cognitive gaps. It is most often delivered by a social worker, mental health professional, or student support specialist who has been specifically trained in this intervention. Although most behavior replacement training intentionally uses a peer group format, we strongly suggest that a student support specialist consider adapting lessons to use in one-to-one coaching or delivering a combination of peer group and one-to-one sessions. The research on most social skills programs for adolescents has been conducted in sheltered programs, residential settings, or juvenile facilities where peer groups meet every day and the delivery is highly saturated. So thirty lessons that cover a breadth of topics, for example, can be delivered to the same peer group in four to six weeks.

In regular middle and high schools, this is an unrealistic program model. It is extremely difficult to schedule the same peer group for multiple weekly sessions during the school day and deliver 20 to 30 lessons. Moreover, the question of transferability of newly learned skills and mindsets from a peer group setting to the classroom presents another challenge. In residential settings, the people who are delivering behavior replacement training are in a position to monitor students' progress in other settings throughout the entire day. In regular schools, a Student Support Team member facilitating one peer group of seven students might need to consult with as many as 30 different teachers who would actually be providing feedback on the classroom performance of those seven students. The logistics make this unlikely.

To make behavior replacement training realistic for students with high needs in the school setting we offer a few suggestions. First, identify a cluster of lessons that address the skills and mindsets that feel most critical for helping the student experience greater success in the classroom. A personalized program of sessions assures that specific desired end-behaviors in the classroom are directly linked to the content of the sessions. Since it is likely that these students have already been assigned a Student Support Coach with whom they have a relationship, we recommend incorporating behavior replacement training into coaching responsibilities and modify lessons to deliver the training as more of a coaching tutorial. And finally, engage the students' teachers in supporting the students' development of the new skills by having them complete direct behavior ratings regularly to serve as relatively simple progress monitoring and feedback tool.

Intervention Recommendations

After reviewing more than 50 social skills curricula/programs, we would like to recommend using one or two resources as the primary curriculum and offer several supplementary curricula for additional topics and materials.

Primary Resources by Arnold Goldstein and John Gibbs:

Teaching Adolescents to Think and Act Responsibly: The EQUIP Approach

Aggression Replacement Training: A Comprehensive Intervention for Aggressive Youth

Both of these curricula/programs address all three social, developmental, and cognitive gaps that students with the most challenging behaviors are most likely to experience.

Supplementary Resources Available from Engaging Schools:

Conflict Resolution in the High School: 36 Lessons

Countering Bullying and Harassment: Skill-Based Lessons to Move from Bystander to Ally

Courage to Be Yourself, and Leaders' Guide to Courage to Be Yourself

Getting Classroom Management Right (Chapter 5: Supporting Students' Social and Emotional Development)

Progress Monitoring: Often the least complicated solution to a problem is the most effective solution. Although progress monitoring is an essential element of all effective intervention plans, progress monitoring, by itself, can serve as a simple and elegant intervention strategy. The quality and efficacy of progress monitoring, however, depends on getting a few things right. Good progress monitoring tools have the following features:

- An academic goal that provides a good reason for learning and using a new behavior
- Explicit description of the desired end behavior(s) that support the academic goal
- A specific place and time for observing behavior(s)
- A consistent, clear, and easily measured rating scale
- An easy to use and quick to complete tool
- A reasonable and appropriate number of weeks that ensures that the student has time to replace the behavior and use the new skills consistently

The adults responsible for monitoring a student's behavior need to provide feedback about the specific desired behavior immediately after the observation period is over and check-in with students regularly to assess progress and lift up positive or negative trend lines. When students are asked to self-assess as part of the process, progress monitoring can have an even greater impact. These intervention tools have other benefits. They foster more positive student-teacher relationships, promote accountability, increase a student's awareness and conscious use of desired behaviors, and strengthen a student's confidence and efficacy by making progress visible. A student's support coach, counselor, or advisor is usually the person who distributes progress monitoring tools to the student, collects the tool, and checks in with the student about overall progress.

Please note that behavior replacement training and progress monitoring are the two most thoroughly researched interventions and have proven to produce significant improvements in behavior. Appendix Q: Identifying Desired Target Behaviors provides a detailed checklist, and Appendix J includes two sample Progress Monitoring Tools. Each illustrates how the tools identify the desired end behavior and utilize some form of "Direct Behavior Rating" (DBR) in which teachers and the student are rating the use of explicit desired end behaviors. As an intervention strategy, DBRs have a history of proven effectiveness in multiple settings with a range of student groups.

The Intervention Process

The intervention process we describe here is grounded in the concept of "systems of care," a coordinated network of school and community-based services and supports that are organized to meet the challenges of children and youth with mental health needs and their families. Systems of care is not a program—it is a philosophy of how care should be delivered. Three important values inform the intervention process within "systems of care." (1) It is child-centered, youth guided, and family driven; (2) it is community-based and comprehensive; and (3) it is culturally competent and responsive. Building the capacity of administrators, student support staff, and teachers to deliver the right array of Tier 2 and Tier 3 interventions within a coherent system of care is a heavy lift when schools shift to a more accountable and restorative model of discipline and student support. It is likely to require more support staff, a reconfiguration of current student support roles, and additional training for student support staff, administrators, and some teachers. Questions about where interventions take place and when interventions are scheduled during the school day must be resolved as well. In addition, schools that have, in the past, depended on out-of-school suspension, alternative placement, and expulsion as the "go-to" responses for students with the most challenges, must now develop in-school interventions and alternative programs for students who need more creative and flexible educational options. Figure 11.2 shows essential steps that need to take place leading up to the implementation of the intervention plan.

Figure 11.2

Intervention Plan Implementation

Data Gathering	Consultation	Desired Outcomes	Intervention Plan	Start-Up Conference
Relevant quantitative and qualitative information from school databases, teachers, parents, and students that capture a holistic portrait of the student to assess root causes and determine student outcomes and the intervention plan	Grade level teacher team, grade level office team, or School Intervention Team consult to review student data, consult with parent and student, and determine student outcomes and the intervention plan or recommend further diagnostics	Clear, unambiguous student outcomes that include desired end behaviors and mindsets that are understood by student, student's teachers, parents, and Student Support Team member who is delivering the intervention	Specific combination of intervention strategies, practices, and activities that enable the student to learn and use desired end behaviors and mindsets	Review with student and teachers what everyone is expected to do throughout the intervention plan

The length of the intervention process is determined, in large part, by the frequency and/or intensity of incidents and issues that a student is experiencing at any given time. In our work, we find that two key elements of an effective intervention are often absent: (1) explicit student outcomes related to a specific intervention or a more comprehensive intervention plan, and (2) consistent progress monitoring to assess whether desired outcomes are being achieved. There is really no way to assess the effectiveness of an intervention or determine when a student should exit an intervention unless teachers, in particular, provide "real time" feedback about whether the student is achieving or not achieving desired outcomes.

A single incident intervention process as shown in Figure 11.3, is most typically used in situations where students are involved in fighting; bullying; harassment; other physical or verbally aggressive acts directed at students or adults; or high profile incidents that have a particularly negative impact on the school community. Most of these incidents are social in nature and involve a student or group doing harm to another student, a group, or the whole school community. They often prompt a student's removal from a classroom or other location because of concerns about safety and order. These incidents need to be investigated and addressed immediately. Thus, this intervention process has a relatively quick turnaround. It begins with a single incident, which prompts an administrator's investigation and assignment of a consequence, and moves to the determination of the short-term intervention (i.e., mediation) related to that specific incident. Even though the intervention process may be completed in a matter of days or a week, monitoring a student's progress during and after the intervention plays the same critical role that it does in longer-term interventions.

Figure 11.3

Single Incident Intervention Process

1) A single incident is serious enough to prompt a behavior referral and an administrator's investigation and assignment of a school sanction/consequence.

2) Administrator consults with School Intervention Team member to determine the right intervention, desired student outcomes, and the person who will deliver it.

3) The short term intervention is likely to involve some kind of restorative conference, mediation, or specific skill building or behavior replacement sessions.

   ▶ **Communication with family/adult ally**

4) The adult who delivers the intervention closes the loop with the referring adult and the student by discussing the intervention, the desired outcomes and how progress will be monitored.

5) The person who delivers the intervention follows up at least once with the referring adult to check progress in meeting desired outcomes and determine if any further steps need to be taken.

   ▶ **Communication with family/adult ally**

If student has achieved targeted desired outcomes, student exits from the intervention	OR	If student has not achieved desired outcomes, the SIT convenes to gather more data and recalibrate intervention plan

A longer-term intervention process, as shown in Figure 11.4, is most appropriate when students have accumulated multiple referrals and/or are experiencing multiple academic, behavior, attendance, mental health and family problems. Students who present multiple risks require a comprehensive student success plan that is likely to involve an extended consultation with the student, family/adult ally, and other staff members, and includes the long-term assignment of a Student Support Coach or case manager.

The referring teacher(s) is the most likely person to initiate the process by either submitting a referral or by requesting a consultation with the grade level team, other colleagues who teach the student, or a student's support coach. The referring teacher remains in the communication loop in order to implement interventions at the classroom level or provide complimentary support to students receiving interventions outside of the classroom.

Figure 11.4

Longer Term Intervention Process

1) Student who is experiencing multiple discipline, academic, and attendance problems that require more intensive support and more complex interventions is placed on the "worry list" or "urgent list" (through screening, school data, and anecdotal reportage).

2) In consultation with student, parent, teachers, and SIT members, a more comprehensive intervention plan and desired student outcomes are developed.

3) Student is assigned a Student Support Coach / case manager who meets with the student regularly and oversees the intervention plan.

   ▶ Communication with family/adult ally

4) The coach or case manager closes the loop with the student's teachers discussing the intervention plan, the desired outcomes, and how teachers can support the plan and monitor student's progress.

5) The student's coach or case manager solicits feedback from teachers every week in order to assess progress and make any adjustments to the intervention plan.

   ▶ Communication with family/adult ally

If student has made significant progress, student exits from the intervention and case manager or coach checks in with student periodically	OR	If student has not made significant progress, the SIT convenes to gather more data and recalibrate intervention plan

Core Intervention Components

Regardless of the length of the intervention, a student's support coach or case manager needs to ensure that the following intervention components are in place. A student's prior history, developmental needs, and the specific academic, behavior, and mental health issues that prompt the intervention will mean that some components are likely to receive greater emphasis and attention than others.

- Adult Collaboration: Ongoing conversations with the right adults to assess receptiveness of the student to the intervention; discuss up, down, or static trend lines; implement any adjustments or modifications to the intervention plan.
- Family / Adult Ally: Engagement: Soliciting consent and support, sharing data, reporting updates, and engaging in collaborative problem solving.
- Quick Check-Ins with Student: Coach or case manager checks-in with the student every day or several days a week to review progress, anticipate and troubleshoot challenges, build trust and confidence, provide encouragement, and communicate, "I'm on your side and on your case." Each check-in conference provides the opportunity to further "suss out" root causes and triggers; identifying student's important needs and wants; discussing impact of unwanted behaviors and benefits of desired behaviors; and listening, reflecting, and processing student's thoughts and feelings about issues that prompted the intervention and are related to other personal challenges.
- Progress Monitoring: Utilizing a progress monitoring tool or system to track student progress on a daily or weekly basis in order to provide data for student feedback, to determine if the outcomes are being met, and assess the effectiveness of the actual intervention plan.

The Process at Work

To further explicate the intervention process we have provided three specific case examples below. Each illustrates the step-by-step processing sequence for a common behavior concern or violation.

Case Study #1

Persistent Tier 1 Concerns: Non-compliance, Back-Talk

The Situation: An English teacher has documented several observation notes that detail the student's refusal to work in class. When the teacher uses friendly prompts and reminders the student responds by staring, mumbling, or saying, "Don't get in my face!" and "I'm not going to do that!" accompanied by passive aggressive gesturing (eye rolling, hostile facial expressions). The teacher has made three unsuccessful attempts to call home and has already met with the student after class for a Problem Solving and Planning Conference. The teacher has not seen any changes in behavior.

Step 1: Referral to Intervention Team and Data Collection. The teacher submits his/her observation notes / Tier 1 referrals about this student to the Grade Level Intervention Team and the student is placed on the "worry list," which triggers a process for collecting and compiling data on Behavior, Attendance, and Grades on the student. Along with compiling data available through school databases, all of her teachers are sent an email asking them to reply with any documented observation notes, current grades, and relative comments.

Step 2: Intervention Team Initial Review and Coach Assigned. The Grade Level Intervention Team conducts an initial review of her case the following week. The data reveal that she is currently failing four out of her six classes, has nearly perfect attendance, has transferred in and out of four schools in the last two years, and is reading slightly below grade level. The student's science and math teachers also had observation data that revealed similar non-compliant behaviors. The student is successful in her art elective and the teacher noted that she always works in his class. The intervention team assigns one of the student support staff to be the student's coach who later schedules a problem solving and planning conference to take place during the student's English period.

Step 3: Problem Solving and Planning Conference with Coach and Development of Intervention Plan. The conference reveals the student feels like she is too far behind in her core classes to catch up and that she feels her teachers do not like her anyway. She also shared how she loves art because she can be creative and "you can't get art wrong." After problem solving together the student and coach decide to sign her up for after school tutoring for the next six weeks, and she agrees to meet with her teacher to identify three specific behaviors that will support her to meet expectations and remain focused during the class period. The coach logs the conference outcomes in the intervention tracking and monitoring system.

Step 4: Communication to Parents and Teachers. The coach, who was able to get the parent's cell phone number, contacts the parent to let them know of the school's concerns, the student's current grades, and the intervention plan. He also updates the student's teachers via an email and recommends four specific strategies to provide classroom support: intentional efforts to build a positive relationship, identify any missing work that the student can focus on during after school peer tutoring, provide specific praise when the student puts forth effort to build the students efficacy, and provide opportunities for the student to use her creative and artistic talents.

Step 5: Intervention Team Reviews the Case and Determines Monitoring Plan. The coach reports back to the Grade Level Intervention Team and a plan is set in place to monitor the student's in class work effort for the next six weeks. Each Wednesday for the next six weeks, the student's teachers get an email from the coach asking them to reply and quickly rank the students effort on a scale of 1-5. The coach will also check-in with the peer tutors weekly to ensure the student is attending and making progress. At the end of each week the coach checks in with the student in a conversation that starts with having the student self-assess her effort in each of her classes and during the peer tutoring.

Step 6: Intervention Team Evaluates Impact of Intervention and Determines Next Steps. After six weeks the student is reviewed by the School Intervention Team and a determination will be made to continue with the intervention, to try a different intervention, or to remove the student from the "worry list" because the student has shown marked improvements.

Case Study #2

Level 3 Violation: Fighting with Minor Bodily Injury: Both students involved engage in hitting or punching the other person.

The Incident: A fight took place in the student parking lot immediately prior to lunch. The school has an open campus rule for juniors and seniors and the two students involved are in the eleventh grade. Student A has no history of fighting and this is the third fight of the year for student B. The assistant principal and security guard were called to the scene and escorted each student separately back to the school. The security guard took student A to the Intervention Center and the assistant principal took student B to small conference room next to his office. Because student B was involved in two other fights earlier in the year, he already had a Student Support Team coach assigned to him. His coach is alerted of the incident and asked to come meet with the student to help him cool down and discuss what triggered the fight.

Step 1: Initial Family/Adult Ally Communication. The assistant principal calls the family/adult ally or allies, informs them of the incident and lets them know that once the investigation is complete there will be a school sanction/consequence and an intervention assigned to each student.

Step 2: Investigation. The assistant principal then begins the investigation by separately conferencing with each student and interviewing other witnesses to uncover the details of the incident.

Student A (first fight, first ODR)	Student B (repeated incidents of fighting)
Step 3: School Sanction/Consequence Assigned. Student is assigned two days of in-school suspension, per guidelines in the Code of Conduct for first offenses.	**Step 3: School Sanction/Consequence Assigned.** Student is assigned 3 days of out-of-school suspension per guidelines in the Code of Conduct because it is a repeat violent offense.
Step 4: Consultation with Student Support Team member. The discipline AP consults with the lead social worker to review the incident report and the student's behavior, attendance, and grades data that has been collected and compiled.	**Step 4: Consultation with Student's Coach.** The discipline AP consults with the student's support coach to review the incident report and the student's behavior, attendance, and grades data that has been collected and compiled.

Step 5: Intervention Plan. The AP meets with the student to conduct a problem-solving and planning conference to develop an intervention plan for resolving the student conflict. Student agrees to a mediation conference with the other student.	**Step 5: Intervention Plan.** The AP meets with the student, his coach, and a parent to conduct a problem-solving and planning conference to develop an intervention plan for resolving the student conflict and supporting the student with reducing aggressive behaviors. The student agrees to a mediation conference with the other student. In addition, the student will attend a Resolving Conflict Peacefully workshop facilitated by an outside community agency. This student will also meet weekly with his coach to ensure the student has regular contact with an adult advocate at school.
Step 5: Communication to Parents. Parents are informed of the results of the investigation, the assigned consequences, and the intervention: a mediation conference.	**Step 5: Tracking and Monitoring the Intervention Plan and Re-entry Conference.** The student meets with the coach upon reentry to discuss the intervention plan. The coach logs updates after meeting with the student each week. The student is placed on the intervention team's calendar for review every 3 weeks.

Step 6: Mediation Conference. When both students have returned to school they participate in a mediation conference facilitated by the Discipline Dean.

Case Study #3

Level 3 Violation: Multiple indicators of crisis including possession of a weapon

The Situation: An administrator learns that a student has possession of five-inch knife. Student has been beaten up at the bus stop and brought a knife to school for self-protection. At first, the student refuses to hand over the knife and curses out the administrator. The student also has chronic absentee issues and is failing most courses. One parent is incarcerated and the other parent is experiencing multiple challenges that make it difficult to serve in a consistent parental role.

Step 1: Cool-Down Conference. The student is removed to the Intervention Center. Because the student is highly charged, his Student Support Coach is called and comes to the IC to meet with him for a cool-down conference. The support coach also helps the student complete the Intervention Reflection and Return Form.

Step 2: Investigation. Later in the same day in the Intervention Center, the student's Student Support Coach and the administrator facilitate the Due Process Investigation/Conference with the student and explain the suspension and hearing process.

Step 3: School Sanction/Consequence Assigned. The student stays in the Intervention Center for the remainder of the day. The administrator assigns a five-day suspension and submits a request for a district hearing.

Step 4: SIT Team Intervention Planning Meeting. While the student is suspended the administrator arranges to meet with the teachers who know the student in order to develop a comprehensive student success plan to be implemented after the five day suspension or long-term alternative placement.

Step 5: District Hearing. The administrator, the student's Student Support Coach, the student, and his parent are all present at the district hearing that renders a decision for a 10-day extended suspension at the alternative placement center. During the extended suspension, the student participates in an anti-violence treatment program co-developed and delivered by the city police department and the adolescent treatment center at the local hospital.

Step 6: Planning Re-Entry Process. The Student Support Coach visits the student at the alternative program and develops a plan with the student to transition back to the sending school and prepares for the Student Re-Entry Process. Before the student returns for a full day of school, the Student Support Coach, the student, parent, and principal meet at the sending school to discuss goals for transition and strategies to avoid circumstances that led to long-term exclusion from school.

Step 7: Return to School-The First Two Weeks. Student transition coach escorts student to all classes on the first day; checks in with student at the end of day to reflect on the first day and set goals for the week; ensures that student participates in any other re-entry/orientation activities that the school provides; progress monitoring that involves weekly feedback from teachers about student's transition; engages in AM check-in and PM check-out every day during first two weeks; and contacts parent or adult ally at least once during each of the first two weeks to discuss students' transition back to school.

Student's teachers complete daily check-in/check-out report daily for the first two weeks.

Step 7: Remainder of the Semester. Student transition coach continues to check-in weekly with student for the remainder of the semester and ensures that student participates in any other support services and youth development opportunities that will support success at school.

Case Management Structure

The previous case studies provide an illustration of the importance of establishing a coherent case management system. We are defining case management as a structure that establishes the systematic process for the delivery of Tier 2 and Tier 3 interventions. This case management structure serves as the container for organizing the work of The Student Support Team. This includes identifying students in need of additional services and interventions; gathering the right data to determine the right intervention or combination of interventions for students; assigning a Student Support Team member to deliver specific interventions or serve as a student's coach; monitoring and tracking a student's progress throughout an intervention plan; and making adjustments to a student's intervention plan as needed. A goal of the case management structure is to "close the communication loop" between administrators, student support staff, teachers, students, and parents throughout the intervention process. The two most typical case management structures are organized at either the schoolwide level or by grade level.

A schoolwide case management structure, shown in Figure 11.5, is driven by the School Intervention Team and the administrators who are assigned to work with the School Intervention Team. This team serves all students in the school.

Figure 11.5

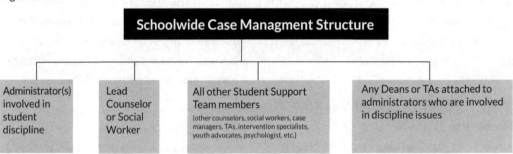

A grade level case management structure, shown in Figure 11.6, is driven by a team of administrators and student support staff who are assigned to work with all students at a specific grade level. Thus, a high school with this structure would have four grade level office teams that each operate like a School Intervention Team, but for one grade only.

Figure 11.6

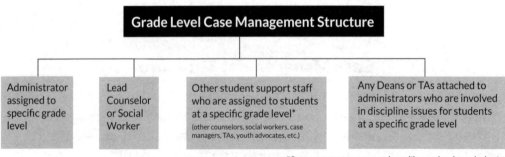

*Some support team members, like a school psychologist, would consult with each grade level office team.

Personalized Program Options for Students With the Most Challenging Profiles

Districts and schools that sincerely aim to support all of their students to stay in school and graduate must confront two sober realities that are seldom discussed honestly and openly. First, public schools include a very small population of students at any given time who simply cannot function at a reasonable level seven periods a day, five days a week in the regularly scheduled educational program. The second reality emerges from the first. Few schools have the necessary resources and capacity to meet the educational, social, and emotional needs of students with severe mental health issues. For decades, the default solutions for students who have the most difficulty functioning within traditional school programs have been expulsion, long-term suspension, and alternative placement or transfer. When these options are eliminated or used on a more judicious and limited basis, schools must anticipate the need to build a more intensive layer of Tier 3 interventions and in-school alternative program options.

Even when interventions are available to address the social, developmental, and cognitive gaps of the students with the highest needs, students may need a modified educational program for some period of time during the school year. Schools need to have the flexibility to personalize schedules and create additional educational options for students:

- Who present pervasive explosive, aggressive, and/or dangerous behaviors that have become a serious safety concern for students and teachers;
- Who have demonstrated absolutely no improvement over an extended period of time after assignment of a coach, home visits, conferences with administrators, and other interventions;
- For whom a seven period day of traveling from one place to another results in too many public space incidents and constant situations where the student is leaving the classroom without permission, and/or;
- Who are returning from extended placement in other settings and need an adjusted schedule in order to make a smooth transition back to a regular school day schedule.

The other rationale for establishing more personalized program options is linked to the regular faculty's capacity to work with seriously troubled young people in ways that are consistently caring, supportive, and effective, day in and day out. Sometimes, student-teacher relationships in regular classes are so damaged that moving forward with the same group of adults will only result in more of the same dysfunction with no genuine improvements, academically or behaviorally. The one thing we absolutely know about conditions that help students who turn themselves around is the constant presence of at least one adult whom they trust, who communicates their respect for them, and who is relentlessly and optimistically on their side and on their case. Establishing fully staffed therapeutic educational programs within most schools is not a likely possibility. However, we have worked with schools that strategically reconfigure staff responsibilities and schedules to accommodate alternative programs within the schools. And, schools can usually identify a few staff people who utilize a more therapeutic pedagogy and will honestly tell you, "These are the kids I love to work with. Give them to me."

The bottom line here is every adult who works with the students who demonstrate the most challenging behaviors needs to be highly skilled and exceptionally patient and compassionate. The teachers who are most effective in alternative settings are likely to utilize what Nicolas Hobbs, a pioneer in supporting troubled youth, calls strength-based principles in the classroom.[5] Although we cannot describe his groundbreaking work in detail, we want to note some of the important principles that help create strength-based learning environments.

1. Every day matters. Every day is a new day. The past is behind us.

2. Trust—in the form of predictable support, understanding, and affection—is the glue that holds teaching and learning together.

3. Competence makes a difference—help students find some academic pursuit that they care about and can get good at.

4. Self-control can be taught and is a step-by-step process of un-learning old habits and mindsets and learning ones that support greater efficacy.

5. Ceremony and ritual give order, stability, and confidence to students whose lives are often in considerable disarray.

6. The peer group is very important and honest talk and sharing can bring out the best in young people.

7. Every student should know some joy in each day—to do well in an academic task, to receive a compliment about engaging in a hard-won behavior, or to express collective laughter in a funny moment—is to know a "sharp delight."[6]

We would like to share a few examples from schools that have taken on this challenge and used very creative scheduling and staffing configurations to implement in-school personalized program options that work.

IN-SCHOOL Personalized Program Options

TA Coaches Who Provide Full or Half Day Support for Three to Six Weeks

Some districts employ a small group of specially trained Teaching Assistants (TAs) who can move from school to school to support individual students in crisis for a period of three to six weeks. The TA works with the School Intervention Team to support implementation of a student's Level 3 comprehensive student success plan through side-by-side coaching in classes throughout the regular school day; daily conferencing, reflection, rehearsal, and feedback; class preparation and homework support; close contact with parent; informal check-ins with student and her/his teachers; and consultation with student's teachers to implement strategies to support students. Depending on the student and TA availability, this program option could work for half days or full days.

Combination Schedule of Independent Learning, Regularly Scheduled Classes, Check-in, and Group Circle

Full day attendance with AM or PM block of independent course work monitored by in-school-suspension supervisor or behavior intervention coordinator and attendance in regular classes during the other block of the school day. The student's coach closely monitors the student's performance in regular classes; consults with student's teachers; checks in with the student at the beginning and close of each day; and meets with the student at least one period a day to check-in on goals, trouble-shoot challenges, and prepare for full participation in regular classes that a student is attending. Ideally, daily check-in includes a group circle time with other students participating in a combination schedule that is facilitated by a Student Support Team member with the charge of helping students to learn and demonstrate more positive group skills and social and emotional competencies. The elimination of so many transitions during the school day eliminates opportunities to get in trouble in public space. The focus on experiencing success in a few, not all, regularly scheduled classes can feel like an attainable goal in which students will invest their motivation and effort.

Abbreviated School Day

For a designated period of time, student attends three to four classes in which the student is most likely to experience some success and begins the day later or leaves school early. The student meets with her/his Student Support Coach every day and is supported to make a gradual return to a regular full schedule over the course of one grading period. In some exceptional situations, providing abbreviated school days for a designated period of time can be most effective.

PM School

Some schools create "flex-time" teaching positions where a few teachers begin their day several hours later, and work with students in a self-contained blended learning program that might run from noon to 5:00 pm. These programs often enable students to take whole courses on-line, engage in credit-recovery, and participate in non-graded competency based small group classes for some required subjects.

Sheltered Learning Program within the School

Students attend school for a full day, but do so in a sheltered learning environment that has a permanent location in the school. This kind of program usually involves a full-time certified teacher who works with 12 to 15 students at a time for a least one grading period up to the remainder of the school year. Successful sheltered learning programs share these common characteristics:

- Most course work involves individually paced computer assisted learning with the teacher providing coaching and feedback. A competency-based curriculum helps to personalize learning for each student.

- At least one or two courses are taught through whole group instruction involving all students in the program. These courses become the laboratory for learning and demonstrating specific skill sets and mindsets that support more cooperative behaviors in the classroom.

- Goal-setting, goal-checking, reflection, and self- assessment are part of the weekly routine.

- Students need to meet a set of academic and behavioral benchmarks before returning to a full day schedule of regular classes.

- Other teachers who have taught the student in the past check-in with them periodically to discuss and validate their progress.

- The program has the flexibility for students to move from attending the program for a full day every day to attending the program for some of the day and attending regular classes for the other portion of the day.

- A Student Support Team member coaches individual students and also facilitates group conversations and social skills training.

- The room is attractive, inviting, and large enough to provide individual student work stations and an area for whole group instruction and small group learning tasks.

Given the new federal guidelines that recommend the development of a more articulated and comprehensive array of interventions, we have we tried to cover the basics in this chapter. We hope that it provides a clearer picture of student support structures, processes, and practices that every middle and high school should consider putting in place.

---

[1] Ballantine, R., & Gaines Pell, A. (2010). Intervention as an Inside Job. Educational Leadership, 68(2).

[2] Boyes-Watson, C., & Pranis, K. (2015) Circle Forward: Building a Restorative School Community. St. Paul, MN: Living Justice Press.

[3] DeBase, A., Gibbs, J., Potter, G., and Blount, M. (2012) Teaching Adolescents to Think and Act Responsibly: The EQUIP Approach. Champaign, IL: Research Press.

[4] Bandura, A. (1986). Social foundations of thought and action: A social cognitive approach. Social Foundations of Thought and Action: A social cognitive approach.

[5] Newman D., "Nicholas Hobbs and Schools of Joy", reclaiming children and youth www.reclaimingjournal.com

[6] Hobbs, N., (1982) The Troubling and Troubled Child, American Re-EDucation Association. https://reclaimingjournal.com/sites/default/files/journal-article-pdfs/21_1_Newman_2.pdf.

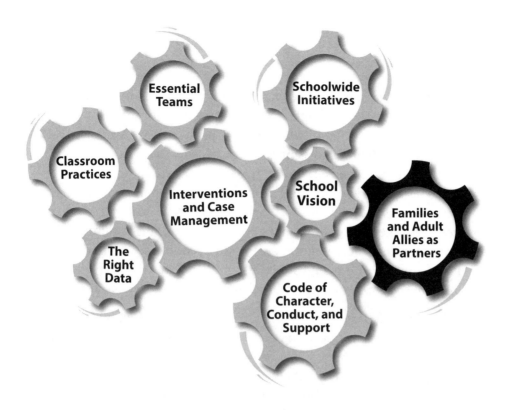

12

Families and Adult Allies as Partners

How can we increase meaningful engagement with adolescents' families and adult allies, when students are on track and when students are experiencing academic, behavioral, and mental health challenges?

CHAPTER OUTLINE

Introduction

Relevant Research About Family as Partners

Tier 1 Schoolwide Family Engagement Strategies

Tier 1 and Tier 2 Classroom-Based Family Engagement Strategies

Family Involvement in Tier 2 and Tier 3 School
Sanctions/Consequences and Interventions

Introduction

On the outset, we want to explain why we chose the chapter title "Families and Adult Allies as Partners" rather than "Family Engagement" or simply "Parents as Partners". The focus of this chapter centers on the relationship between the school, the student, and the adult who serves as primary care giver or advocate for each student. Although distressing to acknowledge, we must take into account that nearly half a million teens in the US live in foster care settings.[1] Of 30 million adolescents (ages 11 to 19) more than eight percent do not live with a parent and in some urban high schools this percentage can soar to almost one in six students.[2] The absence of parents, or circumstances in which a parent is temporarily unable to serve in a parenting role, should never negate a school's commitment to ensure that all students have a designated adult in their lives who fulfills at least some parental roles of support, guidance, and advocacy.

The words "family and parent" are used interchangeably throughout the chapter as broad descriptors that include biological, step, adoptive, and foster parents, grandparents, and other family members, and legal guardians who serve as primary care givers, as well as adult allies who choose to be a reliable and constant presence in a student's life by taking on a role as advocate/coach/mentor.

Almost everyone agrees that family engagement in their children's education leads to improved educational outcomes for students.[3] Yet, conventional wisdom about the benefits of parent involvement needs to be countered by a closer examination of the exact kind of engagement with middle and high school parents that is most likely to generate productive interactions and goodwill between parents and school staff, result in better academic outcomes for students, and maximize parental support and cooperation when students are struggling.

This chapter introduces compelling research that makes the case for developing a more limited, but more strategic and meaningful set of engagement strategies for families of adolescents. As with the rest of the book, we offer a tiered approach for thinking about family engagement, first describing Tier 1 schoolwide strategies that welcome parents as partners, boost parental understanding of their roles in supporting their children's learning, and generate goodwill and relational trust between home and school. Next, we make recommendations about Tier 1 and Tier 2 classroom-based strategies that increase teacher-to-parent communication and hold the greatest potential for improving students' school outcomes. The remainder of the chapter focuses on supporting family involvement in the delivery of Tier 2 and Tier 3 consequences and interventions that require direct school communication to parents, cooperation with parents, and support by parents when their children are experiencing academic, behavioral, or mental health challenges.

Relevant Research About Family as Partners

Shifts in Parental Engagement as Children Get Older

Here is a simple truth. Engaging middle and high school families in school-based activities is challenging. "A spiraling decline of parental support is evident in most high schools around the nation," with more than 70 percent of urban school leaders in one survey citing the near absence of active parental involvement as a major dilemma in their schools.[4] In general, parents' participation in teacher conferences, school sponsored meetings and events, and volunteer opportunities peaks at around fourth grade and dramatically declines when students enter middle school.[5] While 90 percent of parents participate in conferences with their children's teachers in K – 5 schools, this decreases significantly for middle school parents. Less than half of high school parents have any direct contact with teachers.[6] Several factors influence this decline in engagement.

First, and most obvious, parents are simply more "hands on" with younger children whose growth and development are nurtured by a constant exchange of information between parents, the school, and the child's teachers. In contrast, parents of adolescents (ages 11-19) tend to become more "hands off" as children get older, often assuming that teenagers' desire for autonomy becomes a barrier to parent-school connections rather than an expression of what kinds of parent involvement are "okay" and "not okay."[7]

Second, elementary school parents are more likely to actively support a wide range of school-sponsored activities including those that do not necessarily connect to their own children's academic, social and emotional well-being. Most parents of secondary students tend to be far less invested in the school institution and more interested in communication that directly connects to their own children's experience of school.[8]

Parents are quick to point out that when their children enter middle schools and are assigned to six or seven teachers, direct communication about their children becomes more complicated and less frequent. One factor that places obvious limits on direct teacher-parent contact is a secondary teacher's responsibility for 150 students, in contrast to the 30 students for whom a typical elementary teacher has primary responsibility. While elementary teachers expect to serve as the primary school contact with parents, teachers of older students do not generally view direct contact with parents as a primary responsibility. Moreover, the "hands-off" attitude toward parents among many secondary teachers is exacerbated by feelings of fear, anxiety, and inadequacy that they anticipate will accompany their encounters with parents.[9]

One other factor can make family engagement more challenging as children get older. For students who have already experienced years of struggle, a succession of unhelpful or adversarial interactions between parents and school staff may reinforce parental distrust and unease in school settings. This "bad history" can often be accompanied by parents' unpleasant memories of their own schooling.

The result can be an increasing degree of parent unease, and even ill-will when discipline issues arise, making it extremely difficult to secure parents' timely and responsive participation when their children are in trouble.

Parental Impact on Adolescents' School Outcomes and Future Aspirations

Now for the good news. Here is the counterintuitive research finding that surprises everyone. Parents of adolescents remain the most important influence on their children's academic achievement and their future aspirations regardless of race, socio-economic status, and family structure. Interestingly, peers have even less influence on fellow students than their teachers, whose impact on student outcomes ranks second.[10] What is more, the further in school that parents believed their adolescent children would go, the more clearly they communicated their expectations to their children, who, in turn, placed increased value on their parents' expectations that then informed their own expectations to succeed in school.[11]

Meta-researchers John Hattie and Robert Marzano have lifted up another even more counterintuitive finding. Parents have a far greater impact on the variance in achievement from one student to another than all school factors combined.[12] They also agree on the conditions that turn parental influence into an engine that drives increased academic achievement and greater desire for and attainment of a postsecondary education. When parents (1) place a high value on education in general and their children's education in particular; (2) hold high expectations for their children to achieve academically throughout K–12 schooling; and (3) believe their children will attain a postsecondary education, adolescents' academic, attendance, and behavior outcomes all improve. Hattie also reminds us that, *"Meaningful conversations between a school staff member and parent hold the promise of raising parental expectations, strengthening parent beliefs in the value of schooling, and building parents' knowledge of the language of schooling and college and career planning and preparation that support high aspirations."*[13]

What Families Want from their Children's Schools

In 2011, the National School Public Relations Association conducted an extensive survey of parents from 50 urban, suburban, and rural districts to explore the kind of communication parents wanted with their children's schools. The four highest priorities, identified by both elementary and secondary parents, were communication with teachers about their children's progress and how they might improve; timely notification when their child's performance was slipping; information about what their child was expected to learn in their course work; and teachers' grading and homework policies.

Parents in the study also cited their preferences for receiving essential school information: school websites, parent portals, direct email and text message communication from the school or staff members, and automated telephone/voice messaging systems. Text messaging has clearly surfaced as a transformational tool for communicating with parents. During our trainings with hundreds of new principals, they always share how much families love text messaging when administrators and teachers send back timely responses to their questions or provide on-going feedback when their children's academic or behavior progress is being closely monitored.

A new study from Harvard and Brown Universities has also identified the big benefits of prompt, brief, and frequent communication between teachers and parents.[14] Of the 435 underperforming high school students involved in the study, the group of students whose parents received brief, but weekly, text messages or phone calls about actionable steps students could take to improve their grades were 41 percent less likely to fail the course than the control group whose parents received no weekly messages. Researchers speculate that the consistent and predictable communication from teachers served as a catalyst for parents to engage in more frequent and more specific conversations with their children about their progress in the course and their efforts to improve their grades. This study provides convincing evidence that the right kind of parent engagement can make a huge difference in student performance.

Research Implications for Engaging Families in the Middle and High School Years

In summary, research about parent involvement in secondary public schools reveals that administrators and teachers underestimate parental influence, undervalue building relationships with parents, and thus underutilize parents as partners.[15]

We have entered a new era in the field of family engagement in which some researchers and practitioners are urging schools to rethink more conventional approaches to family involvement. Joyce Epsteins's *The Six Types of Partnerships*, accepted as an exemplary family engagement framework, includes six areas of engagement: (1) Parenting to support children's learning; (2) Communications from school to home and home to school; (3) Volunteering at school; (4) Helping students learn at home; (5) Participation in school decision making; and (6) Collaborations with the larger neighborhood/community. However, only the first two, parenting and school communication, appear to generate strong interest from secondary parents and, at the same time, produce improved academic outcomes for students. The other four partnership types simply do not have the same robust returns for secondary school staff, parents, and adolescents themselves.[16] Expending lots of time, effort, and coordination on school-sponsored activities that generate tiny parent turnouts or produce small if any direct benefits to students are just not good investments.

In part, this reassessment of family engagement emerges from reliable findings that low parent participation in school activities is by no means a reflection of parents' lack of interest in their child's education or their desire to be informed about their child's progress in school.[17] For many parents, supporting their children's school success involves more invisible kinds of parental support that center more on family efforts to ensure that their children are attending a good school, limiting children's chores and activities to allow for study time, and communicating the value of education and hard work.[18]

Given the multitude of urgent needs in secondary schools, family engagement often becomes a lower priority. As a result there are limited personnel hours earmarked for parent engagement. Therefore, schools cannot afford to squander time and energy on activities that produce minimal impact. So, how do middle and high school educators invest in family engagement wisely? In Figure 12.1 we are offering schools a 20/50/30 rule for developing meaningful multi-tiered parent engagement strategies.

Figure 12.1

Multi-tiered Parent Engagement Strategies

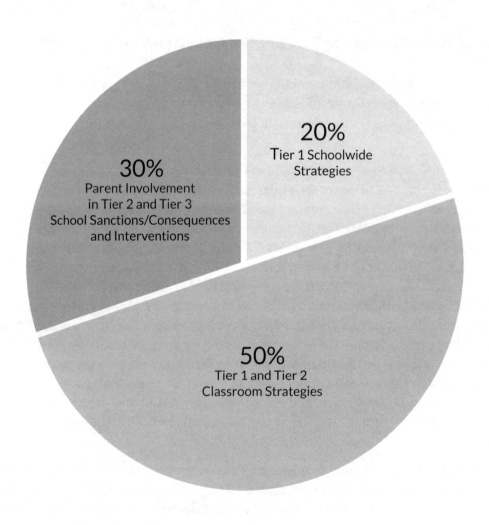

> ### 20/50/30 Parent Engagement
>
> **Tier 1 Schoolwide Strategies:** Use 20 percent of time and resources for crafting important school-home documents, contacting hard to reach parents, and organizing a limited number of schoolwide parent meetings, events, and workshops that welcome parents as partners, boost parental understanding of their roles in supporting their child's learning, and generate good will and relational trust between home and school.
>
> **Tier 1 and Tier 2 Classroom Strategies:** Use 50 percent of time and resources to dramatically increase the kinds of teacher to parent communication that holds the greatest promise for improving students' school outcomes. Schools need to provide the requisite professional learning that will build teacher competence, confidence, and resolve to make parent engagement a meaningful professional responsibility.
>
> **Parent Involvement in Tier 2 and Tier 3 School Sanctions/Consequences and Interventions:** Use 30 percent of time and resources to support parent involvement in the delivery of Tier 2 and Tier 3 consequences and interventions that require direct school communication to parents, cooperation with parents, and support by parents when their children are experiencing academic, behavioral, or mental health challenges.

The 20/50/30 rule means that four out of every five hours devoted to family engagement center on personalized communication between parents and school staff. Our rationale for this distribution of time and effort is informed by three things. First, direct school-home communication is what parents want and need.[19] Second, among the whole range of family engagement activities, meaningful staff to parent interactions provide the highest leverage for improving student outcomes. Finally, making personalized communication the school's number one parent priority, not only builds relational trust and mutual respect; it reinforces the value of parents as partners, and most importantly, lets parents know that there are adults at school who hold a deep personal interest in their child's success.

Tier 1 Schoolwide Family Engagement Strategies

Front load opportunities to connect with families in multiple ways before school opens and during the first month of school.

At the school level, critical information about the school schedule and program, school specific expectations, rules, and policies, and a "go to" directory of school personnel should be mailed home and be available on the school's website. Every attempt should be made to offer multiple dates and times for new student and parent orientation, new student registration, informal welcome and information sessions in which families can meet with school administrators and staff, and scheduled open houses in which parents can follow an abbreviated version of their children's schedule and meet with their children's teachers and grade level administrators and support staff.

All communication, whether written, digital, or in person, should emphasize the role of parental influence on students' school performance and future aspirations. Effective communication affirms the value that the school places on families as partners, and explains the forms of communication families can expect from administrators, teachers, and student support staff. Schools create and disseminate a calendar of important family and student activities that they want them you to attend or to know about and support.

It is important to take advantage of the beginning of the school year when families are eager to receive the right information in order to get their children off to good start. At the district level, dissemination to parents of the district-wide code of character, conduct and support, and other documents that describe parent and student rights and responsibilities, due process protocols related to suspension and district hearings, and "go to" directories of key offices and personnel are absolutely essential. At the beginning of the school year, districts that are parent friendly offer multiple informational sessions across district neighborhoods where parents can receive an overview of code policies, gain a deeper understanding of family advocates and other family-specific personnel, and have their questions answered. If at all possible key documents should be translated into languages other than English that are most frequently spoken by families in the district.

By the end of September, ensure that every student has a designated parent or adult ally who serves as the primary contact for each student and fulfills at least some parental roles of support, guidance, and advocacy.

We cannot and must not give up on identifying that one adult who serves as the primary contact for a student. If, after a couple of weeks, you are unable to reach a parent and/or do not have a reliable phone number, the school staff needs to step up its efforts and make home visits or call parents at their work place to determine who will be the primary contact for each student. Some schools set aside a home visit week, offering staff volunteers a dinner before going out on visits or offering stipends for the home visit push. An orientation and suggestions for scripted conversations should be provided for all volunteers, and home visits should always be done in pairs. If for some students, the school still has no viable parent contact after these efforts, support staff need to check-in with students to discuss whom they would want to serve as their adult ally/advocate.

Provide parent access to a contact number or email address for every staff member.

Ensure that parents can reach every staff member through an email address and a phone number/extension with voice mail during the school day.

Limit schoolwide family meetings, events, or workshops to four topics that maximize parent attendance.

Beyond "first month of school" family activities, a number one priority, limit school-sponsored family events to three other topics: students' academic program in which parents can learn about and discuss what students are learning and how they are doing; and career planning that help parents navigate through and support their children's college and career planning process; and celebrations of students' milestones and accomplishments, which might include end-of year recognitions, step-up nights from one grade to the next, or a half-cap ceremony when students have completed enough credits to become juniors.

Ensure that every school-sponsored family meeting, event, or workshop includes the opportunity for parents to speak with their children's teachers, advisors, or counselors.

If an event is important enough to push parents and families to attend, then it is critical to ensure that staff members are available to welcome and talk with parents.

Schedule well-organized school-sponsored family meetings, events, or workshops and make an effort to ramp up outreach and "perks" that will maximize parent attendance.

Just doing a few things can increase parent attendance exponentially: Provide a meal. Provide child care, perhaps involving the media specialist and older students in developmentally appropriate read-alouds and movie nights. Post flyers in neighborhood locations that parents and families frequent. Use automated phone systems and email for reminders. Ask students to write personal invitations on post cards to be mailed. Encourage staff volunteers and parent liaisons to make personal phone calls to parents. Provide transportation to and from school in key locations where families live.

Develop district-wide, rather than building-based parent education opportunities.

Get a bigger return on your investment in parent trainers and parent outreach coordinators by organizing district-wide "parent university" sessions (singles and series) that offer general parent education topics as well as topics of particular interest to parents of adolescents.

Develop a plan that shapes a family-friendly school environment and meaningful parent-school interactions.

Considering all of the recommendations above, develop an annual family engagement plan for your school. One of the best tools to assess the degree to which a school fully embraces parents as partners is the Family Friendly Partnership School Walk-Through from the Georgia Department of Education.[20]

Tier 1 and Tier 2 Classroom-Based
Family Engagement Strategies

Identify required and strongly recommended teacher-parent communication strategies that all teachers universally implement and document.

This strategy is first because it is the most important thing schools can do to increase meaningful parent engagement. In addition to providing professional learning modules for teachers (see #2 in this section), three other suggestions can help schools make saturated teacher-parent communication a consistent schoolwide practice.

- Allow teachers to choose how they want to contact parents: by phone, by email, text messages, through a face to face conference, or by pre-stamped post cards provided by the school.

- Give teachers the option of keeping a record of their contacts with parents electronically or in a student-parent logbook (one for each class) in which a few pages are set aside for each student in the class to record anecdotal notes about the students, conferences and follow-up goals, plans, and monitoring with students, and all individual parent communication.

- Reach an agreement with the school leadership team and union reps around the expectation that all teachers set aside one hour a week for student conferencing and parent communication. If you do this, the numbers will tell an inspiring story. In a school with 75 faculty, over a period of 40 weeks this one schoolwide practice would translate into 3,000 hours of personalized communication with students and their parents. Figure 12.2 illustrates specific Tier 1 and Tier 2 teacher to parent communication tasks.

Figure 12.2

Teacher to Parent Communication Tasks

Teachers should be prepared to engage in the following tasks:

Tier 1 Teacher-Parent Communication

Welcome and Course Introduction for Parents through a video, on-line parent portal on school website, or print letter communicate your classroom vision, academic and behavior expectations, and overview of the course.

Sunshine Calls, Notes, or Postcards can be a powerful connector between the teacher, the parent, and the student. The goal here is to share with a parent something their child has done well and/or something you appreciate about their child. If it is impossible to get around to making a call to every parent, try to make sure you call the parents of students who do not get the spotlight, students who have made a turn-around, students who you are 95 percent sure have never received a positive call home ever!

Tell Me More Calls are targeted to parents of students about whom you do not have a clue. Parents are thrilled when you say, "I would like to know ____ a little better. What should I know about _____ that will help me support your child to be successful in this class?"

Quarterly Newsletters keep families informed about what students have accomplished, what students will be learning during the next quarter, and what major projects and assessments are coming up.

Parent Sign-offs for specific assignments, projects, and tests are one way to ensure that parents get a sense of the topics that students are learning about as well as the quality of work that students are completing.

End of Grading Period Student Reflections in which students assess their progress, describe what they learned, identify their best efforts, and note their goals for improvement. These are sent home to parents with a "return" form on which parents write their comments.

Student-Parent Interactive Assignments in which students interview parents or other family members about a specific topic or issue.

Mid-Term Parent Check-ins is a way to offer a scheduled time after school when parents can meet with teachers to discuss the academic progress of their children.

Tier 2 Teacher-Parent Communication

Addressing Student Concerns with Parents is never easy, and yet, the vast majority of parents want to be contacted immediately when a concern arises. Strategies that can help make parent calls and conferences more productive include engaging in a problem solving and planning conference with the student beforehand, so that you can share what the student intends to do to rectify the situation or rehearsing and asking the student to call a parent in your presence to explain what the student did that prompts a call home and what the student will do to make it right. For more information, please see Appendix R.

Calls and Conferences to Address Student Concerns with Parents

Failure and Academic "Slippage" Phone Calls and Conferences should be part of a schoolwide protocol that is activated when students are failing a course at mid-term or term. These calls should occur after the teacher and student have had an academic problem solving and planning conference so that the parent can be informed about what the student will do to improve her grade and how her progress will be monitored.

Progress Monitoring Texts, Calls, or Emails related to a student's academic or behavior plan involve brief weekly check-ins with a parent when a student has failed a course or has slipped downward academically. (Please see "Problem Solving and Planning Conference" in Appendix G.)

Calls and Conferences at the Request of a Parent need to be initiated within 24 hours after a parent has requested to speak with a teacher about a child's grade, a class concern, or a particular incident. Be prepared to take notes so that you can focus on identifying the concern clearly and find out how you might help to resolve the situation. (Please see the protocol for "Calls and Conferences at the Request of a Parent" in Appendix S.)

Grade Level Team Parent Conferences usually involve the parent, the student, and several of the student's teachers in a problem solving and planning conference when the student is exhibiting similar behaviors or academic difficulties across classes. The aim is for the student to work on one or two things across classes and for all of the students' teachers to provide prompts, support, and monitoring.

Provide annual professional learning modules and new teacher induction on family engagement.

In her research focused on principals' approach to parent engagement, Margaret Farrar uncovered a glaring missed opportunity: 80 percent of the principals in her study did not provide specific expectations, protocols and professional learning for staff regarding family involvement.[21] Given that professional learning time is very limited in most schools, we suggest beginning with a series of four, 90-minute workshops that address the following topics:

- Understanding relevant family engagement research; acknowledging and discussing staff concerns about direct engagement with parents; presenting a rationale for a 20/50/30 approach to school engagement with parents; and presenting specific expectations for teacher engagement with parents.
- Engaging in culturally responsive communication with families; and strengthening specific communication skill sets (responsive listening, defusing upset and anger, explaining student problems clearly, finding common hopes and values, asking the right questions, collaborative problem solving).
- Practice, role play, and rehearsal of communication scripts.
- Documenting parent contacts, attendance at schoolwide family activities, and participation in grade level, SIT, and administrator convened parent conferences.

Identify someone on the staff who is the resident expert on effective and supportive teacher-parent communication and provide them with a stipend for consulting with staff.

Having access to a supportive colleague who can trouble-shoot and help brainstorm "What do I say when_____?" is a reassuring resource for staff who are on the more reluctant side of the parent engagement continuum.

Schedule student facilitated progress report conferences at least once a year.

Parent report card pick-up increases exponentially when students are facilitating their own progress report conferences. (For specific suggestions and protocols related to student-facilitated grade report conferences, please refer to Engaging Schools' *The Advisory Guide*). This is a fairly manageable proposition when teachers in 6th, 7th, 8th, and 9th grade work in teams. Each teacher on the team serves as the teacher-coach for 25 to 30 students on the team. For 10th, 11th, and 12th graders, the most expedient solution is for students to identify one of their teachers to serve as their teacher-coach for the conference and then schedule a 15-minute conference slot with that teacher.

Create a guide to family engagement for school staff developed by the school leadership team, teacher-leaders, and union representatives.

A guide might include your goals and rationale for the following:

- family engagement
- types of family engagement that have the greatest impact on student outcomes
- the school's role in welcoming parents
- parent rights and responsibilities
- expectations for teacher-parent communication
- expectations for parent communication in disciplinary and intervention processes,
- specific strategies and scripts to increase and improve communication with parents
- a calendar of events and activities that invites families' participation and/or support

Family Involvement in Tier 2 and Tier 3 School Sanctions/Consequences and Interventions

Although the principles of family-driven care, meaning that families have a primary decision-making role in the care of their own children, should be present in all school-home interactions, these principles are particularly important when students are experiencing academic, behavioral, and mental health challenges that require Tier 2 and Tier 3 interventions. Parents should be involved in the discussions and decisions about specific supports, services, and providers; goals for specific interventions; information about how interventions will be delivered; the process and timeline for monitoring student progress; and assessment of the effectiveness of specific supports and interventions.

Provide training and support for administrators to effectively manage disciplinary incidents that require them to facilitate student-teacher-parent conferences, due process investigations to determine the assigned school sanction/consequence, and follow-up -parent conferences.

Principals and district leaders tell us that the most contentious school-parent conflicts arise when parents feel that their children have been treated unfairly or disrespectfully by teachers and administrators. Effective administrators communicate a climate of respect and support immediately by using a transparent process to listen responsively, ask questions, share information, and move beyond consequences to restorative solutions, ensuring that the parent (or child and parent) leave with their dignity intact and fresh hope that things can get better. One strategy that will help defuse upset parents is by immediately providing a family friendly "one pager" that reassures parents of their rights and responsibilities, explains due process protocols clearly, and describes what administrators and teachers will do when parents have a concern or complaint.

Ideally, ensure that every student and their parent /adult ally has a designated staff person who serves as a primary communication point person at school.

This is the "go-to" teacher, advisor, counselor, Student Support Coach, or administrator who holds a holistic knowledge of the students' academic progress, behavior, health, and well-being. At a minimum, try to ensure that students with the highest needs who are receiving Tier 2 and Tier 3 interventions have one adult at school who serves as their conduit between the student and her parent/adult ally and other school staff.

Ensure that long-term interventions always involve at least three conferences with a parent: one on the front-end before the intervention is delivered, another at mid-point to assess student progress, and one at the end of the intervention to support ongoing efforts.

Parental motivation to actively support a school's effort to help improve a student's academic or behavioral outcomes is linked to parents' own sense of self-efficacy, that is "the extent to which parents believe that through their involvement they can exert positive influence on their children's educational outcomes."[22] Consequently, it becomes critical for student support staff to reach out to parents to discuss the goals of the intervention and the things a parent can do to support those goals.

We hope this chapter has provided new information and strategies that reaffirm both the value of engaging families and adult allies as partners and your commitment to rally the entire school staff to have a dialogue and take actions around this effort. Parenting adolescents is never easy, and our parents come with their hopes and their hesitations about partnering with school staff members. Parents need to know that they are perceived as honored partners whose role in supporting their children's education and aspirations is irreplaceable. Successful family engagement will often depend on a school's commitment to:

- Consider cultural perspectives of their families and the community.
- Understand perceptions about power and authority that may influence the dynamics between families and school staff.
- Facilitate access to home language communication whenever possible.
- Ensure that the first staff members that a family member is likely to meet in a school building are ready to welcome them to the school and offer immediate assistance.

Listening to parents with deep regard and open hearts is the cornerstone of family engagement. When we extend the respect and compassion we have for our students to their families and adult allies, we strengthen the circle of care and support to ensure that every child fulfills their promise.

---

[1] Child Welfare Information Gateway. (2015). Foster Care Statistics 2013. Washington, DC. US Department of Health and Human Services, Children's Bureau.

[2] Pew Charitable Trust, FactTank, Dec. 22, 2014. http://www.pewresearch.org/fact-tank/2014/12/22/less-than-half-of-u-s-kids-today-live-in-a-traditional-family/

[3] A New Wave of Evidence: The Impact of School, Family and Community Connections on Student Achievement. (2002) SEDL, Austin, TX.

[4] Ziegler, W. (2000, January). Venturing beyond the schoolyard to bring parents in. The High School Magazine, 7 (5), 22-25.

[5] Child Trends Data Bank: Parental Involvement in Schools, 2013.

[6] "Collaborating for Success" - Parent Engagement Toolkit [Updated 3/25/15] Michigan Department of Education.

[7] Patrikakou, E. (2014 September) Adolescence: Are Parents Relevant to Students' High School Achievement and Post-Secondary Attainment? Family Involvement Research Digests, Harvard Family Research Project.

[8] Gonzalez-DeHass, A. R., & Willems, P. P. (2003). Examining the underutilization of parent involvement in the schools. School Community Journal, 13 (1), 85-99.

[9] Dornbusch, S. M., & Ritter, P. L. (1988). Parents of high school students: A neglected resource. *Educational Horizons, 66*, 75-77.

[10] Patrikakou, E. (2014 September) Adolescence: Are Parents Relevant to Students' High School Achievement and Post-Secondary Attainment? Family Involvement Research Digests, Harvard Family Research Project.

[11] Hoover-Dempsey, K. V. & Sandler, H. M (2005) Final performance report for OERI Grant # R305T010673: The social context of parental involvement: A path to enhanced achievement. IES, US Dept. of Education.

[12] Marzano, R. J., (2000) *A new era of school reform: Going where the research takes us.* Aurora, CO: Mid-continent Research in Education and Learning; and Hattie, J. (2009) Visible Learning: a synthesis of meta-analyses relating to achievement. New York: Routledge.

[13] ibid

[14] Kraft MA, Rogers T. The underutilized potential of teacher-to-parent communication: Evidence from a field experiment. Economics of Education Review [Internet]. 2015;47: 49-63.

[15] Gonzalez-DeHass, A. R., & Willems, P. P. (2003). Examining the underutilization of parent involvement in the schools. School Community Journal, 13 (1), 85-99.

[16] Harris, A., and Robinson, K. (2014) The Broken Compass: Parental Involvement With Children's Education. Cambridge, MA: Harvard University Press.

[17] Watson, Samders-Lawson, and Mc Neal, Understanding Parental Involvement in American Public Education. International Journal of Humanities and Social Science, Vol. 2, No 19, 2012.

[18] Smith, J, & Wohlsetter, P. (2009) Parent involvement in urban charter schools: A new paradigm or the status quo.

[19] A New Wave of Evidence: The Impact of School, Family and Community Connections on Student Achievement, (2002) , Austin, TX: SEDL.

[20] https://www.gadoe.org/School-Improvement/Federal-Programs/Pages/Georgia-Family-Friendly.aspx

[21] Ferrara, M. M. (2009). Broadening the Myopic Vision of Parent Involvement. *School Community Journal, 19*(2), 123-142.

[22] Watson, Samders-Lawson, and Mc Neal, Understanding Parental Involvement in American Public Education. International Journal of Humanities and Social Science, Vol. 2, No 19, 2012

Letter to the reader

Dear Reader,

We want to acknowledge the courage that school leaders and teams bring to the table when they choose to recalibrate their discipline and student support model. That courage is revealed through a willingness to engage senior administrators, faculty, and student support staff in a complex and sustained thinking and problem solving process in order to address what is ineffective and to implement a different approach. Recalibration calls for a rigorous assessment of current systems and the use of a consensus process for developing changes in policies, structures, and practices that closely align to the school's goals for discipline and student support.

Changing your school's model of discipline and student support is what we call a second order change. Second order change calls into question the existing values, philosophy, and practices of an organization. It moves beyond simply adopting a new program and/or implementing a new set of strategies or structures within the larger context of a school reform initiative. Second order change calls for a paradigm shift in which all adults in the school have the opportunity to re-examine their beliefs and assumptions about learning, the nature of human beings, and the kinds of environments and practices that maximize growth for teachers and students.

Guiding a staff and school community through major discipline and student support initiatives requires a clear vision for the work, well-defined goals informed by data, patience and humility on behalf of leadership, a strong collaborative culture, and a commitment to strong individual development. Achieving successful results also requires a reasonable timeline for implementation to ensure attention to the details and to provide saturated professional learning opportunities, which help staff to understand the changes and their impact on their own responsibilities, learn new practices, and strengthen skill sets.

We have partnered with districts and schools that have created conditions that inspire openness and curiosity about the change process and sustain a collective energy to stay with the process until discrete changes are in place. These schools and districts welcome staff members, students, and families into the conversation. Their voices and viewpoints are critical to the momentum, movement, and success of the initiative. Thoughtful teams anticipate the obstacles that might get in the way of change and unpack the dynamics of fear and uncertainty that often accompany major shifts. They are also savvy enough to acknowledge that differences of opinion will remain, even as they galvanize support to move forward.

Most importantly, these schools and districts do not over promise quick and miraculous results. Instead, they invite all stakeholders to view the launch of new policies and practices through a learning lens — documenting small successes and visible positive differences, establishing an inquiry cycle to collect data and assess progress toward achieving intended outcomes, and capturing staff, student, and family perceptions of changes through a continual feedback loop.

District and school leaders who take on recalibrating their model of discipline and student support often do so with a sense of urgency to transform good schools for some into great schools for all. This transformation depends on a school's stance on equity, its commitment to an accountable and restorative approach to discipline, and its capacity to provide the guidance, supports, and opportunities that foster each student's personal development, their academic success, and their hope and confidence in a healthy and productive future. We see you, the reader, as a person who holds a deep regard and respect for the young people in your care and hope that you will become a champion for this important work.

On behalf of all young people, we cannot thank you enough.

The Authors

Appendix A

Recommended Resources for Further Reading

Behaviorist Theory and Practice

Alberto, P. A., & Troutman, A. C. (2003). *Applied behavior analysis for teachers* (6th ed.). Upper Saddle River, NJ: Merrill Prentice Hall.

Kohn, A. (1999). *Punished by rewards: The trouble with gold stars, incentive plans, A's praise, and other bribes* (2nd ed.). Mariner Books.

Mills, J. A. (1998). *Control: A history of behavioral psychology.* New York: NYU Press.

O'Neil, W. N. (1995). American Behaviorism: A Historical and Critical Analysis. *Theory & Psychology, 5,* 285-305.

Skinner, B. F. (1974). *About behaviorism.* Toronto: Alfred A. Knopf, Inc.

Todd, J., & Morris, E. K. (1995) *Modern perspectives on B. F. Skinner and contemporary behaviorism.* Santa Barbara, CA: Praeger Press.

Social-Cognitive Theory and Practice

Bandura, A. (1997). *Self-efficacy: The exercise of control.* New York: Freeman.

Bandura, A. (2001). Social cognitive theory: An agentive perspective. *Annual Review of Psychology, 52,* 1-26.

Pajares, F., & Schunk, D. H. (2001). Self-beliefs and school success: Self-efficacy, self-concept, and school achievement. In R. Riding & S. Rayner (Eds.), *Self-perception* (pp. 239-266). London: Ablex Publishing.

Mental Health Levels of Prevention and Support

Adelman, H., Taylor, L. (2005). *The implementation guide to student learning supports in the classroom and schoolwide: new directions for addressing barriers to learning.* Thousand Oaks, CA: Corwin Press.

Mrazek, P. B., & Haggerty, R. (Eds.). (1994). *Reducing risks for mental disorders: Frontiers for preventive intervention.* Washington, D.C.: National Academy Press.

Osher, D., Dwyer, K., & Jackson, S. (2004). *Safe, supportive, and successful schools: step by step.* Longmont, CO: Sopris West.

Sugai, G., & Horner, R. (2006). A promising approach for expanding and sustaining school-wide positive behavior support. *School Psychology Review*, 35(2), 245—259.

Sugai, G. (2003). Establishing efficient and durable systems of school-based support. *School Psychology Review,* 32(4).

Social Support Theory and the Ethics of Care

Cobb, S. (1976). Social support as a moderator of life stress. *Psychosomatic Medicine, 38(5)*.

Held, V. (2005). *The ethics of care.* Oxford: Oxford University Press.

Lee, V. E., Smith, J. B., Perry, T. E., & Smylie, M. A. (1999). Social support, academic press, and student achievement: A view from the middle grades in Chicago. University of Chicago Consortium on Chicago School Research.

Marks, H. M., Secada, W., & Doane, K. (1996). Social support for achievement: Building intellectual culture in restructuring schools. Washington, D.C.: US Department of Education, Office of Educational Research and Improvement, Educational Resources Information Center.

Nestmann, F., & Hurrelmann, K. (Eds.). (1994). *Social networks and social support in childhood and adolescence.* New York, NY: DeGruyter Press.

Noddings, N. (1984). *Caring: A feminine approach to ethics & moral education.* Berkeley, CA: University of California Press.

Risk and Protection Theory, Psycho-Educational Prevention, and SEL (Social and Emotional Learning)

Durlak, J., Domitrovich, C., Weissberg, R. P., Guilotta, T., & Shriver, T. P. (Eds.). (2015). *Handbook of social and emotional learning: Research and practice* (1st ed.). New York, NY: Guilford Press.

Flay, B. R., & Allred, C. G. (2010). The positive action program: Improving academics, behavior and character by teaching comprehensive skills for successful learning and living. In T. Lovat & R.Toomey (Eds.), *International Handbook on Values Education and Student Wellbeing,* (pp. 471-501). Netherlands: Springer.

Hawkins, D., & Catalano, R. F. (1992). *Communities That Care: Action for Drug Abuse Prevention.* Jossey-Bass

Hawkins, D., Pollard, J., & Arthur, M. (1999). Risk and protection: Are both necessary to understand diverse behavioral outcomes in adolescence? *Social Work Research, 23(3),* 145-158.

Spence, S. H. (2003). Social skills training with children and young people: Theory, evidence and practice. *Child and Adolescent Mental Health, 8(2),* 84–96.

Supportive relationships and active skill-building strengthen the foundations of resilience: Working paper 13. (2015). Harvard University: Center on the Developing Child.

Zins, J., & Weissberg, R. P. (Eds.). (2004). *Building academic success on social and emotional learning: What does the research say?* New York, NY: Teachers College Press.

Choice Theory, Client Centered Communication, Self-Determination Theory

Deci, E., & Deci, R. R. (Eds.). (2013). *The handbook of self-determination research* (1st ed.). Rochester, NY: University of Rochester Press.

Gagne, M. (Ed.). (2014). *The Oxford handbook of work engagement, motivation, and self-determination theory* (Oxford Library of Psychology). Oxford: Oxford University Press.

Glasser, W. (2010). *Choice theory: A new psychology of personal freedom.* New York, NY: Harper-Collins.

Glasser, W. (2010). Choice theory in the classroom. New York, NY: Harper-Collins.

Rogers, C., Lyone, H. C., & Tausch, R. (2013). *On becoming an effective teacher: Person-centered teaching, psychology, philosophy, and dialogues with Carl R. Rogers and Harold Lyon.* London: Routledge Press.

Rogers, C. (1986). *Freedom to Learn: A View of What Education Might Become.* Indianapolis, IN: Merrill Publishing

Restorative Justice

Barton, C. K. B. (2003) *Restorative justice: The empowerment model.* Bellflower, CA: Hawkins Press.

Barton, C. (2000). Theories of restorative justice. *Australian Journal of Professional and Applied Ethics, 2(1),* 41-3.

Braithwaite, J. (2002). *Restorative justice & responsive regulation* (Studies in Crime and Public Policy). Oxford: Oxford University Press.

Costello, B., & Wachtel, T. (2013). *The restorative practices handbook for teachers, disciplinarians and administrators.* Bethlehem, PA: International Institute of Restorative Practices.

Hopkins, B. (Ed.). (2015). *Restorative theory in practice: Insights into what works and why* (1st ed.). Philadelphia, PA: Jessica Kingsley Publishers

Ecological Approach to Classroom Management

Doyle, W. (2006). Ecological approaches to classroom management. In C. M. Evertson & C. S. Weinstein (Eds.), *Handbook of classroom management: Research, practice, and contemporary issues* (97-126). London: Routledge.

Kounin, J. S. (1970). *Discipline and group management in the classroom.* Holt, Rhinehart, and Winston

Osher, D., Bear, G. G., Sprague, J. R. & Doyle, W. (2010). How can we improve school discipline? *Educational Researcher,* 39(1), 48-58.

Conflict Resolution Theory

Coleman, P., Deutsch, M., & Marcus, E. (2014). *The handbook of conflict resolution: Theory and practice.* Jossey-Bass.

Katz, N., & Lawlyer, J. W. (1985). *Communication and conflict resolution skills.* Dubuque, IA: Kendall/Hunt Publishing.

Thomas, K.W. (2002). *Thomas-Kilmann conflict mode instrument.* CPP, Inc.

Moral Development and Character Education

Belenky, M. (2008). *Women's ways of knowing: The development of self, voice, and mind, 10th anniversary edition.* New York, NY: Basic Books

Doris, J. M. (2010). *The moral psychology handbook.* Oxford: Oxford University Press

Gibbs, J. C. (2012). *Moral development and reality: Beyond the theories of Kohlberg and Hoffman.* Thousand Oaks, CA: Sage Publications.

Lickona, T. (2004). *Character matters: How to help our children develop good judgment, integrity, and other essential virtues.* Touchstone Press.

Piaget, J. (1997). *The moral judgment of the child.* New York, NY: Free Press.

Power, F. C., Higgins, A., & Kohlberg, L. (1989). *Lawrence Kohlberg's approach to moral education.* New York, NY: Columbia University Press.

Reamer, J., Paolitto, D., & Hersh, R. (1990). *Promoting moral growth: From Piaget to Kohlberg.* Long Grove, IL: Waveland Press.

Democratic Schools, Authoritative Communities, and Judicious Discipline

Chaltain, S., & O'Connor, S.D. (2009). *American schools: The art of creating a democratic learning community.* Lanham, MD: R & L Education.

Dewey, J. (2012). *Democracy and education: An introduction to the philosophy of education.* Hollywood, FL: Simon and Brown

Dewey, J. (1991). *The School and Society & The Child and the Curriculum*. Chicago, IL: Centennial Publications of The University of Chicago Press.

Gathercoal, F. (2004). *Judicious Discipline*. San Francisco, CA: Caddo Gap Press.

Hardwired to connect: The new scientific case for authoritative communities. (2003). The Commission on Children At Risk. Broadway Publications.

Kohn, A. (2006). *Beyond discipline: From compliance to community, 10th anniversary edition*. Alexandria, VA: ASCD.

Kline, K. K. (Ed.) (2008). *Authoritative communities: The scientific case for nurturing the whole child*. The Search Institute Series on Developmentally Attentive Community and Society. Medford, MA: Springer Press.

Tauber, R. T. (2007). *Classroom management: Sound theory and effective practice*. Santa Barbara, CA: Praeger Press.

Appendix B

Code of Character, Conduct, and Support Essentials Checklist

We have presented this annotated checklist in a sequence of suggested topics for revising district Codes:

Introduction

Resource Directory

Inside the cover page of the Code, provide a directory that includes support services, important phone numbers for students, and hot line numbers.

Message from Superintendent or Principal

The appropriate leader provides a vision and context for the Code. The message should clearly express how the Code fits into the larger mission of the district or school, who participated in the development of the Code, and key differences and improvements from previous codes of conduct. Finally, the leader should endorse the Code as critical for the overall health of the school or district.

Table of Contents

A clearly laid out roadmap for the document. Each section should have the appropriate page number next to the title so that a user can easily find it.

Why do we have a Code of Character, Conduct, and Support?

Provide a statement of purpose that includes an explanation for using the words, "character, conduct, and support" in the title, overarching goals of the Code, and specific goals that prompt Code revisions. The tone of the statement should communicate both your confidence in students to be successful in school and your acknowledgment that when students make mistakes, the school staff is committed to supporting them, to learn from them, and be more skillful with the right supports and interventions.

Beliefs about Children, Learning, and Discipline

Include key statements that communicate the core values that drive the district or school's thinking about children, learning, and discipline. These are the organization's aspirations, i.e., the vision statement, the Code is meant to support.

Guiding Principles of the Code of Character, Conduct, and Support

Provide brief summaries of each principle that underlies the policies, interventions, and overall goals of the Code. This is a space to articulate the thinking that illuminates the "why" of the specific policies and practices.

Promoting a Positive School Climate and Culture

Provide an overview of the features that promote a positive school culture and climate.

The Code is for All School Stakeholders

Include specific messages to students, parents, school staff, administrators, and other district staff that explain reasons for reading, studying, and discussing the Code to support understanding, and commitment to supporting it.

Learning About the Code of Conduct, Character, and Support

Provide a statement that explains how the Code is distributed and describe the activities that the district and schools will implement to ensure that students, staff, and parents have opportunities to discuss the Code.

Acknowledgment of Review of the Code

Include a 'sign-off" page for parents and students that is expected to be signed, returned, and filed at the school.

Rights and Responsibilities of Stakeholders in the School Community

For STUDENTS

Student Rights

Be sure to include the right to remain in school, right to freedom from discrimination, harassment, and bullying, right to information, and right to due process. According to the state, students are citizens, and, as citizens of the U.S., children are entitled to a free public education and the same rights of due process, freedom of expression, and equal protection under the law as adults 21 years of age and older.

Student responsibilities and expected behaviors

Delineating student responsibilities is a logical precursor to exercising good citizenship in the school and in the community. The language of student responsibilities and expectations mirrors the language of public norms of behavior (vs. private norms among family and friends) and often captures the following areas of responsibility: personal conduct and character; cooperating with others and treating others with respect; academic responsibilities as a learner; care of personal and school property; maintenance of a safe school community.

Attendance

Clearly communicate the school, district, and state policies on attendance, including the difference between excused and un-excused absences, the difference between late arrival and tardy during the school day, and the threshold of absences or tardies that require an intervention.

Technology Resource Use

Clearly community policy related to appropriate and inappropriate use of electronic devices in schools.

Student Attire

Clearly and succinctly communicate policies on student attire. Having reviewed dozens of codes of conduct in which dress code policies take up more than three pages, we offer this one that is short, simple, and leaves little room for disagreement.

School is a purposeful workplace for learning and students are expected to dress accordingly. Clothing that creates disruptions or distractions in the learning environment or cause health or safety hazards are not appropriate and not acceptable. Each school will develop its own policies for enforcing the dress code.

- Headwear — Only for health, safety, or religious reasons
- Shoes — No bare feet or flip flops
- Clothing — Cannot show bare skin between shoulders/upper chest and mid-thigh; cannot show profanity, obscenity, violence, or symbols of hate; cannot promote alcohol, tobacco, or drugs; cannot promote gang colors or gang-related signs; cannot show underwear

Bus Conduct

Articulate student expectations for behavior on school transportation.

Getting Help with a Problem

Make clear the different avenues for getting help with the wide variety of problems that the Code addresses. Articulate how a student should seek help for academic, emotional, school, staff, or extracurricular problems. Additionally, this section should make clear the procedures for filing an official complaint and for the student appeals process.

For PARENTS

Rights

Articulate what rights a parent can expect when interacting with the school in issues related to their child and the Code.

Responsibilities

In the same way that the Code expresses norms for the student's public behavior, the Code expresses similar norms for parents and guardians. Examples of these might include: making sure that a child is at school on time and ready to learn, communicating changes in address, and being respectful to school and district staff.

Complaint Procedures

Clearly articulate the steps that a parent should follow for filing a formal complaint and what the school's/district's process for handling the complaint will look like.

Getting Help with a Problem

Make clear the different avenues for how a parent should seek help for academic, emotional, school, staff, or extracurricular problems concerning their child.

For SCHOOL & DISTRICT PERSONNEL

Staff, Faculty, and Administrator Rights

Articulate clearly what rights staff, faculty, and administrators have when working in the school or district. This includes things like the right to be treated respectfully, the right to work in a safe environment, and the right to necessary resources to deliver instruction.

Staff, Faculty, and Administrator Responsibilities

Provide specific and clearly articulated responsibilities the Staff, Faculty, and Administrator have in creating a safe, welcoming, and high-performing learning environment.

District Staff and Superintendent Responsibilities

Clearly articulate the role of District Staff and Superintendent in supporting the Code.

Board of Education Responsibilities

Clearly articulate the role of the Board of Education in supporting the Code.

Tiers of Behavior Concerns, Violations, School Sanctions/Assigned Consequences and Interventions

Determining Disciplinary Interventions and Consequences

Schools must consider the following factors prior to determining appropriate interventions and consequences: the student's age and maturity; the student's disciplinary record; the nature, severity, and scope of the behavior; the circumstances/context in which the incident occurred; the frequency and duration of the behavior; the number of persons involved in the behavior; the student's IEP, BIP (Behavioral Intervention Plan), and 504 Accommodation Plan, if applicable.

Where and When the Code Applies

Lay out the jurisdiction of the Code, providing clarity for potential grey areas (e.g., on the school bus, school events away from the school location).

Tiers of Behavior Concerns, Violations, School Sanctions/Assigned Consequences, and Interventions

Provide an introduction that will frame all of the other text and graphic depictions related to tiers of behavior concerns, violations, school sanctions/consequences and interventions. Be sure to include some version of the following language in an introduction:

> *"These policies apply to all students, including all students with IEPs and 504 plans. Multiple incidents or chronic violations of the same behavior will warrant more intensive interventions and more serious consequences. For more detailed behavior descriptions, please see the Glossary.*
>
> *The interventions and consequences that are aligned with each tier represent a menu of responses. Teachers and administrators can select one or more responses in each tier. Administrators, teachers, and student support teams are not expected to select and use all interventions in each tier. Administrators, teachers, and the student support team may also use a lower tier intervention when it is appropriate."*

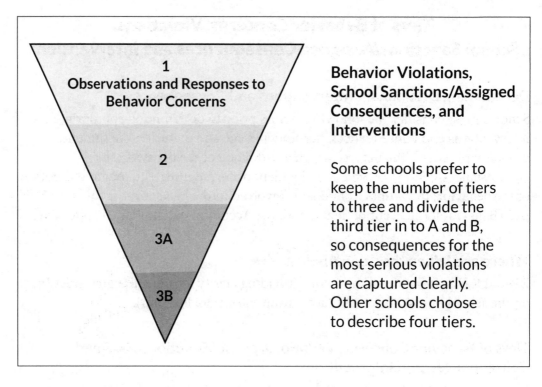

For each tier provide a page that delineates the behavior concerns (Tier 1) or behavior violations (Tier 2 and 3), teachers' responses to Tier 1 concerns, possible school sanctions/assigned consequences for Tier 2 and Tier 3, and possible interventions for Tier 2 and Tier 3. In addition, this section should spell out the policies and step-by-step procedures followed by teachers, deans, and administrators for submission of Tier 1 observation notes; submission of Tier 2 and 3 behavior referrals; removal of student from a classroom or other location to the Intervention Center; short-term in-school and out-of-school suspension (one to three days); five-day suspension with request for district hearing; suspension for students with disabilities, and transition from long-term suspension, alternative placements, or juvenile facilities to sending school.

Summary of Behavior Concerns and Violations

Provide an easy to reference alphabetical listing of all behavior concerns and violations aligned to specific Tier 1 teacher responses and Tier 2 and Tier 3 school sanctions/consequences.

Key Roles of Individuals and School Teams

Provide descriptions of individuals and school teams who play key roles in implementing schoolwide discipline and student support.

Other District Policies

Districts are often required by state law to include these types of policies in the Code.

- Reporting student violations
- Non-criminalization policies related to law enforcement, drugs, weapons, and immigration policy
- Other policies related to exclusion procedures for students without a disability
- Due process for students with a disability
- Enforcement and implementation of Code of Character, Conduct, and Support

Appendix

Glossary of Terms

This is the place to include more detailed descriptions of specific behavior violations and definitions of important terms used throughout the Code.

Index

Provide an index of topics for easy reference in order to *avoid providing an overcomplicated and exhaustive table of contents.*

Reference Documents

We suggest that readers use an array of resources when tackling code revisions. "Framework for Revising School District Codes of Student Conduct," a document created by The School Superintendents Association and the Children's Defense Fund, incorporates code guidelines and exemplary samples of code language from real districts. ("Framework for Revising School District Codes of Student Conduct." 2014. The School Superintendents Association and the Children's Defense Fund). In addition, we invite you to examine district codes from Baltimore, MD; Chicago, IL; New York City, NY; Oakland, CA; and Syracuse, NY. These are accessible on district websites. They each have their strengths and limitations; yet, together they contain language, rich content, and interesting design elements that can easily be mined and adapted for your district's or school's needs and interests. A code of conduct task force can use this document set to compare (1) the sequence of topics, (2) language used in key narratives, (3) explanation of tiers of behavior violations, consequences, and interventions, (4) formatting options, and (5) graphic depictions that can make a revised code more precise, informative, user-friendly, and attractive.

Appendix C

Guidelines for
Student Support Coaches

For many students who are at-risk, consistent face-to-face contact with a trusting adult can serve as the catalyst for showing up to school more often, for taking the role of being a student more seriously, and for engaging in fewer behaviors that result in designation on the "worry list." These guidelines are offered to student support coaches who will be working with the same student for an extended period of time.

1. Facilitate a problem solving and planning conference to identify goals and the actions that the student will take to achieve the goals in order for them to exit from the intervention.

2. Customize the progress-monitoring tool.

3. Determine the length of time that the student will be assigned a student support coach (for a month, a grading period, or even the entire year).

4. Communicate your confidence that they can meet the identified goals.

5. Engage in a "check-in and check-out" protocol at the beginning and end of each day or at least several times a week for at least the first month of the intervention.

6. Review and sign the student's progress monitoring tool every day. Make a copy to place in students' folder at the end of each week.

7. Discuss strategies for "staying under the radar screen," particularly in their encounters with adults with whom they have had conflicts in the past.

8. Discuss strategies for how to "do school" so that a student's day-to-day experiences feel more positive and less frustrating.

9. Check in every week with the student's teachers (grade level team) to get a read on whether the student's trend line is better, the same, or worse.

10. Be prepared to convene informal conferences with the student and other adults to clarify expectations and assess progress when concerns arise.

11. After four weeks or the end of a grading period, facilitate a BAG check (behavior, attendance, and grades) in order to re-set and adjust goals for the next four weeks.

Feedback Questions for Daily Check-in's and Check-out's:

Before the school day begins:

- What is one thing you are going to do in your classes today that will help you have a good day?
- What is one thing you are going to do in public spaces to keep your agreement to stay out of trouble?
- What is one thing you want your teachers to say about you at the end of the day today?
- What is a goal for the day that will help you stay on track?
- When other students bother you or try to get you off track, what might you say?
- If you get upset or frustrated during the day, who are some people you can talk to?
- What can you say to yourself, when you get angry or upset?

After the school day when student is turning in their Daily PROGRESS REPORT:

- What are some things you did today that made you proud of yourself?
- What was your best class today? What would your teacher say about you in this class?
- What is one thing you did today that helped you stay focused an on task?
- What was your toughest or most frustrating class today? What can you do tomorrow that might make this class go better?
- What is one thing you can do tonight that will help you prepare for tomorrow?

Appendix D

Memorandum of Understanding Checklist for Student Support Team and Partners

The Memorandum of Understanding (MOU) checklist includes five major components to consider when crafting MOUs between districts, internal student support staff at the school level, and external student support partners. Much of the information contained in the checklist can also serve as a guideline for developing consistent practices within internal student support teams who represent a wide range of student support positions and responsibilities.

Mission Statement: *The aim of all student support services is to nurture students' healthy development and resiliency, develop and strengthen behaviors and mindsets that will improve students' academic, personal, and social efficacy, and enable all students to be successful in school and the classroom.*

Goals of the MOU:

1. Increase capacity and efficacy to serve all students to ensure their healthy social, emotional, and academic development.

2. Increase family involvement in students' educational success.

3. Create and maintain an infrastructure that links and coordinates all student support functions and services.

4. Improve systems collaboration among partners at the district and school level.

Partnership Values:

- Family Driven — encourage full and meaningful input and participation of the children and families whom we serve.
- Youth Guided — support student voice and students' sense of agency throughout the process.
- Strengths Based — build on and celebrate what is going well.
- Listening Responsively — seek to understand.
- Team Based — support a multidisciplinary approach and shared responsibility for services and outcomes.
- Data Informed — ensure that accurate and holistic information supports decisions.

- Culturally and Developmentally Responsive — seek to understand cultural and developmental differences and respond sensitively to the diverse needs of students and families.
- Persistent Effort — "Do not give up," continue to adapt and modify strategies and interventions with students and families who are experiencing complex challenges.

Communication Expectations among and between the District/School, Student Support Staff, and Partner Agencies:

1. Establishment of a district-wide Student Support Advisory Group comprised of key district and agency leaders and school representatives for the purposes of shared decision-making, assessing needs/gaps, planning, sharing of data, and ongoing program evaluation.

2. Sharing of information to the fullest extent possible in support of students' school success, while respecting family privacy and complying with federal and state regulations.

3. Development of common information sharing protocols and utilizing internal records management protocols to respect each other's confidentiality mandates.

4. Participation in bi-weekly student support team meeting that include cross trainings among student support staff to increase school team capacity to understand and deliver various services, processes, and interventions.

5. Participation in weekly School Intervention Team meetings when requested. Providing an updated roster of "caseloads" to the lead social worker every week.

6. Providing informed consent from parents for supports and services offered to their children.

Accountability and Transparency:

1. Development of clearly defined performance indicators, outcomes, and shared data within the partnership.

2. Use of a standardized electronic database to document work with students and families.

3. Development of criteria that help assess students' experience and the effectiveness of specific services and interventions.

4. Completion of annual audits of effectiveness, relevance, and implementation of partnership services and interventions using data that is disaggregated by race, ethnicity, gender, grade, students with disabilities, English language learners, and students who receive free and reduced lunch.

5. Establishing evidence informed training curriculum and professional development practices for all external and internal partners.

6. Allowing flexibility for times when the School Intervention Team (SIT) may need to meet several times in the same week to accommodate requests for Tier 3 consultations focused on students in crisis and students who are experiencing multiple academic, behavioral, and mental health challenges.

7. Providing and facilitating access to student and participant data and records for the purpose of assessing student achievement and attainment of program goals and objectives as allowed by federal and state privacy regulations.

8. Development of protocols and appropriate support for students and families who transition from more intense to less intense case management or who exit interventions when target goals have been achieved.

9. Identification of the lead school social worker in every school who is the point person for implementing MOU agreements with fidelity and integrity.

Maximizing Resources:

1. Leveraging funds and enhancing resources to meet the goals of the MOU, enhance service provision, and ensure support for highest need students.

2. Keeping the focus on the needs of the school and its students rather than program-specific interests. Supporting innovation and enhancing service delivery whenever possible.

3. Offering trainings to all partners and their staff.

4. Ensuring that 90 percent of case management slots will be filled by the date of _____ in order to maximize utilization of services.

5. Offering flexible case management slots outside of the traditional time frame of year-long services to ensure that opportunities throughout the year for students to be assigned a coach or a case manager on a temporary basis.

6. Commitment to participate in a school's rotation "on call" duty roster for at least two hours every week to ensure that a student support staff member is always available to respond to situations in which a student requires immediate care and attention.

Appendix E

Kid Talk Consultancy Protocol

Gathering for a Student Intervention Meeting/Grade Level Team Meeting

1. Facilitator distributes the coaching list along with the names of students for whom the team has been implementing interventions. Participants jot down on a Post-it note the name of a student for whom they have some "good news" along with a phrase/sentence briefly describing the "good news." (1 min)
   Example: *"Michele has been on time to class every day for four days and has completed most of her assignments."*

2. Share a few "good news" Post-its in a Popcorn style. Participants take Post-its to give to students. (2 min)

Bringing a New Student to the Team

1. Facilitator names the first student whom the team has identified in need of additional supports/interventions.

2. Go-Round: Identify concerns and observable data. (2 min)
   Example: *"I am concerned about James' use of negative speech and distracting and disruptive movement. This sounds and looks like…."*

3. Go-Round: Describe supports and interventions implemented to date for this student that have not been effective. (2 min)

4. Identify the target outcome/desired behavior. (2 min)
   Example: using positive, non-aggressive language to express myself, ask for help, and get what I need.

5. Brainstorm supports/interventions that can be facilitated by teachers and/or Student Support Team moving ahead to support the student. (4 min)
   Example: Provide "scripts" that encourage the student to say and do the right thing: *"When someone is bothering you can say…"* *"When you are angry or upset, ask yourself…"*

6. Prioritize one support/intervention to implement and identify feedback/ progress monitoring tool and process that student and teachers/support staff will use for a specific window of time. (3 min)
   Example: Daily Direct Behavior Rating in all classes around targeted behavior from March 15-March 30.

7. Identify immediate next steps, including the adult who will confer with the student about the plan and create the progress monitoring tool, among other tasks. (2 min)

8. Recorder gives notes to Student Intervention Team or Grade Level Team leader who makes copies and puts them in grade team teachers'/administrators' mailboxes and keeps one copy in a grade team binder/folder.

9. Schedule a date to revisit the student.

Assessing Progress of a Student for Whom the Team has Been Implementing Supports and Interventions

1. Facilitator describes supports and interventions the team has implemented to date to support the student as well as targeted outcomes/desired behaviors of the intervention. (1 min)

2. Team members share observable data and concerns that help assess the student's progress and whether the student's trend line is positive, negative, or about the same. (2 min)

3. Team members share any other information that might help explain a negative or static trend line. (2 min)

4. If the trend line is negative or static, team members discuss any possible modifications to the intervention plan and/or adjustments to the process and tools for monitoring progress. (5 min)

Appendix F

Personal Check-in Protocol

Overview: Students are more likely to trust and be engaged in learning when they feel known, heard, and valued by their teachers. Teachers who use personal check-ins regularly, informally, and systematically get to know students as individuals and learners, build rapport, and create a positive class culture. In addition, personal check-ins often uncover clues that help us understand how to best support students with their emotional, academic, and behavioral needs.

Purpose:
- To connect with students, establish positive relationships, and build trust
- To better understand the lives and learner profiles of each student

What it looks like: (Teacher first scans room to identify student(s) to check-in with)

Option 1: Teacher asks a student a personalized question.
Example: *"Hi Mike. How are you feeling today?"*

Option 2: Teacher makes a comment to communicate to a student that they know and want to know the student as an individual.
Example: *"Hi Maria. I hear from Mr. Tobin that you are quite the athlete. Tell me how soccer tryouts are going."*

Option 3: Teacher checks in with students who look tired, upset, worried, or rambunctious by reflecting back to them what they see and then following up with a question.
Example: *"Hey Arturo. You look a little frustrated. What's going on for you?"*

Option 4: Teacher checks in with the whole group when the energy or vibe seems unusually high or low.
Example: *"Good Afternoon. So how has everybody's day been so far? Show me with a thumbs up, thumbs down, or thumbs sideways."*

Example: *"Hello fabulous fifth period. How's everyone feeling as we head into this 3 day weekend?"*

Opportunities for Implementation:
- Meet and Greet as students are walking into class
- Reflect and Connect at the start of class
- During Independent Student Work Time
- At the close of class while students are packing up

- When class energy is noticeably high or low
- When encountering students outside of class: hallways, lunchroom, etc.

The key to being a good teacher is to know the kids. You have to know, and have a relationship with, every single student. *"I think that one thing that really allows me to work hard is knowing that my teacher knows where I am in life at that moment. If they don't know me, I will tend not to work as hard for them."* – Student quote from Doda, N., & Knowles, T. (2008). Listening to the voices of young adolescents. Middle School Journal, 39(3), 26-33.

Example Personal Check-In Scenario:

The teacher scans the room towards the end of class as students are independently working on an assignment. She notices one of her students, Beth, looks to be finishing up with the task. Beth rarely speaks in class and lately she has not been doing her homework. The teacher decides to take a minute to check-in with Beth in an effort to build a positive relationship with her.

The teacher approaches Beth's desk from the side, bends down to her level, and quietly asks and open-ended question, *"Hi Beth. I notice you are always so focused on your work when you are in class. What kind of things do you do in your free time?"*

Beth responds, *"Uhh. I don't know…I usually just go home and take care of my little brother."*

Teacher paraphrases, *"Ahh, so you have family responsibilities after school." Teacher pauses and asks another open-ended question, "What's that like?"*

Beth replies, *"It is hard. He is only three and he is crazy. I have to feed him and watch him while my mom goes to work at night."*

Teacher paraphrases, *"Wow, so for several hours at night your job is to take care of a toddler."*

Teacher smiles, *"Well, that helps me get to know you a little better. (Pause) Be sure to let me know if you need help with any of your homework assignments… and take care of yourself."*

Appendix G

Problem Solving and Planning Conference

Overview: When unproductive and ineffective behaviors, habits, or mindsets are impeding academic success and high functioning in the classroom, a private problem solving and planning conference is the platform for changing a student's academic and behavior trajectory. Our role is not to fix the problem ourselves and tell the student exactly what to do; rather, our role is to help the student reflect and account for their actions, explore possible strategies and solutions through collaborative problem solving, and create a plan for improvement.

Purpose:

- To support students to engage in behaviors, mindsets, and habits that will ensure their academic success.

Opportunities for Implementation:

- Before or after school
- Lunch
- Part of a prep period
- Team planning time

What it Looks Like: (Identify those students who would benefit from this conference and create a schedule for meeting with them.)

1. Arrange a time to conference and depersonalize to get ready.

2. Thank the student for meeting with you.

3. Share what you have noticed and invite the student to share his perspective too.
   Example: *"I've noticed that you've had a tough time focusing and you've not completed any work tasks this week. I want to support you. What has been going on for you?"*

4. Pause and give the student time to respond. If the student is having a hard time responding, try following up with another question.
   Example: *"How are you thinking or feeling about this? What are some things you think I might be concerned about?"*

5. Paraphrase for understanding and check in with how students are thinking or feeling about the situation. If the student is angry or upset, you may need to acknowledge their feelings to help the student defuse charged emotions.
   Example: *"So you don't like to read and you get frustrated when you don't understand right away. And then it's hard to focus, you stop working, and then start fooling around. Did I get that right?"*

6. Collaborate with the student to identify an academic goal (brainstorm possible strategies together to achieve the goal).
   Example: *"So what might be some things you can start doing to turn things around?*
   "So, you came up with three things that you could start doing that would help with getting your work done and staying on-task. First, you want to start sitting near the front of the room. To help with the reading assignments, you want to try re-reading to summarize and check to see if you understand. You also will try out putting Post-it notes on sections you do not understand and start asking questions."

7. Make a plan for what the student will do to support the desired target behaviors that will help the student achieve the academic or behavioral goal. See Example on next page.

8. Complete daily progress reports for three weeks. See Example on next page.

Weekly Progress Monitoring Report

3 = I did it without prompting.   1 = I didn't do it most of the time.

2 = I did it with prompting.   0 = I didn't do it.

Goal: To complete work tasks and assignments that involve reading.					
What student will do:	M	T	W	Th	F
Sit in the front row.					
Keep reading and thinking when it gets hard.					
Re-read and summarize in my own words.					
Place Post-its where I do not understand the reading.					
Ask for help when I need it.					
Go to Tuesday Homework Hall.	■		■	■	■
Complete my Progress Monitoring Report to assess how I am doing.					

What teacher will do:

- Provide Post-its.
- Provide personal support during Tuesday Homework Hall.
- Provide Daily Progress report.
- Monitor progress every day for three weeks.
- Check in at least once a period to see how you're doing.
- Conference weekly to assess progress and make adjustments.

Student Signature _____

Teacher Signature _____

Supporting Students with Problem Solving

Often, students have a tough time naming exactly what behaviors are getting them off-track and identifying exactly what replacement behaviors will help get them back on track. Consider using cards or Post-it notes with behavior descriptions that you can place out on the table in front of the student as a way to scaffold the self-reflection and problem solving process.

Behaviors that are getting me Off-Track Card Sort Examples (on red paper)		Behaviors that will help me get back On-Track Card Sort Examples (on green paper)	
Talking during whole group instruction	Cursing and using disrespectful language	Following routines and procedures	Saying, "Okay," when I am asked to do something.
Refusing to follow directions	Arguing, yelling, and back-talk to teacher	Working cooperatively in small groups	Working by myself without bothering others
Teasing, taunting, name calling	Fussing and arguing with peers	Keeping my hands to myself	Working silently when required
Making noises and movements that distract others	Getting mad when I am asked to do something	Making a good effort to complete every assignment	Asking for help respectfully when I need it
Playing around with others	Not listening carefully to instructions	Sitting somewhere else in the classroom	Writing a note to myself when I am angry or frustrated

Problem Solving and Planning Conference Note Tracker

Student: _____   Teacher:_____

Teacher	Initial observations or concerns that prompted the conference.	
Student	Response to observations and concerns. What are you thinking/feeling about this?	
Teacher and Student	Agreement on what is getting in the way of learning and being okay in class.	
Teacher and Student	Agreement on an academic goal.	
Teacher and Student	Behaviors that are getting me off-track and behaviors that would help me get back on-track.	
	Off-Track:	On-Track:
Student	Summarize what you will do. What might the teacher do to support your efforts?	
Teacher	Summarize the plan, what you will do, what behaviors will be monitored, and how progress monitoring will work.	
Teacher and Student	Close the conference by sharing one thing you feel better about or one thing you are feeling hopeful about.	

Student Signature_____ Date_____

Teacher Signature_____ Date_____

Appendix H

Behavior Check-in Protocol

Overview: When a student is off-task, a quick informal behavior check-in can gently guide students to self-assess and redirect their behavior. These one-to-one, question based check-ins communicate care, respect, and high expectations for on-task, respectful behavior in your classroom. The question format keeps the conversation positive and is helpful for immediately diagnosing and addressing the actual cause of the misbehavior.

Purpose: To help a student re-engage in learning by:
- Addressing low-impact off-task or negative behavior;
- Understanding the reasons behind students off-task behavior;
- Helping students become more self-aware and able to self-regulate; and
- Normalizing mistakes and missteps using a respectful, matter-of-fact, no drama voice and tone.

Opportunities for Implementation:
- When you notice a student is disengaged or off-task
- When a student is not following a classroom procedure
- When one or more students are goofing off or engaging in sidebar conversations
- When a student blurts out an inappropriate statement
- When you notice a student acting frustrated, emotional, upset, or angry

(NOTE: If the behavior check-in is not sufficient for calming the student down, begin implementing the Defusing Protocol.)

What it Looks Like:
(While scanning the room, the teacher observes a behavioral situation that warrants a check-in.)

1. Try to get eye contact with the student and point to any written cues, procedures, or directions. (This might be all it takes to get the student back on-track.)

2. Use proximity and nonverbal cues next. Move close to the student and make it clear that you are observing their behavior.

3. If the behavior persists, approach the student for a one-to-one conversation by moving to their side, positioning yourself at the same level as the student, and greeting the student by name.

4. Ask an open-ended question that encourages the student to think for themselves about their behavior and what they could be doing differently.

    Off-task behavior Example: *"Hey, Matt and Arturo. What might you need to do to get back on track and stay focused on this assignment?"*

    Emotional Behavior Example: *"Hi Jackson. What are some things you might need in order to get yourself in a better space so you can rejoin your group?"*

Example Behavior Check-In Scenario:

While the rest of the class is busy working on the Do Now, Veronica walks into class one minute late, dancing around and humming a popular song.

The teacher catches Veronica's eye and points to the Do Now instructions that are posted on the whiteboard.

Veronica sits down but continues to just "hang out."

The teacher approaches Veronica from the side, bends down to be at eye level and quietly asks an open-ended question, *"Hey Veronica. What is our class routine during the first five minutes of class?"*

Veronica responds, *"Oh, I forgot my notebook so I don't have anything to write in."*

The teacher paraphrases, *"So you have not started working because you do not have your materials."* (Pause) The teacher questions, *"When you forget your materials, what are your options?"*

Veronica replies, *"I guess I could ask Margo for a piece of paper."*

Teacher nods, *"Good option—Sounds like you solved your problem. There are three minutes left for you to complete the Do Now task."*

The teacher follows up with Veronica towards the end of class and asks an open-ended question, "Hey Veronica. What can you do tomorrow to make sure you are ready to do the Do Now the minute the bell rings?" Veronica, *"Oh, I need to find my notebook. That's why I was late today. I couldn't find it in my locker. I am so disorganized."*

The teacher nods—and after pausing—paraphrases, *"So your locker is a bit of a mess and that resulted in you being late."* (Pause) Veronica nods. The teacher questions again, *"So what might you do to make sure you are on time tomorrow so you have the whole five minutes to complete the Do Now?"*

Veronica thinks for a moment and then responds, *"Well I guess I could clean my locker out today after school."*

The teacher asks, *"How long do you think that will take?"*

Veronica pauses and then says, *"Probably twenty minutes or so. It will be worth it though cause it's so messy and it is stressing me out."*

Teacher smiles encouragingly, *"Sounds like you have a plan."*

Situational Considerations:

If the student does not re-engage within a minute or two and appears really stuck or emotionally paralyzed, offer to help them assess what is getting in the way of their learning.

Example: *"Jackson, I'm noticing that you seem really frustrated right now. What can I do to help?"*

If a student's emotional state is making it difficult for them to think, consider offering them a few options.

Example: *"Ok Jackson. I can tell you are really upset. Let's consider some options for you. You could take the hall pass and go get a drink of water and give yourself a minute to collect yourself OR you can take the RE-SET Pass and go check in with Mr. Edwards. Which of these options might work for you?"*

If a student challenges you, be prepared to deliver a neutral statement about what you observed.

Example: *"Matt, I listened to you and Arturo talking about the football game for the last four minutes and noticed that neither one of you had your articles out to work on. Sounds like an interesting game. Time to get to work."*

Appendix I

Academic Check-in Protocol

Overview: The informal, academic check-in used daily as a tool for formative assessment allows teachers to assess what a student is learning, doing, or thinking at a particular point in the lesson or unit. The one-to-one simple three-question format is intended to help students practice metacognition and gain confidence in their capacities as independent learners. Academic check-ins also help teachers target their academic supports and interventions, resulting in a class culture where high levels of thinking and learning are both expected and supported.

Purpose:

- Determine what students are learning, doing, or thinking related to academic skills and content.
- Help students practice important metacognitive skills.
- Provide opportunities to address confusion, misunderstandings, or support the correction of errors.
- Provide specific positive feedback when a student's thinking is on track.

What it Looks Like: (Teacher first scans room to identify student(s) to check-in with)

1. Inform the class that you will be moving around and checking in with students to hear their smart thinking and questions, which will help you support their learning.

2. Build Rapport: Approach the student for a one-to-one check-in by moving to their side, positioning yourself at the same level as the student, and greeting the student by name.

3. Open Ended Questions: Ask some version of the following three questions:
   - What are you working on?
   - How is it going?
   - What are you going to do next?

     Example:

     Hi, Renee. Where you are in the lab?
     How did you determine what was the independent variable?
     Describe for me what you are going to work on next.

4. If necessary, follow up by addressing any areas of confusion. When appropriate, point to any written cues, procedures, or directions that would support the student being self-directed and figuring things out for themselves.

Opportunities for Implementation:

- While students are completing the Do Now at the start of class
- After your mini-lesson, when students are working independently on an assignment or a project
- When pairs, trios, or small groups are working on an assignment, project, or lab
- When students are packing up at the end of class
- When you have handed back a graded assignment, test, or a quiz

Example Academic Check-In Scenario:

The teacher is walking around the room while students work on a close reading of *A Letter from a Birmingham Jail*. The teacher wants to check in with each student at least once a week, and he has identified six students to do informal academic check-ins with today.

The teacher informs the class of his next move to prepare the students and support their focus and attention for the task: *"I am going to move about the room and check-in with several of you to hear your smart thinking and answer any questions you might have."*

First on his list is Myra, so once he sees everyone has made the transition to settle in to work he moves over to Myra's desk, grabs a chair so he can sit beside Myra and starts the check-in with an open-ended question, *"What are some strategies you use when doing a close read?"*

Myra shares, *"I'm re-reading this sentence to try and figure out what King is trying to say. It is really long and has a bunch of names and words I don't know."*

The teacher nods and paraphrases, *"So this sentence is confusing and you are re-reading to try and understand the meaning."* He pauses and then asks an open-ended question, *"How is this strategy working for you?"*

Myra, *"Well I re-read this part a couple of times and it still didn't make sense so I skipped ahead to the end of the sentence and now I think I understand that he is just giving a bunch of examples of why he is feels he should be in fighting in Birmingham."*

The teacher pauses and paraphrases, *"Ahh, so you didn't let unfamiliar vocabulary hold you back. You went ahead and skimmed to try and get the gist of the whole paragraph."* (Pause) The teacher then asks a follow up open-ended question, *"What might you do next?"*

Myra replies, *"Well, I'm going to mark up the text the way you showed us to highlight the main point and then read the next paragraph."*

Teacher wraps up check-in, *"Sounds like you know exactly what to do. Thanks for sharing your thinking with me."*

Appendix J

Progress Monitoring Tools

Daily Progress Monitoring Tool—Sample #1

Name_____ Dean_____

Coach/Advisor_____Course_____

Period_____ Teacher_____

Start-up Date_____ Number of Weeks _____

Please write in the number each day 0 – I did not do it. 1 – I always needed prompting 2 – I did it with some prompting 3 – I did it without prompting.		Current Week:				
		M	**T**	**W**	**Th**	**F**
Behavior Focus: Social, Self-regulation, Moral/Ethical, Academic	**Student**					
Desired Target Behavior:	**Teacher**					
Behavior Focus: Social, Self-regulation, Moral/Ethical, Academic	**Student**					
Desired Target Behavior:	**Teacher**					
Behavior Focus: Social, Self-regulation, Moral/Ethical, Academic	**Student**					
Desired Target Behavior:	**Teacher**					

Notes and Comments:

Daily Progress Monitoring Tool—Sample #2

Name_____ Dean_____

Coach/Advisor_____Course_____

Period_____ Teacher_____

Start-up Date_____ Number of Weeks _____Current Week_____

Behavior Focus: Social, Self-regulation, Moral/Ethical, Academic

Desired Target Behavior:_____

Monday

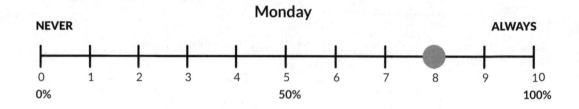

Tuesday

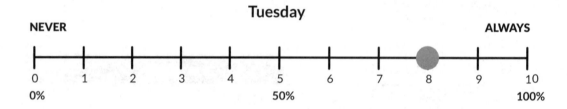

Wednesday

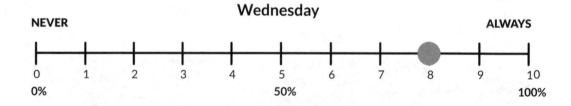

Thursday

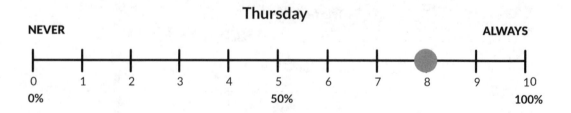

Friday

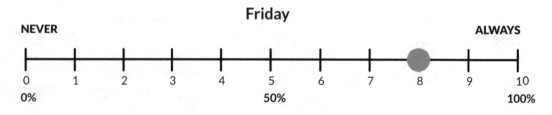

Appendix K

Defusion and De-escalation Protocol

Overview: When a student is overtly upset, frustrated, aggressive, or angry, our immediate goal is to defuse their emotions and help them calm down. These strategies and protocols will help students work their way to an improved emotional state so they can access the reasoning, problem solving, and cognitive part of their brain.

Strategies For Defusing Highly Charged Situations:

👁 **Depersonalize ("Don't pick up the rope.")**

🧍 **Use Mindful Proximity**

↑↑ **Acknowledge Feelings**

⚑ **Communicate Care**

🗨 **Give Firm Directives to Establish Safety**

When an emotional situation is more volatile, it often requires additional strategies to effectively manage the student(s) and maintain a safe classroom.

- **Depersonalize:** ("Don't pick up the rope.") A student's emotional state is not about you or your class. Therefore, it is important to not take their behaviors personally. Instead, take a deep breath and ground yourself with the knowledge that you have the skills and strategies to support this student.

- **Use Mindful Proximity:** When a student is highly emotionally charged, his brain (specifically the amygdala) has triggered an automatic "fight, flight, or freeze" response. For many students, getting too close to them will elevate this response and could put others and you in harm's way. So avoid getting too close, touching the student, or standing above him so he does not see you as a threat. Your goal here is to try to talk to him privately.

- **Acknowledge Feelings:** Reflecting and/or acknowledging the emotions the student is expressing shows the student that you are tuned in and care about her. This enables the student to calm down and step into a verbal exchange.

- **Communicate Care:** Verbalize that you are concerned for the student and that you want to support him. If a situation is unsafe, acknowledge that the situation is not safe with a calm, compassionate tone and tell the student that you want to help.
- **Give Firm Directives to Establish Safety:** If a situation continues to be unsafe, give simple instructions telling the student(s) what to do to make the situation safe. For example, *"I need you to walk with me to the other side of the room."* Or if two students are involved, "I need you to move away from each other and return to your seats."

A. When you notice a student is emotionally charged/upset/angry
Immediate Goal: Defuse upset feelings and help student re-engage

Protocol:

1. Scan to assess the situation, and depersonalize to get ready.

2. If you are at the front of the class and engaged in whole group instruction, your first critical step is to give the class an independent task so you can speak more privately with the student.

3. Approach the student for a one-to-one conversation by moving to their side, position yourself at the same level as the student, and greet the student by name.

4. Reflect/acknowledge the emotion you think you see or hear and ask the student what is going on.
   Example: Hey, Amelio. You seem pretty upset. What's going on for you?

5. Paraphrase, pause, and follow up with questions to discover the cause(s) of the elevated emotional state.
   Examples: What's not working for you right now? Is there anything else bothering you? What else might help me understand?

6. Ask the student what they need to get themselves into a better space.
   Examples: What are some things you might do to feel better? What are some things you could do so you are able to rejoin the class? What are some things I could do to help you get yourself feeling ok?

Example Defusing Protocol Scenario:
The teacher notices that when Ben entered the class, he threw his backpack on the ground, sat in his seat, and immediately put his head down. After getting the class started on the Reflect and Connect, the teacher approaches Ben, who still has his head down and quietly asks an open-ended question, *"Hey, Ben. I notice you have had your head down since you entered class. What's up?"*

Ben mumbles, *"Leave me alone."* The teacher paraphrases, *"So you want a moment to yourself right now?"* Ben pops his head up and says, *"Yes! All you teachers are always on my case! Mr. Franklin already yelled at me today. I guess it is your turn now!"*

The teacher pauses for thinking and then calmly paraphrases, *"So Mr. Franklin yelled at you today and you are upset about it and think I might do the same thing?"* (Pause) Ben does not respond, but continues eye contact with the teacher and starts to look a little calmer.

The teacher shares, *"Well, Ben, it sounds like you have had a tough morning. Thank you for explaining what is going on.* (Pause) Teacher asks another open-ended question, *"What do you need in order to feel better so you can focus on the lab we are going to do today?* (Pause) Ben responds, *"Nothing. Just leave me alone for a minute."*

The teacher replies, *"Ok. Take a minute or two to regroup. When you are ready, pull out your notebook and write down a quick response to the Reflect and Connect question. And, let me know if you want to talk later about what happened in Mr. Franklin's class. Maybe I can help."*

B. When a student is physically explosive

Immediate Goal: Remove student to a more private space and keep other students safe.

Protocol:

1. Scan to assess the situation, and depersonalize to get ready.

2. Do not directly confront. Move to a spot that gives the student space and enables you to communicate with them.

3. Acknowledge the unsafe situation and communicate care in a calm and assertive voice.
   Example: *"Russ, this is not safe and I want you to be safe. Walk with me out into the hallway for a minute."*

4. Tell the rest of the class to remain in their seats and communicate care.
   Example: *"Class - I need you to stay in your seats for a moment. I want to take care of Russ and I will be right here at the door."*

5. At the doorway, thank the student for making a good choice, acknowledge their emotional state, and communicate care again.
   Example: *"Thanks Russ. You made a good choice stepping out of the class with me. I know you are very angry right now and I want you to be okay."*

6. Follow your school's code of conduct for responding to physically explosive unsafe behavior.
   Example: *"We can talk about what is going on later. Right now I need you to go _____ so you can speak with _____ and she will help you."*

C. When a student is being argumentative, hostile, resistant or confrontational

Immediate Goal: Depersonalize, avoid or de-escalate the power struggle and move on.

Protocol:

1. Scan to assess the situation, and depersonalize to get ready.

2. <u>Do not</u> pick up the rope and argue back, explain yourself, answer questions or draw student into a conversation. When a student is agitated, confrontation will likely just increase their aggressive behavior and escalate the problem.

3. Say one statement that respectfully communicates that you will not engage right now and then move away.
   Examples:
   "You said _____ and I would like to talk with you about that later."

   "I have heard what you said and I will think about it."

   "I know you are upset about this and we will get a chance to discuss it later."

   "I am not going to argue about this with you."

   "You are right. I cannot make you..."

4. Later, follow up with the student with a Behavior Check-In or a Problem Solving Conference.

Appendix L

Intervention Center Coordinator: Roles and Responsibilities

The Intervention Center (IC) is a separate place that is supervised by a coordinator who oversees the intake and processing of all students who are assigned to IC. The coordinator also serves as a kind of broker who contacts others who need to meet with a student immediately. For example, the IC coordinator contacts an administrator when a student has been escorted to the IC for committing a serious behavior violation that requires investigation and processing by an administrator. Or the IC coordinator contacts an "on call" student support team member to facilitate a brief "cooling off" conference with a student who is highly charged and explosive. Or the IC coordinator contacts a student's support coach who can pick up the student and work with the student in a more private location.

The coordinator works with four different groups of students who may be assigned to the IC:

1. Students who have committed Tier 2 and Tier 3 behavior violations that warrant immediate removal from a classroom or public space.

2. Students who have been traveling in public spaces without permission during class periods are temporarily removed to the IC for processing before returning to class.

3. Students who have received a RE-SET Pass to meet briefly with a student support team member to cool off and regain their equilibrium so that they can return to class ready to learn.

4. Students who report to IC for a designated period of time (from a class period, to a half day, to a whole day) during which they participate in scheduled conferences or assigned interventions with administrators, student support team members, and/or teachers.

Essential Responsibilities

Every Day, the IC Coordinator:

1. Establishes and implements expectations, rules, and procedures for students who report to the IC.

2. Processes and logs in all students who are assigned to the IC and records all data electronically.

3. Ensures that students who are upset have a space where they can sit and restore their sense of calm and equilibrium.

4. Ensures that all students assigned to the IC participate in a reflection/planning conference with a counselor, social worker, other student support staff, or IC coordinator before student returns to regular classes.

5. Contacts an administrator when serious incidents must be investigated immediately.

6. Communicates with the student support staff members who will meet with students directly.

7. Supports all students to complete assigned work through personalized coaching and conferencing.

8. Ensures that students document what they have completed in the Work Log.

9. Connects students with the assigned student support staff member.

Every Week, the IC Coordinator:

1. Collects and summarizes all the IC student data on a weekly basis and submits weekly data summary to the AP responsible for discipline and the lead social worker.

2. Coordinates any and all interventions during the IC time with SPED Coordinator and SPED liaisons and other counselors and student support staff.

3. Participates in case conferences during the weekly School Intervention Team meeting when asked to share observations about a specific student.

4. Gathers informal data from students about their experience of school, barriers that may get in the way of learning and behaving appropriately, and what students say they need to do to turn around their behavior.

Appendix M

Intervention Center Referral Form

When a student would benefit from a referral to the Intervention Center, the adult needs to complete a very brief referral slip that goes with the student to the Intervention Center. We have found that providing a clear "check the box" list makes this easy to do in the moment and it also reminds the adult of the specific conditions under which a student can be removed from the classroom or other location. The IC referral slip does not replace the official discipline referral that the adult is expected to complete later when they are not teaching or supervising students.

Name: _____

Grade: _____ **Course:** _____

Time: _____ **Date:** _____

Referring Adult: _____

Student Action that Prompted this Referral:

- ☐ Intentional disruption of learning through <u>excessive</u> distracting or disruptive movements, noises or voices
- ☐ Teasing, taunting or name-calling
- ☐ Bullying or harassment
- ☐ Physical or verbal aggression towards another
- ☐ Dangerous, reckless, or explosive behavior that jeopardizes safety
- ☐ Emotional distress

Teacher Comments:

Appendix N

Intervention Center
Reflection and Return Form

When a student is referred to the Intervention Center, Part 1 of the Reflection and Return form is completed by the student (and, at times, with the help of an adult) after the student arrives at the Intervention Center. Part two is completed during a brief conference between the student and the referring adult within 48 hours of the student's return to class. Administrators, deans, and teachers like this type of form because it keeps all relevant information on one document and closes the loop about the incident with the referring adult.

Name: _____

Grade: _____ **Course:** _____

Time: _____ **Date:** _____

Referring Adult: _____

Part 1

Getting the Story Out

What happened?

_____

_____

What are some feelings you have about what happened?

_____

_____

Taking Responsibility

How did your actions impact your learning? I was not able to:

_____

_____

In what ways did your behavior impact others or the learning environment?

_____

_____

Problem Solving and Moving Forward

When a situation like this comes up again, what do you want to pay attention to and do?

_____

_____

Preparation and Rehearsal

What might be some things you can say or do to restore your good standing in class and repair your relationship with the teacher?

_____

_____

Part 2

Getting Support and Keeping on Track

What are two to three things that your teacher(s) might do to support you?

_____

_____

What are two to three things that you can do for yourself to stay on track?

_____

_____

Specific Actions to Be Monitored

_____

_____

Date _____

Appendix O

Restorative Group Conference Protocol

Overview: A formal restorative group conference is typically used in situations when an individual is clearly identified as an aggressor/offender who has harmed others in a specific incident. Participants in the protocol include co-facilitators, parties directly involved in the immediate incident, parties directly impacted by the incident, and parents and other allies of both the person who was harmed and the person who committed the offense. Schools are most likely to use restorative group conferencing for high impact incidents that have seriously harmed or threatened the safety and well-being of individuals and groups or jeopardize the safety, functioning, and reputation of the entire school community.

Restorative group conferences require plenty of advanced planning and a time frame of 60 to 90 minutes for facilitating the actual protocol. The process usually incorporates time for key participants to prepare and rehearse what they want to say before they enter the restorative group conference. In addition, some or all participants may also need a brief preview of the goals, the step-by-step process, and their role in the conversation (providing support, being an attentive listener/ witness, sharing perspectives and ideas). The seating format is always a circle which promotes equal voice and shared accountability. Because of its complexity, this protocol, in its full form, should be convened with a specific set of conditions and criteria in mind and should be used sparingly. Specific components and language of the restorative group conference protocol will vary to fit different community needs, cultures, and time constraints.

Purpose:

The goal of restorative group conferencing is to empower the targeted person(s) who was harmed by the incident, community members, families, and the offenders to seek a constructive resolution to the incident by giving all participants a voice and encouraging shared accountability for the outcome. The intent is to address the underlying causes of offending behavior, foster awareness and understanding of the human impact of his or her behavior, and ensure that offenders take responsibility for making amends for their actions. Adults (including family) or students who serve as the offender's support network are expected to follow up and follow through in helping a student keep their commitments to engage in restorative actions that are part of a final agreement. Restorative group conferencing provides opportunities to promote and share community values by strengthening a sense of connectedness and building the community's capacity and commitment to resolve conflicts constructively.

Restorative Group Conference Protocol:

The protocol assumes that one facilitator or two co-facilitators will prepare for, schedule, convene, and facilitate the restorative group conference. It is critical that facilitators take thorough notes during the conference in order to paraphrase, review, and summarize what has been said at key points in the process. Throughout the protocol we use the word "targeted" instead of "victim" to identify the person who has been harmed and use the word "offender" to identify the person who has harmed the targeted person.

Pre-Conference Rehearsal:

If appropriate, the facilitator meets with the offender(s) separately and targeted person(s) separately to do three things:

1. Explain the process and how they are expected to participate.

2. For the offender, rehearse what she/he might say when asked, *"What happened?"* And *"How does the offender think her/his behavior impacted others?"* Before the group conference can be convened, the offender must verbally accept responsibility for their role in the incident.

    For the targeted person, rehearse what he/she might say when asked, *"What were you thinking or feeling during or after the incident?"* And *"What impact did the incident have on you and others?"*

3. For the offender, rehearse *"What do you think you can do to make things right?"* and/or *"What might you say to others that will convince them that you want to make amends for what happened?"*

    For the targeted person, rehearse *"What do you need from _____ to make things right?"* and/or *"What do you need to move past this incident and feel okay?"* and/or *"What would you like to see happen that will convince you that _____ wants to make things right?"*

Welcome and Set-Up:

1. Welcome parties to the circle and have each person introduce themselves. *"Welcome. My name is _____ and I will be facilitating this restorative group conference."*

2. Invite each person to introduce themselves and share their relationship to the targeted person and/or the offender or their connection to the specific incident.

3. Explain the goals and how the process will work. *"This conference will focus on an incident that happened* (state the date, place and nature of offense very briefly). *_____ has accepted responsibility for her role in the incident, so we will look at what happened and how her actions affected others. Our aim is to develop an agreement for repairing the harm done and support _____ to follow through with the agreement. Everyone who wishes to*

speak will have opportunities during the conference. What questions do you have about the goals?"

4. Review ground rules as needed: (1) Treat each other with respect. (2) No name calling, blaming, or personal attacks. (3) Be as honest as you can. (4) Listen without interrupting each other.

Offender's Story:

1. Ask the offender to respond to the following questions:

    "What happened?"

    "What were some of the things you were thinking and feeling at the time?"

    "What have you thought about since the incident?"

    "Who do you think has been impacted by your actions?"

    "How did your behavior impact them?

2. Summarize what the offender said.

Targeted Person's Story:

1. Ask the targeted student to respond to the following questions:

    "What was your reaction at the time of the incident?"

    "What are some feelings you have about what happened?"

    "What impact did the incident have on you?

    "How did others react when they heard about the incident?"

2. Summarize what the targeted student said.

Story from Others Impacted by the Incident:

Some incidents impact the functioning of other adults or students in the school or impact the safety and reputation of the entire school community. In these situations, specific students or adults may be asked to represent particular concerns from their perspective in the group conference.

1. *"_____, would you share how this incident has impacted you here at school? What has been challenging for you since this incident?"*

2. Summarize what participants have shared.

Targeted Person's Support Network:

This is the time for the targeted student's parents, advocates, allies, or friends to share their thinking.

1. *"What are some of the things you were thinking or feeling when you heard about the incident?"*

2. *"What has been challenging for you since this incident?"*

3. Summarize what participants have shared.

Offender's Support Network:

This is the time for the offender's parents, advocates, allies, or friends to share their thinking.

1. *"What are some of the things you were thinking or feeling when you heard about the incident?"*

2. *"What has been hard for you since the incident?"*

3. Summarize what participants have shared.

Offender's Response:

Ask the offender, *"Is there anything else you might like to say at this time?"*

Identifying and Responding to the Needs of Targeted Person:

1. Ask the target person: *"What do you need from_____ to make things right?"* and/or *"What do you need to move past this incident and feel okay?"* and/or *"What would you like to see happen that will convince you that _____ want to make things right?"*

2. Ask the offender: *"How does that sound to you? Is there anything else you might say or do that can help make things right between you and repair the harm?"* In some situations, the following questions might be appropriate to ask: *"What might you say to others that will convince them that you want to make amends for what happened?"* or *"How can you show others that you regret what happened?"* or *"What might you do to restore your good standing in the community?"*

3. Summarize what has been agreed to so far.

Developing an Agreement:

1. Invite other participants to offer their suggestions: *"Does anyone else have some thoughts about how to make things right?"* It is important for the offender to respond to each suggestion before the group moves to the other suggestions by asking *"What do you think about that?"*

2. Summarize what has been suggested and accepted by the offender. Ask the offender to paraphrase what she/he has agreed to do.

3. Ask the targeted person if these actions meet their stated needs. *"Do the actions that _____ has agreed to meet the needs you stated earlier?"*

4. Ask the offender what kind of support will help him/her keep the commitment to take the agreed upon actions.

5. Invite others to share any other ideas that might support the offender to stay on track.

6. As the agreement develops, clarify each item so that the written document is as specific as possible, including details, deadlines, and follow-up arrangements. As you sense that the agreement discussion is drawing to a close, say to the participants: *"Before I prepare the written agreement, I would like to make sure that I have accurately recorded what has been decided."* Read the items in the agreement aloud and look to the participants for acknowledgment. Make any necessary corrections. You may also need to review any other school sanctions that a student needs to carry out as a result of the incident.

Closing the Conference:

1. Invite the offender and the targeted person to share their final thoughts, hopes, or appreciations. *"Would you like to share any final hopes, thoughts, or appreciations as you close the past and move forward?"*

2. Invite any others in the group to share final hopes, thoughts, or appreciations. *"Before I formally close this conference, I would like to provide everyone with a final opportunity to speak. Are the any hopes, thoughts or appreciations you would like to share?"*

3. Appreciate everyone's participation and thank everyone for coming. *"The final agreement will be written up and available for you to read at your request. We will follow up with _____ to make sure the agreements are met. Thank you all for participating in today's group conference. As a group you have shown the value you place on working through tough issues and your commitment to supporting _____ and _____ as they move forward."*

Appendix P

Mediation Protocol

Overview: Mediation is the appropriate protocol when students are involved in protracted interpersonal conflicts or have been involved in a physical or verbal fight in which neither party has engaged in an unprovoked attack. Mediation is also an ideal protocol for teacher-student conflicts because the third party mediator ensures that both the student and the teacher get to share their perspectives and participate in the solution. Perspective taking, the capacity to understand and restate the other person's feelings, needs, and interests, is a critical component of the protocol. Mediation is always voluntary. You may need to review the goals, the process, and the norms beforehand with each disputant. Mediations usually take 20 to 30 minutes and need to be conducted in a place that is quiet and private where participants can sit at a table in the following configuration: mediator(s) sit at the center of the table and disputants sit on opposite sides of the table.

Purpose: The goal of mediation is for the disputants to work out differences constructively in a way that solves the problem and preserves the relationship. Disputants agree to have a mediator facilitate a process in which the disputants reach a win-win solution and agreement. Win-Win solutions are non-violent, meet important needs and interests of both parties, feel positive and satisfying to both parties, and repair and/or maintain relationships. A mediator does not offer solutions or advice. The mediator's role is to encourage problem solving between the disputants so that disputants generate their own solution. Disputants sign an agreement at the close of a mediation.

Protocol:

We use the acronym **START** to divide the protocol into five major steps. (**S**et up; **T**ell your story; **A**ssess needs; **R**eview and choose best solution; **T**hink and thank.)

Set Up

1. Welcome parties to the mediation and reassure each party that they will have a chance to speak and share his/her perspective.

2. Ask, *"Are each of you ready to work on the problem?"*

3. Review norms as needed: (1) Treat each other with respect. (2) No name calling. (3) Be as honest as you can. (4) Listen without interrupting each other. (5) Mediation is confidential, so what you say here stays here.

Tell Your Story:

4. Ask disputant #1, *"What happened?"* **Restate.** *"How did you feel about this and why?"* (Ask clarifying questions that show you are listening and draw out specifics.) **Restate.**

5. Ask disputant #2, *"What happened?"* **Restate.** Ask, *"How did you feel about this and why?"* (Ask clarifying questions that show you are listening and draw out specifics.) **Restate.**

6. Ask each disputant to **Restate** how the other person feels and why.

7. Ask *"Is there anything else you want to say?"* Then **Summarize** the whole problem, including key facts and feelings.

Assess Needs

8. Ask disputant #1: *"What do you need to solve the problem or make things right?"* **Restate.**

9. Ask disputant #2: *"What do you need to solve the problem or make things right?"* **Restate.**

10. *"Is there anything else you want to say or ask each other?"* **Summarize** what both people need.

Review and Choose Best Solution

11. *"What is the best solution that will work for both of you?"* (Each disputant makes suggestions about who does what, when, how, where...) If they get stuck...ask, *"Any other ideas? What would you tell someone else to do who had a similar problem? How would this solution work? What are some other things you might do or say? Can you say more about your idea?"*

12. **Summarize** the solution and what each person will do. Is the solution **reasonable?** (*"Is it fair? Are you both okay with this?"*) Is it **realistic?** (*"When, where, how will you do this?"*) Is it **responsible**? (*"Is it safe, legal, moral?"*)

Person A	Person B

Ask, *"Is the problem solved?"*

Think and Thank

13. Ask, *"When a situation like this comes up again, what might you say and do differently?"* **Restate.**

Person A	Person B

14. *"What do you want to say to each other that communicates that the problem is solved?"* (If appropriate also ask: *"What can you do to let others know that the problem is solved?"*) **Restate.**

15. Congratulate parties on solving the problem successfully.

Name_____

Name_____

Date_____

Follow-up Check-in_____

Appendix Q

Identifying Desired Target Behaviors

Social Behaviors that Support Cooperation and Positive Participation

- getting along with others in class, even if they have different opinions or disagree with me
- encouraging people to have their say
- working cooperatively with others
- doing my fair share of the work
- taking on leadership or more responsibility in a group
- helping others
- demonstrating friendliness through smiles and positive responses to others
- carrying out different roles and responsibilities in small-group learning activities
- working effectively with different students listening respectfully without interrupting or making sidebar talk

Self-regulation Behaviors that Support Personal Efficacy

- accepting feedback, correction, and 'No' from adults without a fuss
- sustaining my focus throughout the activity or task
- persisting in my effort to complete work even when the work is hard (not giving up)
- working silently when it s required
- working independently without bothering others
- handling mistakes, setbacks, anger, and frustration constructively
- asking for help when I need it
- showing up on time every day
- making transitions from one activity to another easily
- keeping my hands to myself

Moral/Ethical Behaviors that Support Respect and Caring

- calling people by the name they wish to be called
- greeting people in a friendly manner when they say 'hello' to me
- focusing my attention on people who are speaking to me
- saying 'please' and 'thank you' as a normal courtesy
- not pressuring others to do things they don't want to do
- not using or borrowing other people's stuff without asking permission
- making a best effort to be courteous even when people are unpleasant
- responding to incidents of disrespect without becoming threatening, aggressive, or hostile
- using positive, nonaggressive language to express myself, ask for help, and get what I need
- accepting other viewpoints and opinions respectfully recognizing and appreciating individual and group similarities and differences

Academic Behaviors that Support Engagement in Learning

- following classroom guidelines, agreements, routines, and procedures
- bringing all necessary materials to class
- ready and organized to learn
- asking questions when I do not understand
- correcting, proofing, editing, and revising work until completed with quality
- attempting each part of the question, task, assignment, or test
- expressing curiosity, enthusiasm, or personal interest in what I was learning
- accepting challenges, taking academic risks, and pushing myself to excel
- completing homework routinely
- organizing, managing, and prioritizing time and tasks
- using a range of learning and problem-solving strategies to complete tasks
- demonstrating strong work ethic
- persisting when tasks are new, difficult, or ambiguous
- assessing and monitoring performance accurately

Appendix R

Calls and Conferences to Address Student Concerns with Parents

Overview: Parents need to be notified when a student's unproductive and ineffective behaviors, habits, or mindsets are impeding academic success and high functioning in the classroom. Calls and conferences to address student concerns with parents are never easy, and yet, the vast majority of parents want to be contacted immediately when a concern arises. Strategies that can help make parent calls and conferences more productive include engaging in a problem solving and planning conference with the student beforehand, so that you can share what the student intends to do to rectify the situation or rehearsing and asking the student to call a parent in your presence to explain what the student did that prompts a call home and what the student will do to make it right. Using a script will help you keep the conference to 10 to 15 minutes.

Purpose:

The goals for most parent calls or conferences include describing the situation that prompted the call or conference; sharing the plan for addressing the current situation, and garnering the parent's support in implementing the plan.

Protocol:

1. Introduce yourself and the course for which you are the student's teacher. Ask the parent if it is a convenient time to talk for a few minutes. *"Hello Ms. Green, my name is _____ and I teach Delvin in my 3rd period _____ class. Is this a convenient time to speak for a few minutes?"*

2. Share something that indicates that you know the student—a positive quality that she or he brings to the classroom, something he or she does well, something unusual that she or he knows about, etc. *"First, I want to say that I'm glad to have Delvin in my class. He is energetic and likes to participate. He has told me about his interest in _____. That is really impressive."*

3. Get right to the point and state the problem simply. Be clear about what the unacceptable or unproductive behavior is and how it impacts the student, you, and the classroom. Close by inviting the parent to share information or ask questions. *"Here is the situation I would like to discuss. Our class has been working hard on learning when to work silently and when it is okay to talk. Delvin's chatter and blurting out during times for silent attention or silent work*

keep him from focusing on the task and other students who are trying to listen carefully or work silently find this distracting. Is there anything you would like to share or any questions you might have about the situation?"

4. Inform the parent of the plan for improving behavior and academic performance and invite parent to respond to the plan. *"Delvin and I have spoken and we have a plan for getting him back on track. Delvin has agreed to change seats so he is sitting at the front of the room and is less distracted. He has also agreed to post his "Help" card when he needs to ask a question during silent work time. We have both agreed to monitor his behavior during silent times for three weeks using a daily progress card and I will call you to let you know how he is doing at the end of every week. How does that sound?"*

5. If the parent is upset, acknowledge their feelings and try to find a common concern or hope that you share about their daughter/son. *"I hear your concern and I hope we can work together on this." or "I know this is upsetting to hear and I have confidence that Delvin can correct this."*

6. Share how much you would appreciate it if the parent would talk to their son/daughter about the situation and the plan for improvement. Reassure the parent you are calling now so that the student can practice behaviors and habits that will improve the student's performance. *"I would really appreciate it if you could speak with Delvin about this and let him know that you will be expecting to see improvement on his progress card. I am calling now because learning when and how to be silent in class will help Delvin be a better student. And I want him to have a great year in this class."*

7. Pause to invite any last words from the parent and thank them for their support. *"Ms. Green, thank you so much for you concern and support. I will let you know how Delvin is doing at the end of the week."*

Appendix S

Calls and Conferences at the Request of a Parent

Overview: When a parent requests a call or conference with at teacher about their child's grade, a class concern, or a particular incident, it is important to respond with 24 hours. If a parent is angry or upset, defusing a parent's charged emotions is a critical aspect of the call or conference. Taking notes as you listen can help you keep focused on the parent's needs and concerns.

Purpose:

The primary goal of this kind of call or conference is to ensure that the parent's concerns are understood and their feelings about the situation are acknowledged. A second goal is to agree on next steps in order to move past what happened and resolve the situation in ways that support the parent and the student.

Protocol:

1. First, thank the parent for taking the time to speak with you. *"Ms. Grey, I want to thank you for taking the time to speak with me"*.

2. Invite parent to share exactly what the concern is. *"I understand that you want to discuss _____. Tell me a little about your concern."*

3. Paraphrase what the parent said to communicate your understanding. *"So it sounds like _____. So you're thinking/wanting _____."* Check for accuracy of understanding and invite correction. *"Let me make sure I understand. You said that you_____. Did I get that about right?"* Acknowledge the parent's feelings in ways that reflect the person's emotional state and the feelings he or she attaches to the issue being discussed. *"I can see you're upset about this. It sounds like you felt _____ when_____."* **If the speaker is extremely upset or agitated, continue to reflect her feelings first, in order to defuse highly charged emotions to help the speaker regain equilibrium.**

4. Ask open-ended questions to help clarify the parent's thinking. *"What else should I know about _____? "How has this affected your child?" "What do you find troubling about what happened? "Is there something you wish had been done differently?"* Continue to paraphrase what parent says.

5. Summarize the concern and then identify a common hope or interest you share with the parent. *"It sounds very important to _____. I also want to make sure that _____."*

6. Offer ways to help or problem solve. *"How might I help?" "What would you like to happen next?" "What might a good solution look like?"*

7. Reach agreement on next steps and ask parent, *"What feels important to discuss when I conference with the student tomorrow?"*

8. Summarize the plan of what you will do and how you will follow-up with the parent (phone call, note, email, etc.). *"So tomorrow, I will _____. Then I will call you on _____ and let you know how it's going."*

9. Thank the parent for the conversation, express your appreciation for the parent's concern, and express your confidence that the situation can be resolved positively. *"Thank you so much for bringing your concern to me. I have a clearer sense of what I need to do to support your daughter. I'm confident that this plan can make things better for her. Please stay in touch and call me with any other thoughts or questions you might have."*

Index

D

T

About the Authors

Carol Miller Lieber got the call to teach as a teenager and never stopped. Exploration of the art, craft, and science of teaching and learning has been her driving passion for over forty-five years as an urban educator in the roles of middle and high school teacher, school founder, principal, curriculum writer, and clinical professor in teacher education. She is a national leader in integrating principles of personalization, schoolwide and classroom discipline, and youth development into everyday practices and structures for middle and high schools. Carol is the author of many books and publications including *Making Learning REAL: Reaching and Engaging All Learners* and *Getting Classroom Management Right*. She is also a longtime professional development consultant, and program designer for Engaging Schools. Carol has recently moved to Lancaster County in rural Pennsylvania.

Michele Tissiere has extensive experience as a classroom teacher and senior administrator in secondary schools. As director of program for Engaging Schools, she oversees the implementation of the Schoolwide Discipline and Student Support Program. Michele has extensive experience partnering with district leaders, school leaders, and teachers on aligning their vision, mission and core beliefs with their policies, systems, structures, and processes to support effective and sustainable change. Michele is committed to co-constructing strategic and differentiated professional learning opportunities to maximize adults' capacity to carry out the complex work of school change, helping to shape healthy faculty, peer, school and classroom cultures. Michele is co-author of *Getting Advisory Right: Tools for Supporting Effective Advisories*, a four-disc DVD set published in 2011, and several articles. Michele lives in Denver, Colorado.

Nicole Frazier supports middle and high schools across the country in the areas of instruction, data-driven decision making, professional development, advisory, postsecondary supports, and freshman orientation and intervention programs. Her experience is wide-ranging; in addition to serving as a high school educator for 13 years in diverse high schools in large and small cities, Nicole has worked with urban youth at-risk, rural schools, English language learners, high-performing large comprehensive high schools, and small turnaround schools. With Engaging Schools, Nicole helps leadership teams and faculty develop schoolwide systems and practices that support teaching and learning to build an intentional academic culture. Nicole is the producer, director, and co-author of *Getting Advisory Right: Tools for Supporting Effective Advisories*, a four-disc DVD set published in 2011, and *Activators: Classroom Strategies for Engaging Middle and High School Students* published in 2013. Nicole lives with her family in Denver, Colorado.

About Engaging Schools

Engaging Schools is a nonprofit organization that collaborates with educators to create school communities where each and every student develops the skills and mindsets needed to succeed and make positive contributions in school, work, and life. We specialize in work with middle and high schools to integrate academic, social, and emotional learning and development, and create a positive climate and learning-focused culture. We offer professional development and resources with practical strategies for instructional practice, classroom management, discipline and student support, and advisory programs — all grounded in the values of equity, community, and democracy. Engaging Schools was founded in 1982 as Educators for Social Responsibility and changed its name to Engaging Schools in 2014.

Schoolwide Discipline and Student Support Services

Engaging Schools partners with district leaders, school administrators, school-based student support teams, and other staff to recalibrate discipline and student support policies, systems, and practices in order to maximize each and every student's opportunity for success. We collaborate to reduce the use, overuse, and disproportional use of punitive and exclusionary discipline, and develop a more equitable and supportive approach to discipline grounded in larger efforts to foster a positive climate and culture in schools. Staff members strengthen their ability to implement restorative practices, provide scaffolded academic and behavioral supports and interventions for all students, respond productively to a wide range of behavior challenges, create optimal conditions for leaning, and increase engagement in the classroom. Students develop habits and skills to support greater self-management, self-discipline, responsibility, and academic success.

Engaging Schools has provided high-quality services and practical expertise for districts and schools nationwide for over 30 years. We have a proven track record of facilitating positive change in middle and high schools. Within the district and/ or school, Engaging Schools identifies and leverages existing assets to address specific challenges. Our work includes a needs assessment, planning, consensus building, implementation, and preparation for sustainability that is informed by current research and the best practices in educational leadership, instruction, discipline and student support, and youth development.

Visit us online at www.engagingschools.org for more information about additional Engaging Schools products and services, to sign up for our monthly e-newsletter, and to connect with us via social media.

Engaging Schools
23 Garden Street
Cambridge, MA 02138
www.engagingschools.org

Notes

Notes

Notes

Notes

Notes

Notes